The Influence of Values on Consumer Behaviour

Substantial progress has been made in the conceptualization of values within psychology. The importance of values is also acknowledged in marketing, and companies use values to describe the core associations of their brand. Yet despite this, the values concept has received limited attention in marketing theory. *The Influence of Values on Consumer Behaviour* aims to bridge the gap between the conceptual progress of values in psychology, and the current practice in marketing and branding literature. It proposes the 'Value Compass', a comprehensive value system that is cross-culturally applicable to consumer behaviour and brand choice.

The values concept is used in psychology to identify the motivations underlying behaviour, a concept that marketers have borrowed to define brand values. This has led to conceptual confusion. Whereas in psychology the values system is perceived as an integrated structure, in marketing, values are treated as abstract motivations that give importance to the benefits of consumption. Attention in marketing has shifted away from brand values toward brand personality, a set of human characteristics associated with a brand. Despite its popularity, brand personality has limitations in explaining consumer behaviour, while the potential merits of a brand values concept have remained largely unexplored.

The book presents a meaningful alternative to the brand personality concept and promotes the benefits of using the Value Compass for assessing the effects of brand values and personal values on consumer choice. As such, it will be essential reading for academics and postgraduate students in the fields of marketing, consumer psychology, branding, consumer choice behaviour and business studies.

Erik Kostelijk is Senior Lecturer of Marketing at the International Business School of the University of Applied Sciences in Amsterdam, the Netherlands. Alongside that, he works as Project Leader Research for Marklinq, the research institute of the Hanze University of Applied Sciences in Groningen, The Netherlands, and he has been engaged in teaching and research projects in a number of other countries, among them China, the USA, Lithuania, France and Italy. By doing market research on image and market potential, he has advised many profit and not-for-profit organizations on their positioning strategy.

The Influence of Values on Consumer Behaviour

The Value Compass

Erik Kostelijk

Routledge
Taylor & Francis Group

LONDON AND NEW YORK

First published 2017
by Routledge
4 Park Square, Milton Park, Abingdon, Oxon OX14 4RN
605 Third Avenue, New York, NY 10017

First issued in paperback 2017

Routledge is an imprint of the Taylor & Francis Group, an informa business

British Library Cataloguing in Publication Data
A catalogue record for this book is available from the British Library

Library of Congress Cataloging in Publication Data
Names: Kostelijk, Erik, author.
Title: The influence of values on consumer behaviour: the value compass /
Erik Kostelijk.
Description: Abingdon, Oxon; New York, NY: Routledge, 2016. |
Identifiers: LCCN 2016002733 | ISBN 9781138676473 (hardcover) |
ISBN 9781315560045 (electronic)
Subjects: LCSH: Consumer behavior. | Values. | Marketing—
Psychological aspects.
Classification: LCC HF5415.32 .K668 2016 | DDC 658.8/342—dc23
LC record available at http://lccn.loc.gov/2016002733

ISBN 13: 978-1-138-48955-4 (pbk)
ISBN 13: 978-1-138-67647-3 (hbk)

Typeset in Bembo
by Florence Production Ltd, Stoodleigh, Devon, UK

This book is dedicated to my parents,
Lourens Jan Kostelijk and Everdina Johanna Kostelijk-Kruis.
Without their love and support, I would not have been the
person who I am today.

Contents

Chapter 1

Introduction

We start our exploration of consumer values in the sixth century BC, with Aesop. Aesop was a storyteller credited with a number of fables now collectively known as *Aesop's Fables*. One of these is 'The Cock and the Jewel' (original sixth century BC, translation provided by Townsend, 1867):

> *A cock, scratching for food for himself and his hens,*
> *found a precious stone and exclaimed:*
> *'If your owner had found thee, and not I,*
> *he would have taken thee up, and have set thee in thy first estate*
> *but I have found thee for no purpose.*
> *I would rather have one barleycorn than all the jewels in the world.'*

The cock in this fable is motivated by the practical concern of a full stomach. This concern made him look for food, not for jewels. Values such as prestige or wealth did not seem important to this cock.

Values have been referred to as 'a conception [. . .] of the desirable' (Kluckhohn, 1951, p. 395), 'an enduring belief that a certain mode of conduct or end-state of existence is personally or socially preferable' (Rokeach, 1973, p. 5), or 'desirable [. . .] goals, varying in importance, that serve as guiding principles in the life of a person or other social entity' (Schwartz, 1994, p. 21). In the Oxford Dictionary of English (2005), values are defined as 'principles or standards of behavior'. Despite differences in emphasis, these definitions share a common principle: values define what is important to the individual, and guide him or her to make choices. The cock values a full stomach, and behaves accordingly. A young family visits IKEA if they believe IKEA offers the modern yet cosy family life that they desire. A just-married couple might cherish values such as intimacy and romance, values that lead them to look for a candlelit Italian restaurant to enjoy their Saturday evening together.

In his definition, Rokeach pointed out an important distinction: '*personally or socially*'. Within the context of a society or a (sub)culture, values refer to behaviours or beliefs that *ought to be* preferred to alternative behaviours or beliefs.

Personal values, on the other hand, refer to the individual belief that a certain goal in life (e.g., taking care of others) is to be preferred to another goal (e.g., having a successful career). These personal values do not *prescribe* any cultural or social norm as to which type of behaviour should be preferred to other types of behaviour. They are personal guidelines that help to make personal choices. Throughout this study, the latter viewpoint – values as personal guidelines – is adopted.

Values guide people when they make choices. Consumers, for instance, will be looking for products or services that express those values that are important to them. If there is a signal, a certain 'flag', telling consumers which values are implied by the product, it will help them to make choices. Brands can perform this signalling function. The values profiled by the brand (e.g., the Italian restaurant represents romance) motivate the consumer to behave in a certain way (the young couple visits the Italian restaurant) to achieve certain goals (a romantic evening together). A brand with clearly defined values will attract those people who are motivated by these values. The young family shops at IKEA, if they are convinced that IKEA represents a modern yet cosy lifestyle. The brand IKEA then is the 'flag': it signals the values represented by the IKEA brand, and tells consumers what they can expect.

Hence, brand values indicate what the brand stands for; they stimulate consumers to have certain associations with the brand. These associations are the essence of the added value of a brand: '. . . *what distinguishes a brand from its unbranded commodity counterpart and gives it equity is the sum total of consumers' perceptions and feelings about the product's attributes and how they perform, about the brand name and what it stands for, and about the company associated with the brand'* (Keller, 2008, p. 5). We can expect brands to express those associations that are looked for by the consumers in their target group. These associations are expressed by the brand's value proposition: '*A brand's value proposition is the set of benefits or values it promises to deliver to consumers to satisfy their needs'* (Armstrong & Kotler, 2013, p. 37). That brands contain an important monetary value can be illustrated by rankings such as the Interbrand Best Global Brands (Interbrand, 2015). This ranking, published annually, depicts the 100 most valuable brands in our world. The most valued brand in this ranking, Apple, contains a brand value of nearly $100 billion (Table 1.1).

Because of the importance of a strong value proposition, many corporations spend a lot of money and effort in associating their brands with certain values. Multinational corporations, for instance, often profile their core value(s) prominently. For instance, the core value of Unilever is '*vitality'* (Unilever, 2012). Its competitor Proctor & Gamble profiles with the values '*integrity, leadership, ownership, passion for winning, trust'* (Proctor & Gamble, 2012). Other examples are '*respect, enjoyment and a passion for quality'* (Heineken International, 2012), '*simplicity, cost effectiveness and meaningfulness'* (Ikea, 2012), and '*respect, dignity, care for community and environmental sustainability'* (Starbucks, 2012).

Table 1.1 The world's most valuable global brands

2015 rank	2014 rank	Brand	Country of origin	Sector	2015 brand value ($m)	Change in brand value
1	1	Apple	United States	Electronics	170,276	+43%
2	2	Google	United States	Internet Services	120,314	+12%
3	3	Coca Cola	United States	Beverages	78,423	−4%
4	5	Microsoft	United States	Computer Software	67,67-	+3%
5	4	IBM	United States	Business Services	65,095	−10%
6	8	Toyota	Japan	Automotive	49,048	+16%
7	7	Samsung	South Korea	Technology	45,297	0%
8	6	General Electric	United States	Diversified	42,276	−7%
9	12	Intel	United States	Computer Hardware	37,257	−5%
10	9	McDonalds	United States	Restaurants	39,809	−6%

Source: www.interbrand.com

The relevance of values as a major determinant of brand equity has been acknowledged in marketing literature. The core brand values are considered the '*abstract associations that characterize the most important aspects or dimensions of a brand*' (Keller, 2008, pp. 45, 151), hence, an important asset for the brand (Kapferer, 2008). In a more popularized overview of the current and future developments in marketing, Kotler, Kartajaya and Setiawan (2010) signal the emergence of what they call values-driven marketing: in order to capture the hearts and minds of the consumers (or other stakeholders), and to create a meaningful relation with these stakeholders, they emphasized that brands ought to be associated with values.

Marketing theory uses values to describe brands, relying on values classifications developed in the 1970s and 1980s: the Rokeach Value Survey (Rokeach, 1973), the List of Values (Kahle, 1983) and the VALS method (Values, Attitudes and Lifestyles), a method that relates values to lifestyle (Mitchell, 1983). However, these classifications conceptualize values as a list of unrelated items, whereas the current interpretation of the values concept within psychology and sociology emphasizes the interrelations between values in a value system (Hitlin & Piliavin, 2004; Maio, 2010; Rohan, 2000; Schwartz, 1992). A value system is a dynamic interrelated structure in which actions in the pursuit of any value have consequences that conflict with some values, but are consistent with others. But the use of a dynamic value system in assessing consumer choice has been limited, so far. A couple of marketing studies used a dynamic value system (e.g., Allen, Gupta & Monnier, 2008; Torelli, Özsomer, Carvalho, Keh & Maehle, 2012; Zhang & Bloemer, 2008, 2011). These studies were based on Schwartz's value system (1992), a value system that was designed to evaluate the influence of values on life in general. Values, however, were shown to affect behaviour only when they are activated (Verplanken & Holland,

2002). Value activation is context-specific: we can expect that a marketing context such as the choice for a holiday destination or for a new car activates a specific (sub)set of values. Application of a value system in a consumer choice context, therefore, necessitates the use of a values approach specifically geared toward consumer choice, not the replication of a system applied to (human) psychology in a more general sense.

With the introduction of the brand personality concept (Aaker, 1997), the major focus in marketing shifted away from brand values toward brand personality. Aaker introduced the brand personality concept to incorporate the symbolic use of brands in consumer behaviour literature. Brand personality, the set of human characteristics associated with a brand (Aaker, 1997), was based on the Five-Factor Model (Costa & McCrae, 1992; Goldberg, 1981), the theory that states that personality traits are organized in five factors. Both brand personality and brand values focus on the associations produced by a brand. However, the brand personality construct has been developed specifically for a branding context, whereas a values construct adapted toward branding does not exist. This has favoured the use of brand personality in marketing literature. Keller (2008, p. 369), for instance, mentions values and brand personality as important determinants of brand image, but in his elaboration of the topic he turns to the brand personality concept, leaving brand values untreated. The distinction between brand values and brand personality is not always clear, judging the following citation in Keller's introduction on brand imagery, where brand values are explained as brand personality traits: '*Brands may also take on values. Five dimensions of brand personality (. . .) are sincerity (down-to-earth, honest, wholesome, and cheerful), excitement (daring, spirited, imaginative, and up-to-date), competence (reliable, intelligent, successful), sophistication (upper-class and charming) and ruggedness (outdoorsy and tough)*' (Keller, 2008, p. 66). Due to the popularity of brand personality, the potential merits of a brand values concept have remained largely unexplored. A recent article of Torelli, Özsomer, Carvalho, Keh & Maehle (2012), however, suggested that the use of a values concept for marketing purposes has advantages, compared with the brand personality construct. A couple of recent studies (Kressmann, Sirgy, Herrmann, Huber, Huber & Lee, 2006; Torelli *et al.*, 2012; Zhang & Bloemer, 2008) explored new roads for application of the values concept in a marketing setting. This study intends to progress along these lines.

Summarizing, we can state that, despite the attention and substantial progress in the conceptualization of values within psychology and sociology, despite the acknowledged importance of values in current-day marketing, and despite the widespread use of brand values to describe the core associations of a brand, the elaboration of the values concept has received limited attention in the marketing context. Instead, concept confusion has lead to the use of brand personality, a *personality instrument*, as indicator for brand *values*. With this research, we intend to bridge the gap between the progress in the values concept in psychology, and the current practice in marketing and branding literature, which, so far, has not yet fully taken advantage of this progress. The aim is to generate a comprehensive value system activated toward consumer choice:

The development of a value system that can be cross-culturally applied to assess the effect of brand values and personal values on consumer choice.

This purpose implies the following three objectives:

1   Development of a value system activated toward consumer choice.
2   Assessment of the effect of values on consumer choice.
3   Test of the cross-cultural validity of the value system.

The value system that we propose in this study is labelled the Value Compass. The Value Compass is a comprehensive value system applicable to consumer behaviour and brand choice. As specified above, the Value Compass intends to bridge the gap between the conceptual progress in psychology and the current practice in marketing and branding.

We believe it is important to establish the added value of the Value Compass as compared with existing brand concepts. Accordingly, a fourth objective is added, stressing the added value of using brand values instead of the currently most dominant brand concept, Aaker's brand personality framework:

4   Demonstration of the conceptual difference between brand values and brand personality.

This study is organized into four sections. These sections cover an extensive overview of the development and validation of the Value Compass. The sections are briefly introduced below.

Part I. Literature review

We start by providing the theoretical foundations of this study. Chapter 2 presents an overview of relevant literature.

Part II. Values and the consumer

Part II addresses the first objective of this book: the development of the Value Compass – the value system that is activated toward consumer choice. The Value Compass will be developed through a stepwise approach. This development process is described in Chapter 3. The structure and components of the Value Compass are outlined in Chapter 4. The following questions are addressed in these two chapters:

- Which values are relevant for consumer choice?
- To what extent can these values be organized into a meaningful value system?
- To what extent is the Value Compass, and the values it contains, compatible with existing value typologies?

Part III. Values and branding

In Part III, the Value Compass is applied to consumer behaviour and brand choice. Chapter 5 uses the Value Compass to test the influence of brand values on brand choice and Chapter 6 focuses on value congruence – the match between brand values and consumer values – and the influence of value congruence on choice. Chapters 5 and 6 address the following questions:

- How do brand values influence consumer choice?
- How important is the influence of brand values on consumer choice?
- How, and to what extent, does a match between the brand values and the personal values of the consumer influence consumer choice?
- Adoption of a brand values concept in a marketing context implies that this concept should have an added value as compared to existing brand concepts. As stated above, the main 'competitor' is the brand personality framework. Chapter 7 presents the comparison of brand values and brand personality. This chapter attempts to answer the following question:
- To what extent does the brand values concept provide a meaningful alternative to the brand personality concept?

Part IV. The Value Compass and culture

A theory that has been developed in one country is not necessarily applicable in other cultural contexts. Cross-cultural validation is needed to test the extent to which a theory can be used across different cultures. In a cross-cultural analysis of the Value Compass, the following questions need to be answered:

- Does the Value Compass have the same structure across cultures?
- Is it possible to identify cross-cultural differences in the importance of the values that motivate consumer choice?

Cross-cultural validity of the Value Compass is tested by submitting the Value Compass to respondents in a number of different countries, using a similar test design for each country. Chapter 8 presents the outcomes of this test. This chapter also presents similarities and differences of value priorities across a number of selected countries. Chapter 9, finally, summarizes the main conclusions of this book.

References

Aaker, J. L. (1997). Dimensions of brand personality. *Journal of Marketing Research, 34*(8), 347–356.

Aesop. (original sixth century BC). *Aesopus – De Gallo et Iaspide.* Retrieved 7 July 2011, from http://la.wikisource.org/wiki/Fabulae_(Aesopus)_-_1._De_gallo_et_iaspid

Allen, M. W., Gupta, R. & Monnier, A. (2008). The interactive effect of cultural symbols and human values on taste evaluation. *Journal of Consumer Research, 35* (8), 294–308.

Armstrong, G. & Kotler, P. (2013). *Marketing: An introduction* (11th global edition). Edinburgh Gate, Harlow (UK): Pearson Education Limited.

Costa, P. & McCrae, R. (1992). *Revised NEO Personality Inventory (NEOPI-R) and NEO Five-Factor Inventory (NEO-FFI) Professional Manual.* Odessa, FL: Psychological Assessment Resources.

Goldberg, L. (1981). Language and individual differences: The search for universals in personality lexicons. In L. Wheeler, *Review of Personality and Social Psychology* (pp. 141–165). Beverly Hills, CA: Sage.

Heineken International (2012). *Heineken: governance.* Retrieved 7 September 2012, from Heineken international website.

Hitlin, S. & Piliavin, J. A. (2004). Values: Reviving a dormant concept. *Annual Review of Sociology, 30,* 359–393.

Ikea (2012). *IKEA: about us.* Retrieved 7 September 2012, from IKEA corporate website: www.ikea.com/ms/en_US/about_ikea/index.html

Interbrand (2015). *Best global brands 2015.* Retrieved 1 December 2015, from Interbrand corporate website: http://interbrand.com/best-brands/best-global-brands/2015/ranking/

Kahle, L. R. (1983). *Social values and social change: Adaptation to life in America.* New York, NY: Praeger.

Kapferer, J.-N. (2008). *The new strategic brand management* (4th edition). London, UK: Kogan Page Limited.

Keller, K. L. (2008). *Strategic brand management: Building, measuring, and managing brand equity* (3rd edition). Upper Saddle River, NJ: Prentice Hall.

Kluckhohn, C. (1951). Values and value orientations in the theory of action. In T. Parsons & E. A. Shils, *Toward a general theory of action.* Cambridge, MA: Harvard University Press.

Kotler, P., Kartajaya, H. & Setiawan, I. (2010). *Marketing 3.0.* Hoboken, NJ: Jon Wiley & Sons, Inc.

Kressmann, F., Sirgy, M., Herrmann, A., Huber, F., Huber, S. & Lee, D.-J. (2006). Direct and indirect effects of self-image congruence on brand loyalty. *Journal of Business Research, 59*(9), 955–964.

Maio, G. R. (2010). Mental representations of social values. *Advances in Experimental Social Psychology, 42,* 1–43.

Mitchell, A. (1983). *The nine American life styles.* New York, NY: Warner.

Pearsall, J. & Hanks, P. (2005). *Oxford Dictionary of English* (2nd edition). London, UK: Oxford University Press.

Proctor & Gamble (2012). *P&G: our foundation.* Retrieved 7 September 2012, from Proctor & Gamble corporate website: www.pg.com/en_US/company/purpose_people/pvp.shtml

Rohan, M. J. (2000). A rose by any name? The values construct. *Personality and Social Psychology Review, 4*(3), 255–277.

Rokeach, M. (1973). *The nature of human values.* New York, NY: The Free Press.

Schwartz, S. H. (1992). Universals in the content and structure of values: theoretical advances and empirical tests in 20 countries. In M. Zanna, *Advances in Experimental Social Psychology (25, pp 1–65)*. New York, NY: The Free Press.

Schwartz, S. H. (1994). Are there universal aspects in the structure and contents of human values? *Journal of Social Issues, 50*(4), 19–45.

Starbucks (2012). *About us: our Starbucks mission statement*. Retrieved 7 September 2012, from Starbucks corporate website: www.starbucks.com/about-us/company-information/mission-statement

Torelli, C. J., Özsomer, A., Carvalho, S. W., Keh, H. T. & Maehle, N. (2012). Brand concepts as representations of human values: Do cultural congruity and compatibility between values matter? *Journal of Marketing, 76*(7), 92–108.

Unilever (2012). *About us: Vitality*. Retrieved 7 September 2012, from Unilever corporate website: www.unilever.co.uk/aboutus/-introductiontounilever/vitality/

Verplanken, B. & Holland, R. W. (2002). Motivated decision making: Effects of activation and self-centrality of values on choices and behavior. *Journal of Personality and Social Psychology, 82*(3), 434–447.

Zhang, J. & Bloemer, J. M. (2008). The impact of value congruence on consumer-service brand relationships. *Journal of Service Research, 11*(2), 161–178.

Zhang, J. & Bloemer, J. M. (2011). Impact of value congruence on affective commitment: Examining the moderating effects. *Journal of Service Management, 22*(2), 160–182.

Part I

Literature review

Chapter 2

Values, brands and culture

2.1 Introduction

Values are guiding principles that motivate action to achieve desirable goals. As such, they represent what is important to the individual: a certain value can be very important to one individual but hardly important to somebody else. A major goal of values research has been to relate (differences in) individual value priorities to (differences in) attitudes or behaviour (Schwartz, 1996). In this study, we focus on the influence of values on consumer attitudes and consumer behaviour. By synthesizing recent developments in the psychological field and in marketing literature, we construct a model that relates values to consumer behaviour. This chapter provides an overview of the relevant theory. It includes an overview of values theory, mainly from sources originating from psychology, and an overview of relevant branding and consumer behaviour theory. The main conclusions of this overview are summarized in the form of a number of propositions. The implications of these propositions are tested in the following chapters.

The first three sections of the literature review introduce the values concept. Section 2.2 gives a historical overview of the treatment of values in literature. Then, we continue with a detailed description of the currently most influential value theory: the value system developed by Schwartz. Section 2.4 examines the relation between values and quality of life. People focus many of their activities on realizing higher quality of life. Since values motivate action to realize desirable goals, a link between values and the struggle to achieve a higher quality of life is expected. The importance of values as guiding principle in realizing a higher quality of life is further explored in this section.

In this study, the relation between values and behaviour is explored for a specific context: the influence of values on consumer behaviour. The theoretical aspects of context-specific value activation are discussed in Section 2.5. Section 2.6 then presents an overview of the current use of values in marketing and consumer behaviour literature. The influence of values on consumer behaviour is discussed in Sections 2.7 and 2.8. These sections show the relevance of the use of brand values, however, without making a comparison with other brand concepts. This comparison is provided in Section 2.9. In this section, the use of values as brand concept is compared with the currently prevailing brand personality construct. Finally, the value system as universal framework is explored in the last section of this chapter. Universality of a value system implies that human behaviour all over the world is motivated by the same set of value types.

2.2 A history of the values concept

In the early twentieth century, Max Weber interpreted values as individual, but culture-bound, points-of-view that motivates action (Bruun, 2007). To Weber, value analysis involved the analysis of the ideas or motivations behind a certain action. In Weber's analysis, this mainly concerned religious or political ideas. The structure of Weber's value system is hierarchical, containing a vertical goal-oriented element, and a horizontal element involving a choice between alternative values:

> Values lead to actions, as means to achieve a desired goal: 'All serious reflection about the ultimate elements of meaningful human conduct is oriented primarily in terms of the categories 'end' and 'means.' We desire something concretely either 'for its own sake' or as a means of achieving something else which is more highly desired'.
>
> (The Methodology of the Social Sciences, 1904, p. 52)

To achieve a certain goal a number of alternative values could theoretically be appropriate: '*Exactly the same end may be striven after for very divergent ultimate reasons*' (*The Methodology of the Social Sciences*, 1904, p. 12). It is up to the individual – in his cultural context – to make choices. This existence of – potentially conflicting – alternatives makes the analysis of values relevant for our understanding of individual choices.

The idea that values motivate action was further developed in action theory. In action theory, behaviour is a motivated, goal-oriented activity, organized in three systems: the personal system, the social system and the cultural system. The cultural system includes a set of standards, '*the organization of the values, norms, and symbols which guide the choices made by actors and which limit the types of interaction which may occur among actors*' (Parsons & Shils, 1951). Value orientations in action theory provide a more or less normative framework for behaviour (Spates, 1983), delineating the individual's commitment to the cultural standards. The anthropologist Kluckhohn, a representative of action theory, defined values as something desirable, motivating the choice between alternative courses of action: '*A conception, explicit or implicit, distinctive of an individual or characteristic of a group, of the desirable which influences the selection from available modes, means and ends of action*' (Kluckhohn, 1951, p. 395). He developed a value theory serving as framework to analyse cultural differences between groups (Kluckhohn & Strodtbeck, 1961). He used this model to analyse differences between native American culture and the mainstream American culture.

Allport (1961) defined value orientations as ways to live. He designed a personality test – the Study of Values – based on six ideal value types constructed by the German psychologist Eduard Spranger in 1928: the theoretical man, the economic man, the social man, the aesthetic man, the political man and the religious man. In Allport (1961), the notion of value priorities emerges. He stated that a value is a *'belief upon which a man acts by preference'* (Allport, 1961, p. 454). This emphasizes that an individual holds different values, not all of them equally important. This makes it possible to establish a hierarchy of values, showing the relative importance of individual values. Different individuals can be expected to hold different value hierarchies, with behavioural preferences being determined by their most important values.

It is important to distinguish between a value system and value priorities. A value system refers to the way that values are structured. Value priorities are the relative importance of values to an individual, within his or her value system. For instance, we can consider the values *power*[1] and *equality*. In a value system these are two different, to a certain extent perhaps even conflicting values: pursuing *power* might conflict with a need for *equality*. Within someone's value system, *power* can have a higher value priority than *equality*. This person then considers *power* to be more important than *equality*, and part of his choices and actions are focused on achieving *power* (e.g., a powerful position in the workplace). But for another individual, *equality* can be the more important value.

The number of values is not a constant in literature. By some it was ascerted that *'we will probably never develop a complete list that will encompass all possible human values'* (Beatty, Kahle, Homer & Misra, 1985, p. 185). Kluckhohn & Strohbeck (1961), on the other hand, developed a system with only five values, and Hofstede (1980) conceptualized cultural differences based on a structure of four cultural (value) dimensions (a fifth and a sixth dimension were added later). Rokeach (1973) assumed a value system consisting of 18 terminal and 18 instrumental values. He considered values to be guiding principles in an individual's life: a value was defined as *'an enduring belief that a specific mode of conduct or end-state of existence is personally or socially desirable to an opposite or converse mode of conduct or end-state of existence'* (Rokeach, 1973, p. 5). The distinction between mode of conduct and end-state of existence reflects the 'means-to-an-end' element as referred to by Kluckhohn. Some values can be seen as lower-order, instrumental values serving to achieve the higher-order, terminal values desired 'for their own sake'. Rokeach distilled the terminal values in his value system from a literature review, in combination with interviews with individuals representative of American society (Rokeach included himself as one of the respondents). He selected his instrumental values by making his own, intuitive choice out of an extensive list of personality-trait words derived from the work of Allport and Odbert (1936). With this system of instrumental and terminal values, Rokeach developed the Rokeach Value Survey (RVS). The RVS is a ranking method, asking the respondent to '*arrange the values in order of importance to YOU, as guiding principles in YOUR life*' (Rokeach, 1973, p. 27). Table 2.1 gives an overview of the values in the RVS.

Rokeach's conceptualization of values differs significantly from the values concept in action theory. In action theory, a value is seen as a moral, *culturally determined* belief about the most appropriate rationale for action. For Rokeach, a value is an *individually determined* belief directing a preferred way of behaviour. A related method, the List of Values (LOV), was developed from Rokeach's work on values (Beatty *et al.*, 1985; Kahle, 1983). The purpose of the LOV was to create a set of values related more closely to life's major activities (e.g., marriage, work, daily consumption) than the values in the RVS. As a consequence, the LOV is more related to behaviour based on individual choice than the RVS.

Both the value system developed by Rokeach and the List of Values represent, as literally expressed by the latter, a 'list of values'. Rokeach does distinguish between instrumental and terminal values, but he does not provide additional insight into how these two types of values relate to each other. His value system does not describe other interrelations between values. By not

Table 2.1 The values in the Rokeach Value Survey

Terminal values	Instrumental values
A comfortable life (a prosperous life)	Ambitious (hard-working, aspiring)
An exciting life (a stimulating, active life)	Broadminded (open-minded)
A sense of accomplishment (lasting contribution)	Capable (competent, effective)
A world at peace (free of war and conflict)	Cheerful (lighthearted, joyful)
A world of beauty (beauty of nature and the arts)	Clean (neat, tidy)
Equality (brotherhood, equal opportunity for all)	Courageous (standing up for your beliefs)
Family security (taking care of loved ones)	Forgiving (willing to pardon others)
Freedom (independence, free choice)	Helpful (working for the welfare of others)
Happiness (contendedness)	Honest (sincere, truthful)
Inner harmony (freedom from inner conflict)	Imaginative (daring, creative)
Mature love (sexual and spiritual intimacy)	Independent (self-reliant, self-sufficient)
National security (protection from attack)	Intellectual (intelligent, reflective)
Pleasure (an enjoyable, leisurely life)	Logical (consistent, rational)
Salvation (saved, eternal life)	Loving (affectionate, tender)
Self-respect (self-esteem)	Obedient (dutiful, respectful)
Social recognition (respect, admiration)	Polite (courteous, well-mannered)
True friendship (close companionship)	Responsible (dependable, reliable)
Wisdom (a mature understanding of life)	Self-controlled (restrained, self-disciplined)

considering the interrelations between values, these value systems are, essentially, more a list of unconnected value words than a true value *system*. In the next stage of the development of the values concept, conceptualization evolved from listing values as more or less unrelated words or categories of words toward modelling these values into a 'real' value system, a structure providing insight into how values relate to each other. This stage in the development of the values concept was accomplished by the work of Schwartz (1992).

2.3 The value theory of Schwartz: a coherent stucture of compatible and conflicting value types

Weber already acknowledged the horizontal interrelations between values, by pointing out that different, potentially conflicting, values can result in striving for the same goal. The emphasis on the relations between values, and the notion of viewing a value system as a structure of interrelated values, is central to the work of Schwartz (1992): '*Consistent conflicts and compatibilities among values (. . .) point to a meaningful structure that underlies relations among single values*' (p. 3). The structure of his value system has become the standard in current-day thinking about values.

Six features of values are central to Schwartz's conceptualization of values (Schwartz, 1992, 2006; Schwartz & Bilsky, 1987):

1   Values are beliefs. When values become activated, they create feelings. For instance, if *independence* is an important value to someone, he or she will become aroused if his or her independence is threatened.
2   A value is a guiding principle, referring to a desirable (end) goal. Values motivate action to pursue these goals.
3   Values transcend specific actions and situations. *Independence* as value would be relevant at work, but also with family, in sports or in political opinions. This feature distinguishes values from narrower concepts like norms and attitudes that usually refer to specific actions, objects or situations.
4   Values serve as standards or criteria; they enable the selection or evaluation of actions, policies, people and events. People decide what is good or bad, or worth doing or avoiding, based on possible consequences for their cherished values. This often is an unconscious process.
5   Values are ordered by importance relative to one another. This hierarchical feature also distinguishes values from norms and attitudes.
6   The relative importance of multiple values guides action. The trade-off among relevant, compatible and conflicting values is what guides attitudes and behaviour.

It is important to highlight the difference between values and needs. Both needs and values motivate action. The need, as motive for action, was elaborated on by Maslow (1954).[2] A need is a drive for an organism, either human or animal. As opposed to needs, people are not born with their values. In contrast, values represent learned beliefs about preferred ways of acting or being (Olver & Mooradian, 2003). These behavioural preferences reflect the strategies the individual adopted to cope with the three universal requirements with which all individuals are confronted (Schwartz, 1994; Schwartz & Bilsky, 1987): biological needs (organism), social motives (interaction) and institutional demands (society). In other words, needs can translate into values, but societal or psychological norms might stimulate or constrain this development. Consequently, values are susceptible to social or cultural influences.

As was pointed out above, Schwartz emphasized the interrelations between values. A key aspect of his value theory is the assumption that some values reinforce each other, while other values have a conflicting impact. For example, an individual who values *power* likely also favours compatible values such as *leadership,* or other values emphasizing the possibility of having influence over another person. *Equality*, on the other hand, does not agree with having power and is likely to be a conflicting value. Individual behaviour is a trade-off of the interplay of compatible and conflicting values. Schwartz hypothesized that the conflicts and compatibilities among value types constitute universal inter-relations. Schwartz tested his value theory with what is now called the Schwartz Value Survey. For his value survey, Schwartz (1992) took values from Rokeach's survey, and combined these with values that he derived from instruments developed in other cultures, for instance, the Chinese Culture Connection (1987) and Hofstede's cultural dimensions (1980). Out of these sources, Schwartz selected 56 values. In a cross-cultural study, he submitted these values to a sample, which encompassed at first 20 countries (Schwartz, 1992) and was later on gradually expanded to 67 countries (Schwartz, 2006).

In the cross-cultural study, Schwartz found evidence for 10 value types. Each of the 10 value types represents a number of values whose meaning and motivational goal match with the corresponding value type. The value types are mentioned in Table 2.2. In this table, the individual value items that Schwartz used as indicators for these value types are presented in the last column.

Schwartz (1992) demonstrated that these values are related to each other, and that these relations can be represented as a circular structure. The closer the values located in this circular structure are, the more similar their underlying motivations. The more distant they are positioned, the more conflicting their underlying motivations. Schwartz (1992) suggested that two motivational dimensions structure the value system:

1   *Self-enhancement versus self-transcendence*: the conflict between values with a primary focus on the pursuit of the individual interest and values focusing on the well-being and interest of others.
2   *Openness to change versus conservation*: the contrast between people's motivation to follow their own intellectual and emotional interests, versus the motivation to preserve the status quo and the certainty it provides in relationships with close others, institutions and traditions.

Table 2.2 The value types of Schwartz's value system

Value type	Defining goal	Corresponding value items
Self-direction	independent thought and action – choosing, creating, exploring	Creativity, freedom, choosing own goals, curious, independent
Stimulation	Values of this value type derive from the need for variety and stimulation in order to maintain an optimal level of stimulation. The defining goal of this value type: excitement, novelty, challenge in life	A varied life, an exciting life, daring
Hedonism	Pleasure or sensuous gratification for oneself	Pleasure, enjoying life
Achievement	Personal success through demonstrating competence according to social standards	Ambitious, successful, capable, influential
Power	Attainment of social status and prestige, and control or dominance over people and resources	Authority, wealth, social power
Security	Safety, harmony, and stability of society, of relationships and of self	Social order, family security, national security, clean, reciprocation of favors
Conformity	Restraint of actions, inclinations, and impulses likely to upset or harm others and violate social expectations or norms	Obedient, self-discipline, politeness, honouring parents and elders
Tradition	Respect, commitment and acceptance of the customs and ideas that one's culture or religion provides	Respect for tradition, humble, devout, accepting my portion in life
Benevolence	Preserving and enhancing the welfare of those with whom one is in frequent personal contact	Helpful, honest, forgiving, responsible, true friendship, mature love
Universalism	Understanding, appreciation, tolerance and protection for the welfare of all people and for nature	Broad-minded, social justice, equality, world at peace, world of beauty, unity with nature, wisdom, protecting the environment

Figure 2.1 presents the structure of the human value system, as uncovered by Schwartz. As an example, we can see in this figure that *equality* (value type *universalism*) and *power* indeed represent conflicting motivations, whereas, for instance, *power* and *achievement* are neighbouring value types, hence representing more compatible motivations.

With his cross-cultural studies, Schwartz (1992, 1994) found supportive evidence that the structure of the human value system, as presented in Figure

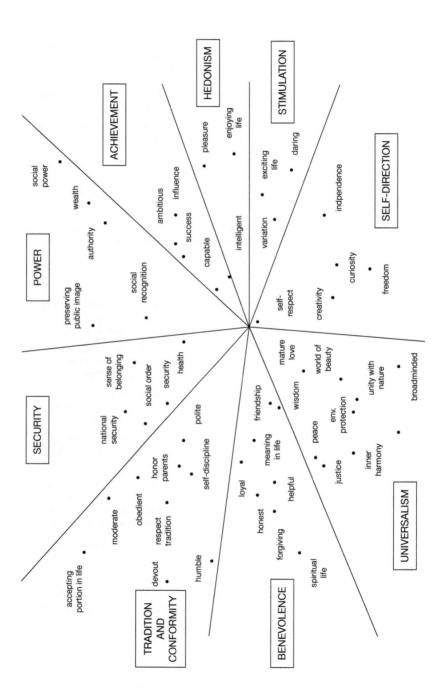

Figure 2.1 The structure of Schwartz's value system (adapted from Schwartz, 1992)
Reprinted with permission from Elsevier.

2.1, provides a near-universal representation of human values. This implies that the values of individuals from different cultural backgrounds can be described according to this structure. However, this does not imply that the importance of all these values is the same across individuals. Although, for instance, for everybody *equality* and *power* are conflicting motivations, people differ in the relative importance they place on these (or on other) values. If a person is gifted with strong inner needs for dominance or recognition, then he might consider power and status important values in his life. If this individual was raised in a society that appreciates power distance, then his tendency to value power is likely to be reinforced, whereas it might be restrained to a certain extent in an egalitarian society. In short, individual differences in value priorities derive from each person's unique combination of biological endowments, in combination with the demands placed on the individual by his environment.

Although Schwartz's theory identifies distinctive value types, it also postulates that values form a continuum of related motivations. In empirical studies, values from adjacent types may intermix. For example, we see in Figure 2.1 that *exciting life* and *enjoying life* belong to different value types, although they represent related motivations. In contrast, values and value types that express opposing motivations are clearly distant from one another. For instance, values expressing the desire to make a difference with others, for instance, *power* or *achievement* values, oppose universalist values such as *equality* or *unity with nature*.

Finally, it is relevant to point out that, although Schwartz emphasized relations between values, he did not find evidence for a distinction between instrumental and terminal values, as was assumed by Rokeach. Hence, as opposed to Rokeach, Schwartz's value theory does not differentiate between terminal and instrumental values.

2.4 The ultimate motivation: a higher quality of life

As was expressed previously, individual value priorities reflect the strategies the individual adopted to deal with the requirements of life. This might imply a conception of values as guidelines for survival, either in a Darwinistic sense, or in coping with societal demands. But, although survival certainly is a minimum requirement, the concept of values as guidelines for choice optimization assumes that more than basic survival is at stake. Actually, many views relate values to achieving the optimum, as opposed to surviving life's necessities. For instance, human behaviour has been demonstrated to correlate with values as a means to achieve one's personal well-being (Levy, 1990). Rohan (2000) similarly conceptualized value priorities as guidelines to best possible living. This notion can also be retraced in the two major value systems discussed so far. Rokeach (1979, p. 147) identified values as meaningful indicators for the quality of life. In a similar style, Schwartz (1992, p. 8) observed that the value *happiness* is positively correlated with all other values, and can be attained through the successful pursuit of the individual's value priorities.[3]

The notions of happiness, quality of life and well-being can be traced back to the concept of *eudaimonia* in ancient Greek philosophy. Best possible living was recognized by Aristotle and his contemporaries as eudaimonia, the ultimate goal toward which all human action is directed. In ancient philosophy, a lot of attention was devoted to the type of virtues or activities that would enable the realization of eudaimonia. Box 2.1 provides an extensive background.

The concept of quality of life is widely used across disciplines including economics, ecology, psychology, law, political science and social welfare. It was already a matter of debate among the ancient Greeks, and still the ever-returning question is: *what makes for a good or satisfying life?* Two different types of indicators are used nowadays to define and measure quality of life (Diener & Suh, 1997):

- 'Objective' or social indicators: indicators reflecting people's objective circumstances in a given cultural or geographic unit (e.g., welfare, health, education or human rights indices).
- Subjective well-being (SWB): the individual's judgement of his own well-being. SWB is typically measured by using one or more of the following indicators (Deci & Ryan, 2008; Diener, 2000): life satisfaction, feelings of positive and negative affect and unpleasant emotions like sadness, depression and stress.

Although literature on SWB often proposes *happiness* as a key element, happiness – up to a certain extent – has an association with more hedonic pleasure. The discussion in Box 2.1 highlights the difference between happiness and the more eudaimonic *best possible living* (see also Deci & Ryan, 2008; Waterman, 1993). Although the discussion is partly semantic, it is important to point out that a higher quality of life can be attained in various ways. If we consider values as guidelines to a higher quality of life, then the different values in the individual's value system – and hedonic pleasure can be one of them – form alternative ways of attaining a higher quality of life.

'Objective' economic indicators such as Gross Domestic Product (GDP) often prevail as an indicator for the quality of life. But in many western societies, over the past 50 years, the per capita income levels have at least doubled, whereas subjective well-being has hardly changed (Diener & Suh, 1997). The rewards of an increase in per capita GDP seem to level off at a threshold of around $10.000.[4] Above this threshold, a further increase in material progress does not lead to a significant increase in subjective well-being (Inglehart, 1997). Other studies confirm that external influences such as income, age or education explain only up to a maximum of 20 per cent of someone's quality of life (Diener, Suh, Lucas & Smith, 1999), and that quality of life is primarily enhanced by satisfying psychological needs (Deci & Ryan, 2008). This stresses the importance of SWB, in measuring quality of life, as opposed to 'objective' motivations such as per capita income. Results from the World Values Survey confirm this tendency: in developed countries, values emphasizing economic growth and achievement lose importance, whereas values related to subjective well-being (e.g., self-expression, individual autonomy, diversity) become more prominent (Inglehart, 1997). In accordance with this development, in July 2011, the General Assembly of the United Nations recognized the importance of happiness and well-being, and advocated the use of measures of well-being instead of GDP-related indicators (f, 2011). Bhutan, so far, is the only country profiling itself with the use of 'Gross National Happiness' as indicator, instead of other (economic) indicators.[5]

Box 2.1   Eudaimonia

The concept of quality of life is grounded in classical philosophy. The word eudaimonia is a combination of 'eu' (good) and 'daimon' (spirit). Although often translated as 'happiness', the meaning of the word is more closely related to 'flourishing' (Cooper, 1975), or 'well-being', 'the feelings accompanying the realization of one's goals and purpose in life' (Ryff, 1989). A more or less similar expression can be found in Maslow's Motivation and Personality (1954), when he addresses self-actualization, the highest need in his hierarchy of needs:

> What a man can be, he must be. [. . .] Self-actualization [. . .] refers to man's desire for self-fulfilment, namely, to the tendency for him to become actualized in what he is potentially
> (Motivation and Personality, p. 46)

In ancient times, realizing this full potential, and what this actually means, was a matter of what we would call now fierce debate. In his Nicomachean Ethics (fourth century BC), Aristotle considers eudaimonia 'the highest good for human beings' (Nicomachean Ethics, 1095a, 15–17), the ultimate human goal of each and every individual:

> For eudaimonia we choose always for itself and never for the sake of something else, but honour, pleasure, reason and every virtue we choose [. . .] them also for the sake of eudaimonia. Eudaimonia, on the other hand, no one chooses for the sake of these, nor, in general, for anything other than itself.
> (Nicomachean Ethics, 1097a, 1–7)

> For, in a word, everything we choose we choose for the sake of something else – except eudaimonia, which is an end.
> (Nicomachean Ethics, 1176b, 36–38)

If eudaimonia represents best possible living, the ultimate goal toward which all other human action is directed, then people live and strive in order to realize their full potential. Hence, all human activities, wishes, or desires, can be considered means to achieve eudaimonia. Then, it becomes relevant to determine which of these means serve this purpose best:

> Verbally there is very general agreement; for both the general run of men and people of superior refinement say that it is eudaimonia [. . .] but with regard to what eudaimonia is they differ, and the many do not give the same account as the wise. For the former think it is some plain and obvious thing, like pleasure, wealth, or honour.
> (Nicomachean Ethics, 1095a, 17-24)

Where the 'many' (i.e., the quite ignorant majority of people) consider happiness the result of wealth or pleasure, the 'wise' hold a different opinion. Both Plato, and through him Socrates, are quite normative in the guiding principle to achieve eudaimonia. They consider that happiness and virtue are inseparably linked. Only a virtuous life will lead to eudaimonia, e.g., in the following citation from The Republic (4th century BC):

> And the same may be said of lust and anger and all the other affections, of desire and pain and pleasure, [. . .] they ought to be controlled, if mankind are ever to increase in eudaimonia and virtue.
> (The Republic, X, 606d)

Plato believes that each part of the soul pursues its own pleasure. The highest quality of life can be realized if the three parts of the soul are harmoniously in balance, governed by the virtue[1] of wisdom in the rational part, the virtue of courage in the spirited part, and the virtue of moderation (control over bodily pleasures) of that part of the soul governed by our desires. When considering best possible living, also Aristotle acknowledges the importance of moderation:

> Virtue is a state of character concerned with choice [. . .] It is a mean between two vices, that which depends on excess and that which depends on defect (Aristotle, Nicomachean Ethics, 1107a, 1–5). For eudaimonia does not lie in [bodily pleasures], but [. . .] in virtuous activities.
> (Nichomachean Ethics, 1177a, 9–10)

The highest virtue can be realized when a man lives according to its nature. According to Aristoteles (agreeing with other contemporaries, e.g., Anaxagoras, Plato), this is 'nous', intellect, also translated as reason, or common sense:

> That which is proper to each thing is by nature best and most pleasant for each thing; for man therefore, the life according to intellect is best and most pleasant, since intellect more than anything else **is** man. This life therefore is also the most eudaimonious.
>
> (Nicomachean Ethics, 1178a, 5–9)

In Stoicism, like for Aristotle, pleasure is seen as contrary to nature (Cleanthes, 3rd Century BC), consequently, not as a virtue. Best possible living can be characterized by control over emotions, specifically control over pleasure (Arrian's Discourses of Epictetus, 108 AD), to live consistently with nature (Cleanthes), or to live in accordance with one's own human nature, as well as that of the universe (Chrysippus, 3rd Century BC).

Democritus, around 400 BC, also favors intellect and moderation, but he asserts that the motive of our actions is the pursuit of pleasure and the avoidance of displeasure:

> The best thing for a man is to live his life as cheerfully as possible, and with the least distress.
>
> (Democritus, fragment 53, Stobaeus III, 1, 46)

The pursuit of pleasure, and the avoidance of pain becomes central in hedonism. Epicurus (around 300 BC) recognizes that pleasure ('hedone') is the end goal of human existence, the way to reach the highest quality of life, a notion opposite to the Stoic view. This is evident in the following text:

> For this reason we call pleasure the alpha and omega of eudaimonious life. Pleasure is our first and kindred good. It is the starting-point of every choice and of every aversion, and to it we come back, inasmuch as we make feeling the rule by which to judge of every good thing.
>
> (Epicurus, Letter to Menoeceus 128–129)

Where many of his contemporaries see virtues as a condition for, or even as a constituent of eudaimonia, for Epicurus virtues are only one of the means to achieve 'best possible living':

> Let beauty and virtue and suchlike be honoured, if they provide pleasure; if they do not provide pleasure, let them go.
>
> (Epicurus, Fragments 12)

The moralistic element in Epicurus appears to be absent, as opposed to, for instance, Plato who considers some roads to eudaimonia evidently superior to others (e.g., intellect or wisdom superior to wealth or sensual pleasure).

1   The Greek 'arete' is commonly translated as virtue. The meaning is best conveyed by 'excellence': for a Greek virtue pertains to all sorts of desirable qualities as in, for instance, 'speed is virtue to a horse'.

In assessing someone's feeling of well-being, goals serve as an important standard of reference (Diener & Suh, 1997). People react in positive ways when making progress toward goals and react negatively when they fail to achieve goals. But not all goals are related to SWB. It was demonstrated that SWB is only enhanced by progress toward goals that are in line with individual motivations (Brunstein, Schultheiss & Grassman, 1998). This highlights the importance of values: values define these individual motivations. Consequently, an increase in SWB is most likely to be experienced when people make progress toward achieving personal goals that are derived from their most important values (Diener & Suh, 1997). As a consequence, attempts have been made to develop a value-based index to assess quality of life (Diener, 1995).

The importance of values as guides to a higher quality of life brings us to the first proposition of this study. We propose that quality of life can be enhanced by any of the values in an individual's value system.[6]

Proposition 1:
Values are guiding principles. Values motivate people to make choices that improve their quality of life.

2.5 Value activation

Specific value priorities lead to preferences of an individual, a society, culture or subculture. The notion of peace and love in the 1960s and 1970s, or the emphasis on ambition in the 1980s (iconized by Gordon Gekko in Oliver Stone's 1987 movie *Wall Street*), illustrate this: relative importance of certain value priorities set the direction of thought and action within a given context. This general principle is expressed in the following quotation of Max Weber:

every history is written from the standpoint of the value-interests of the present and that every present poses or can pose new questions to the data of history because its interest, guided by value-ideas, changes.

(Weber, 1904, p. 157)

In the Schwartz Value Survey, individuals are asked to rate the importance of values *as a guiding principle in MY life* (Schwartz, 1992, p. 17). This way of asking creates no reference to any particular situation. The hidden assumption is that the importance of values does not depend on the context: the assumption of the stable value system. This is in line with one of the central features of values: values transcend specific actions and situations (Feather, 1975; Schwartz, 2006).

The citation of Weber, on the other hand, suggests that value priorities are not a constant. This was affirmed by a number of studies: values affect behaviour only when they are activated. Activation is context-specific, and depends on the situation or the information with which a person is confronted (Verplanken & Holland, 2002; Verplanken, Trafimow, Khusid, Holland & Steentjes, 2009). For example, suppose an individual watches a charity show on tv, and is confronted with images of people being victims of war and hunger. This activates his values for a world at peace, or equality, and these values motivate a certain behaviour (e.g., he donates money). The next day, the competitive environment of his office activates his sense of ambition, motivating him to work harder than his co-workers in order to earn a bonus. Apparently, the individual ordering of his value priorities is situation-specific. Additional empirical support was provided by Seligman and Katz (1996). Individuals were found to show different value priorities for different target issues. In one of their studies they observed changes in value priorities when people judged abortion. For those favouring the pro-choice stance, the values *freedom* and *sanctity of one's own body* increase in importance when they think about abortion, as compared to the importance of these values in their lives in general. For the anti-abortionists, the values *sanctity of life* and *inner harmony* have a higher priority when they specifically judge abortion. These results are in line with Rokeach's observation (1973) that a value system is never fully activated. He considered a value system as a mental blueprint, of which different subsets are activated in different situations. Any given situation may activate a number of different values, but not all values in a person's value system are simultaneously activated in any choice situation.

The above-mentioned studies do not directly challenge the value system structure as proposed by Schwartz. However, they do challenge one of the six features of values mentioned in Section 2.3: the assumption that values transcend specific actions and situations. The above-mentioned studies demonstrate that external influences change the order of value priorities in a value system. As a consequence, the importance of values does not fully transcend specific actions and situations. Hence, we can conclude that values motivate behaviour, but the relative importance of value priorities depends on the extent to which they are activated by the situation.

This book is focused on consumer choice. Following the proposition developed in Section 2.4, values motivate the individual to make those choices, which maximize his perceived quality of life. Thus, we can expect values to motivate consumer choice decisions as well. In line with this observation, a limited number of recent studies used Schwartz's value system to assess the impact of values on brand preferences and brand loyalty (Torelli *et al.*, 2008, 2012; Zhang & Bloemer, 2008). However, the previous overview highlighted value activation as being context-specific, whereas Schwartz's value system refers to life in general, not toward consumer choice. Within a consumer choice context, the importance of certain values is not necessarily the same as their importance as a guiding principle for life in general. Some of the values defined by Schwartz might not be applicable to the brand context at all. In a general marketing textbook (Shimp, 2010), for instance, the value types of conformity, tradition, benevolence and universalism were not assumed to typify usual consumer behaviour for most products or services. On the other hand, it has also been suggested that brand values not covered by Schwartz's value system might exist (Gaus, Jahn, Kiessling & Drengner, 2010; Lages & Fernandes, 2005).

It is important to note here that similar observations were made with respect to the relation between attitude and behaviour (Ajzen, 1991; Ajzen & Fishbein, 2005; Fishbein & Ajzen, 1975): a general attitude failed to correlate with context-specific behaviour. To counter the lack of correspondence between attitude and behaviour, the theory of reasoned action was developed. This theory emphasized the importance of defining more situation-specific attitudes when one wants to link attitudes with behaviour.

There is another reason why the values of Schwartz's value theory might be less suitable for consumer choice. This involves the abstract nature of these values (Maio, 2010). Because they apply to all aspects of life, some values were described in a more general, abstract sense, so that these values actually have the potential to cover all aspects of life. But when more abstract words are used to describe a value (e.g., in a survey), it might become more difficult for consumers to attribute a specific motivation to this value. For instance, Schwartz's value system contains values such as *equality, reciprocation of favours*, or *accepting my portion in life*. Even though these values could be applicable to a certain consumer choice situation, it might be difficult for consumers to relate these values – without further specification – to specific buying motives in this choice context. The abstract nature of values complicates their assessment and leaves room for various interpretations among individuals.

The above-mentioned complications seem to point to the necessity of a more specific value measurement, activated toward the behaviour of interest. Hence, if we want to use values to assess consumer choice, we need a value system that is activated toward consumer choice.

Proposition 2:
A consumer choice situation, being a specific choice context, activates a specific (sub)set of values. This set of values is structured as a dynamic value system of compatible and conflicting values.

2.6 Brand values

As we noted in the introduction, many corporations profile their brands by emphasizing the values that the brand is supposed to represent. Values represent motivations of human beings, but apparently it also makes sense to associate brands with values. The following sections provide a deeper understanding of the importance of brand values. We will show that brand choice can be seen as a process in which consumers somehow try to find a match between their own values and the values proposed by the brand.

A brand is a set of mental associations

Brands are an essential element in current day society. In the introduction, we referred to a brand as the set of mental associations, held by the consumer, that add to the perceived value of the branded product or service. The added value of the brand then can be seen as the consumer's reaction to the brand, in comparison to his reaction to a non-branded version of the product or service. This added value, which has been labelled 'brand equity' (Keller, 2008), occurs when the consumer is familiar with the brand and holds some favourable, strong and unique associations about the brand. It can imply that the consumer is enticed to like the brand, to prefer the brand, or even to buy or to continue buying the brand, simply because of these positive associations. For instance, even though Coca Cola is essentially a dark-coloured soft drink with a lot of sugar, with the help of marketing activities this brand now represents happiness to some people, and this − conscious or subconscious − association stimulates them to buy Coca Cola.

Brand awareness and brand associations can be conceptualized as an associative network (Keller, 1993). When memory or knowledge is modelled as an associative network, it is considered to consist of a set of nodes and links. Nodes are stored information connected by links that vary in strength. As an example, for instance, the associative network of a brand such as 7-Up can include the features of the brand (*7-Up has no colour*), or aspects independent of the product, like benefits (*refreshing*), previous experiences (*I didn't like it*), or values associated with the brand (*pure, healthy*).

Brand benefits

Brands (products or services) have features or attributes. In the case of a car, for instance, these attributes include size, engine capacity, the design of the car, the colour, and so on. Consumers derive benefits from these tangible or intangible attributes (Gutman, 1982). Benefits are the consequences consumers enjoy from the consumption of products and services. For a car, these benefits might include a comfortable drive, arriving quickly at the destination, or safe means of transportation. In Gutman's means-end chain model, benefits are linked to values (Gutman, 1982). According to this model, consumers choose actions that produce desired consequences and minimize undesired consequences. Values determine the desirability of these consequences: benefits are considered favourable (attractive) or unfavourable, depending on the value priorities of the consumer. For example, a consumer who values safety will think the benefit of a safe means of transportation is more important than comfort.

Marketing literature provides a number of classifications of benefits. Holbrook and Hirschman (1982) distinguish two types of benefits of consumption by contrasting two views of consumer behaviour, the – more or less – rational information-processing model and a view focusing on consumer experience. The information-processing model regards the consumer as a logical thinker who solves problems to make purchasing decisions. This results in a focus on the tangible benefits of goods and services: products perform functions based on relatively objective features. The success of a purchasing decision is primarily evaluated by utilitarian criteria: one asks how well the good or service performs its proper function or achieves its intended purpose. According to the experience-focused view, the consequences of consumption relate to the overall consumer experience – the enjoyment that it offers and the resulting feeling of pleasure that it evokes. This creates a focus on the symbolic, hedonic and aesthetic nature of consumption, by considering aspects such as amusement, fantasy, arousal, sensory stimulation or enjoyment. With respect to the experiential view, hedonic consumption is defined as '*those facets of consumer behavior that relate to the multisensory, fantasy and emotive aspects of one's experience with products*' (Hirschman & Holbrook, 1982, p. 92).

In the same vein, Batra and Ahtola (1990) recognized two basic motivations that drive consumer behaviour: affective (hedonic) gratification and instrumental, utilitarian reasons. They showed, through several empirical studies, that attitudes toward brands have both a hedonic and a utilitarian component. This two-dimensional conceptualization was also found by Voss, Spangenberg and Grohmann (2003). They suggested that the hedonic and utilitarian components are two distinct dimensions. The utilitarian dimension in their model is derived from functions performed by products, and the hedonic dimension deals with sensations derived from the experience of using products.

The interplay between utilitarian and hedonic benefits has gained importance in recent years. It has been related to, for instance, shopping motivations (Arnold & Reynolds, 2003; Babin, Darden & Griffin, 1994), product preferences (Chitturi, Raghunathan & Mahajan, 2007), consumer attitude toward brand extensions (Czellar, 2002), consumer choice (Dhar & Wertenbroch, 2000; Okada, 2005) and post consumption experience (Chitturi, Raghunathan & Mahajan, 2008). In her article on brand personality, Aaker (1997) used a framework similar to the hedonic-utilitarian distinction. She distinguished between symbolic product categories (e.g., jeans, cosmetics), utilitarian product categories (e.g., computers, appliances) and product categories with both utilitarian and symbolic aspects (e.g., automobiles, beverages or athletic shoes). Keller (2008) made a similar distinction, by identifying more functional, performance-related brand aspects and more intangible, image-related aspects. The brand performance aspects are related to the intrinsic properties of the brand, the attributes by which the product or service attempts to meet consumers' more functional needs. Brand imagery deals with the more intangible aspects of the brand, the ways in which the brand attempts to meet psychological or social needs. Psychological needs refer to the feelings or sensations the individual experiences through using the product; social needs involve the relation the individual wishes to express with respect to others. Whan Park, Jaworski and MacInnis (1986) used the distinction between psychological and social needs to distinguish three types of benefits:

1   A brand with functional benefits is designed to solve consumption-related needs, for instance, solve a current problem, prevent a potential problem, resolve conflict or restructure a frustrating situation.
2   Experiential needs create a desire for products that provide sensory stimulation, variety and/or cognitive stimulation. A brand providing experiential benefits is designed to fulfil these hedonic desires. This type of brand was emphasized in Pine and Gilmore's influential publication *The Experience Economy* (1999). Central to this publication is the notion that a brand ought to provide an experience to people by entertaining or engaging customers, and by connecting with them in a personal, memorable way.
3   Symbolic benefits are outer-directed. These benefits enable people to express how they relate to each other: a brand expressing symbolic benefits is designed to associate the individual with a desired group, or role. Consumers may value the prestige, exclusivity or fashionability of a brand to express a certain status position. Alternatively, a consumer can pursue brands to express group membership, to stimulate social connections or the consumer may value brands because these brands help him to express that he cares for friends or family.

Whan Park *et al.* (1986) argue that, although product classes are often assigned to one of these three categories, any brand can be positioned with a functional, symbolic or experiential image. For instance, cars can be seen as functional, but car brands can also profile experiential benefits ('fun to drive') or symbolic benefits (e.g., the exclusivity or prestige value of the car).

Brand values

Keller (2008, p. 66) explicitly stated that brands can take on values similar to people. These brand values have been considered the primary building blocks of the brand image (Kotler, Kartajaya & Setiawan, 2010). Brand values have become essential in the profiling of many brands, as was evident from the examples we mentioned in the introduction. But how should we interpret these brand values?

In its traditional sense, marketing focuses on an exchange process: people spend scarce resources (money, time) in exchange for goods (products or services) because of the benefits they expect to receive from these goods. These benefits are related to functional attributes or to image-related characteristics of the product, and can be functional, experiential or symbolic. As we saw in the previous section, the desirability of these benefits is determined by consumer values (Gutman, 1982): benefits are considered favourable (attractive) or unfavourable, depending on the value priorities of the consumer.

Vargo and Lusch (2004, 2008) argued that a shift in marketing logic is emerging, from the exchange of tangible resources toward what they call the service-dominant logic. In this logic, products or services do not supply any value, only a value proposition. Within this logic, the vision on the brand was further developed in the brand value co-creation model (Merz, He & Vargo, 2009). Central to this model is the idea that a brand constitutes a collaborative, value co-creation activity involving the firm and its stakeholders. For instance, Gillette is not relevant to the consumer because it is a supplier of razor blades: the razor blade in itself does not create a smooth skin. Gillette is relevant because the brand promises a smooth skin: the razor blade enables the user to create a smooth skin by shaving himself. In doing so, it replaces the direct service provided by a barber. Consequently, value is created because of the interaction between the consumer and the product. Only by using the razor blade, the customer 'co-creates' the value (smooth skin) proposed by the firm. Therefore, a firm cannot deliver value, but only offer value propositions. It is up to the consumer to use the good in order to create something that is valuable to him.

In the example, Gillette, as the supplier of razor blades, promises the potential of a smooth skin to the consumer. This proposed value can be of importance to the consumer, for instance, if he believes that a smooth skin makes him more attractive, or gives him the professional looks needed for his professional life. If impressing others by attractive or professional looks are important values for the consumer, then the proposed smooth skin is relevant. This relevance motivates the consumer to buy the razor blades, and subsequently to use them to co-create the desired value: the attractive, smooth-skinned appearance. Hence, the values proposed by Gillette (attractive appearance, professional looks) are relevant to the consumer if they match the values he considers important in his life.

The example illustrates the importance of a match between the values proposed by the brand and the values central to the consumer. Consumers can be expected to look for brands that embody the values they consider relevant. Hence, a brand can be described in terms of the values it promises:

Brand values form the perceived value proposition of the brand. They represent the values that are promised by the brand.

Values were defined previously as guiding principles, motivating people to make choices in order to achieve desirable goals. Brand values then represent the perceived contribution of the brand in achieving these goals: the consumer is motivated to buy or use a brand if he believes that its brand values are in line with the goals he wishes to achieve.

The brand value profile

Schwartz (1992) demonstrated that values are related to each other, and that they can be systematically organized in a value system. A value system is a psychological structure, referring to the organization of the values that people use to judge or motivate their behaviour. Brands, however, do not qualify as living beings. They are inanimate, and, obviously, do not exhibit any kind of value-motivated behaviour. But then, why does it make sense to consider brand values? And even if it makes sense, is it possible that brand values can be organized into a meaningful value system?

We already showed that brands propose values, which can be 'released' when the consumer uses the brand, as was illustrated with the example of the razor blade. Research has also shown that consumers perceive brands in human terms. They attribute human characteristics or human goals to brands based on their observations of and experiences with the brand over time (Aaker, 1997; Aggarwal & McGill, 2007). The personification of brands can become so strong that people engage in a relationship with brands, wherein they perceive the brand as a viable relationship partner (Aaker, Fournier & Brasel, 2004; Fournier, 1998). Personification can be illustrated with examples such as the description of the brand Absolut Vodka: '*A cool, hip, contemporary 25-year old*' (Aaker, 1997, p. 347).

If consumers attribute human characteristics or human goals to brands, then we can also expect them to perceive human values in brands. The attribution of human values to other entities was illustrated by Rohan (2000). She argued that individuals hold perceptions of the value systems of others, based on their judgements of others, and that these value systems are expected to be organized in a structure similar to their own value system. She highlighted that the others can be other individuals, but that also groups can be described in terms of the values they endorse or promote. Groups were broadly defined by Rohan; they comprise '*clubs, religious congregations, corporations, societies, cultures*' (p. 265). Although she didn't include brands in this description, the examples she gave suggest that the definition of group can be extended to brands as well. This implies that brands can be described in terms of their value system. An example of how brands can be perceived as a group is the brand community. A brand community is a specialized community based on a structured set of social relationships among admirers of a brand (Muniz & O'Guinn, 2001). In a brand community, for instance, the Facebook community of Harley Davidson, the brand can be considered a platform embodying the values shared by the members of the community.

Concluding, we expect consumers to hold perceptions of the brand value system, and perceive it along similar lines to their own value system. Hence, we expect this brand value system, the perceived value proposition of the brand, to be structured like the consumer's value system.

Proposition 3:
The structure of the brand value system, the perceived value proposition of the brand, is similar to the structure of the consumer's value system.

A number of marketing studies attempted to conceptualize brand values. In a qualitative study on shared values in brand communities of Australian extreme sports subcultures, the involvement with the subculture was assessed by examining the degree to which brands reflect certain core values of individuals (Quester, Beverland & Farrelly, 2006). Another study assessed the taste perception of individuals (Allen, Gupta & Monnier, 2008). One's impression of the tastiness of a food or a beverage could be an objective assessment: the chemical properties of the product stimulate taste receptors in the mouth, resulting in taste perception. This study showed, however, that people experienced a better taste and aroma, and developed a more favourable attitude and behaviour intention, when the values symbolized by the product corresponded with their own value priorities. A study by Limon, Kahle and Orth (2009) demonstrated that consumers derived brand values from the packaging of the brand. This study showed that purchase intentions were based on these inferred brand values. Alsem, Wieringa and Hendriks (2007) demonstrated that newspaper subscriptions in the Netherlands are related to a match between the values of the subscriber and the values profiled by the newspaper. In services marketing, a couple of studies used the values associated with mobile phone services (Lages & Fernandes, 2005), or financial services and clothes stores (Zhang & Bloemer, 2008, 2011) to assess the relationship between the consumer and a brand.

The previously mentioned study of Torelli et al. (2012) gave an empirical confirmation of Proposition 3. This study showed that brand values follow the same structure of compatible and conflicting values as was derived by Schwartz for the human value system. In their study, Torelli et al. grouped a number of brands according to the two dimensions of Schwartz's value system. For instance, Gucci and BMW were profiled as brands with a self-enhancement concept. Torelli et al. showed that values are useful in predicting which brand meanings can be added to an already existing brand structure, for instance, adding a slogan with self-enhancement aspects such as status and prestige strengthens a brand with a self-enhancement concept. The study also demonstrated that a match between brand concept and personal value orientation made people like the brand more. For instance, an individual higher in self-enhancement values will have a higher liking for a brand with a self-enhancement concept such as BMW or Gucci.

Some of the studies mentioned above point out that the presence of brand values influences the perception of the brand, and thus the attitude toward the brand, or that they influence the purchase intention. The relation between brand values, brand attitude and brand behaviour, is addressed in the next section. But, before turning to this section, we would like to point out that the studies mentioned here used unmodified versions of Schwartz's value system (Allen, Gupta & Monnier, 2008; Torelli *et al.*, 2012; Zhang & Bloemer, 2008, 2011) or the List of Values (Lages & Fernandes, 2005; Limon, Kahle & Orth, 2009) to conceptualize brand values. In Section 2.5, however, we argued that, for the analysis of consumer behaviour, it is preferable to use a value system activated toward consumer choice. And Proposition 3 concludes that brand values are also perceived according to the structure of this value system.

2.7 The relation between brand values and consumer behaviour

Several marketing studies link characteristics of a brand (e.g., its hedonic or utilitarian aspects), the overall evaluation of the brand (through indicators of attitude or attitude-related concepts), and the resulting behaviour or behavioural intention. Examples of these studies include Brakus, Schmitt and Zarantonello (2009), Carroll and Ahuvia (2006), Chaudhuri and Holbrook (2001), Dick and Basu (1994), Edson Escalas and Bettmann (2005), Grundlach, Achrol and Mentzer (1995), Kressmann *et al.* (2006), McAlexander, Schouten and Koenig (2002), Sprott, Sandor and Spangenberg (2009), Thomson, MacInnis and Whan Park (2005), Yoo and Donthu (2001) and Zhang and Bloemer (2008).

The conceptualizations used in these studies often follow a mechanism resembling the attitude-behaviour relationship as described in the reasoned action approach (Ajzen, 1991; Ajzen & Fishbein, 2005; Fishbein & Ajzen, 1975). Therefore, we briefly describe the reasoned action approach below. Figure 2.2 presents a schematic representation of this approach.

In the theory of reasoned action, the intention to engage in a certain behaviour is determined by the overall evaluation (*attitude*) toward the behaviour. This attitude depends on the expectations about the outcomes of the behaviour (*behavioural beliefs*), which vary from person to person, and from situation to situation, as a result of a wide range of *background factors*, including individual (e.g., personality, mood, personal value priorities, age), social (e.g., education, culture) or informational (e.g., knowledge, influence through media) aspects. *Subjective norms,* resulting from *normative beliefs,* influence the extent to which the overall attitude translates into an intention: perceived social or societal approval (or disapproval) exerts pressure to engage in (or refrain from) the behaviour.

The following example illustrates this theory for a consumer choice context. An individual needs to travel to his job. He considers himself environmentally responsible, but lack of public transport implies that he needs to have a car

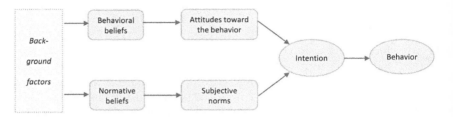

Figure 2.2 Theory of reasoned action

(background factors). He believes, partly due to media exposure and a visit to the showroom, that driving a Toyota Prius would fulfil his needs (behavioural beliefs): The Toyota Prius is a safe, functionally styled hybrid car with a relatively low level of gas consumption. Therefore, he develops a positive attitude toward buying a Toyota Prius, resulting in an intention to buy the car. This intention is positively influenced by the approval of his wife and his friends, but also by the importance of environmental-conscious behaviour in our society (subjective norms).

Buying intention serves as a proxy to real behaviour. In the example, the translation of intention into actual behaviour depends on constraints such as the availability of the desired car or the availability of the necessary budget. It is beyond the scope of many studies to measure the actual behaviour of individuals. The intention to engage in a certain behaviour then is frequently used as a proxy for real behaviour, under the assumption that this behaviour can be predicted with reasonable accuracy from the intention (Ajzen & Fishbein, 2005). Despite the existence of a wide variety of interfering external factors, the assumed intention-behaviour relation is supported by empirical evidence. A meta-analysis of a large number of studies shows an average correlation of 0.53 between intention and behaviour (Sheeran, 2002).

Marketing studies that try to explain behaviour often focus on the relationship between the customer and the brand. The operationalization of this relationship follows a mechanism similar to the one specified in the theory of reasoned action: a stronger relation with the brand implies a more favourable attitude toward the brand, resulting in a more positive (re)purchase intention. In Chaudhuri and Holbrook (2001), for instance, favourable brand attitude results in a certain level of commitment of the consumer toward the brand. The behavioural intention – the intention to purchase or use the brand – is a consequence of this commitment. Other studies focusing on the attitude-behaviour relationship include Bandyopadhyay and Martell (2007), Carroll and Ahuvia (2006), Kressman *et al.* (2006), and Thomson, MacInnis and Whan Park (2005). The attitudinal and behavioural component of the customer–brand relationship is discussed in the following overview.

Brand attachment: indicator for the attitude toward the brand

The level of commitment of the consumer toward a brand reflects the relation between the consumer and a brand. Brand commitment has been defined as the enduring desire to maintain a valued relationship with a brand (Chaudhuri & Holbrook, 2001), or an attachment to the goals and values of the brand (Grundlach, Achrol & Mentzer, 1995). Attachment reflects an affective bond between a person and a specific object (Bowlby, 1979). The stronger one's attachment to an object, the more likely one is to maintain proximity to the object. Emotional attachment is used here as indicator for the relationship toward the brand: people can develop a relationship with a brand if they feel attached to the brand (Thomson, MacInnis & Whan Park, 2005). A stronger attachment results in a higher purchase intention, which in turn increases the chances that the actual purchase takes place. Thomson *et al.* (2005) showed that brand attachment consists of three dimensions: affection, passion and connection. A stronger attachment is associated with stronger feelings of connection, affection and passion. These dimensions have received frequent attention in recent literature, and are discussed below.

Brand affect

Brand affect reflects the warm feelings a consumer has toward a brand (Thomson *et al.*, 2005), and has been shown to be an important predictor of brand loyalty (Chaudhuri & Holbrook, 2001). The affect toward an object (e.g., brand) can be measured by a unidimensional attitude scale reflecting the overall like or dislike to the object (Wilkie & Pessemier, 1973). Interpreting brand affect in terms of *like* or *dislike* parallels the use of these words in Facebook and other social media. Facebook, for instance, created the possibility of expressing the overall evaluation toward an object, organization, or person, by clicking the like-button.

Brand passion or brand love

Brand love is defined as the degree of passionate emotional attachment that a satisfied consumer has for a particular brand (Carroll & Ahuvia, 2006). Brand love is a more intense emotional response than brand affect, involving an integration of the brand into the consumer's sense of identity. Carroll and Ahuvia demonstrated that brand love is positively related to both purchase intention and positive word-of-mouth.

Brand connection

Consumers sometimes create strong connections between themselves and a brand. Brands can be used to create and reinforce the consumer's identity (Belk,

1988; Richins, 1994). They can also serve a social purpose: individuals can present themselves to others through their brand choices (Edson Escalas & Bettman, 2005). The following two constructs express the connection between the self and the brand:

1 Brand community: The relation between the brand, the individual and other users or buyers of the brand.
2 Brand engagement: The relation between the brand and the individual.

A brand community has been defined as 'a specialized, non-geographically bound community, based on a structured set of social relationships among admirers of a brand' (Muniz & O'Guinn, 2001, p. 412). A community is made up of its member entities and the relationships among them (McAlexander, Schouten & Koenig, 2002). The first and most important element of a community is consciousness of kind: members of a brand community feel an important connection to the brand, but also a strong connection toward other users of the brand (Muniz & O'Guinn, 2001). Through communities, members share essential resources that may be cognitive, emotional or material in nature. An example is Lugnet, the global community of Lego User Groups (Lugnet, 2012). In these user groups, Lego enthusiasts share ideas or experiences, exchange Lego toys, or share their passion for the brand. McAlexander et al. (2002) recognized that, with the rise of mass media, communities are no longer bound by geographic restrictions. The rising importance of social media increases the importance of (virtual) communities. This emphasizes the importance of inclusion of brand community in the brand attachment construct.

Brands can do more than create a connection with others; they also have the potential to become an integrated part of one's identity (Edson Escalas & Bettman, 2005). The study of Edson Escalas and Bettman demonstrated that these self-brand connections exist and that they lead to favourable brand attitudes. Self-brand connections have been referred to as brand engagement (Keller, 2003; Sprott, Sandor & Spangenberg, 2009). Brand engagement is the extent to which individuals include important brands as part of their self-concept. Sprott et al. (2009) demonstrated that brand engagement affects important aspects of brand-related consumer attitudes and behaviour.

Intention to buy or use the brand

Brand attachment is expected to increase behavioural intentions toward the brand: a stronger relationship with the brand increases the probability that one is willing to buy the brand, or talk in a positive way about the brand. Indicators of brand behaviour include the intention to buy or use the brand, as well as items referring to word-of-mouth (Carroll & Ahuvia, 2006; Kressmann et al., 2006). Word-of-mouth is mentioned by Dick and Basu (1994) as an important consequence of the consumer-brand relationship. Carroll and Ahuvia (2006) demonstrated that brand love results in positive word-of-mouth. Since the publication of the article *The one number you need to grow* (Reichheld, 2003), the concept of word-of mouth has received a lot of managerial attention. Reichheld advocates that the Net Promoter Score is the most important indicator that a manager needs to know to measure customer loyalty. The Net Promoter Score is measured by one question: '*How likely is it that you would recommend our company to a friend or colleague?*'

Brand values and brand behaviour

This study focuses on the relevance of values for consumer behaviour. Brands can be characterized by their brand values, which were defined as the perceived value proposition of the brand. Framed in the context of the theory of reasoned action, the values proposed by the brand can be considered behavioural beliefs: consumers believe to acquire these values through buying or using the brand. If the values promised by the brand are important to consumers, then we expect them to develop a favourable attitude toward the brand, which in turn motivates them to buy or use the brand. We proposed buying intention and word-of-mouth as proxy to consumer behaviour.

Proposition 4 expresses the proposed relation between brand values and the consumer-brand relationship:

Proposition 4:
Brand values stimulate the relationship between the consumer and the brand by creating an emotional attachment to the brand. Brand attachment, in turn, results in an intention to buy or use the brand.

2.8 Value congruence stimulates consumer behaviour

Following the publication of Rokeach's value system, a couple of articles suggested that values, being deep rooted beliefs, influence consumer behaviour through their impact on the evaluation of product attributes (Valette-Florence, 1986; Vinson, Scott & Lamont, 1977). This can be illustrated with the example of a sturdy SUV such as a Land Rover. A person who values excitement, independence and freedom, will appreciate the four-wheel drive and sturdy appearance of a SUV. The positive evaluation of these product attributes results in a positive attitude toward SUVs, which in turn will influence choice behaviour.

In Section 2.6, Gutman's means-end chain model was introduced. This model comprises two central linkages: the linkage between product attributes and benefits, and the linkage between benefits and values. Benefits are derived in this model from product attributes. They are the desirable consequences consumers wish to enjoy from the products they consume. Consumer values provide these consequences with meaning: benefits are considered more desirable or less desirable (or even undesirable), depending on the value system of the consumer. Consumers choose brands that produce desired consequences and minimize undesired consequences. Since value priorities are ordered by importance (Rokeach, 1973; Schwartz, 2006), values also give importance to benefits. Some benefits have a more central (positive or negative) meaning to the consumer than other benefits. The extent to which certain benefits are important and desired influences the selection of brands.

Two approaches help to understand the influence of values on behaviour:

1   An approach derived from expectancy-value theory. According to expectancy-value theory, a choice alternative in a decision situation is evaluated by a number of beliefs one has concerning the outcomes of the alternative.
2   An approach used in marketing literature, based on self-congruence. Self-congruence refers to the match between the consumer's self-concept, and the image of a given product or brand (Sirgy, 1982).

In Section 2.7 we found that brand values stimulate the relationship between the consumer and the brand. In this section, we create a deeper understanding of the mechanism through which values stimulate the consumer-brand relationship, by exploring the expectancy-value approach and the congruence approach.

Expectancy-value theory and values

Expectancy-value theory explains how attitudes are formed. It stipulates that a choice alternative in a decision situation is characterized by a number of beliefs one has concerning its outcomes (Fishbein & Ajzen, 1975). In a consumer context, for instance, the choice for a certain brand involves beliefs about the benefits that this brand will generate. The attractiveness of the brand then is characterized by the perceived likelihood that each benefit results as an outcome, combined with the perceived attractiveness of the benefit. This results in the following equation (Fishbein & Ajzen, 1975):

The attractiveness of a choice alternative involving n salient beliefs is proportional to

$$\sum_{i=1}^{n} \left(b_i \times e_i \right)$$

Where: b_i = the strength of belief i (the perceived likelihood of the occurrence of belief i),
e_i = the evaluation (perceived attractiveness) of belief i.

Means-end theory can be considered a variant of the expectancy-value theory (Reynolds & Gutman, 1988). The common premise of both theories is that consumers prefer alternatives believed to contain attributes leading to desired consequences. Means-end theory, however, specifies the reason that certain consequences are more desirable than others, namely, personal values: as mentioned above, means-end theory stipulates that values provide consequences (benefits) with meaning. In other words, means-end theory specifies that personal values determine the perceived attractiveness of the beliefs about a brand.

As we saw in the previous section, brand values can be considered behavioural beliefs; they represent the likelihood that a certain value actually is 'released' when the consumer uses the brand. The strength of a brand value then is the strength of the belief that this value is embedded in the brand. Not all brand values are equally desirable. As suggested by means-end theory, whether the brand value is considered as more or as less favourable to the consumer will depend on his value system. For instance, a brand such as Disney can be expected to promote family values. A person who values family life (or other family values) will then likely consider Disney a more attractive brand. Concluding, the attractiveness of a brand for a consumer is characterized by the brand values it promises, combined with the perceived attractiveness of each value to the consumer. This leads to the following adaptation of the equation:

The attractiveness of a brand that proposes n brand values is proportional to

$$\sum_{i=1}^{n} \left(b_i \times e_i \right)$$

Where: b_i = the strength of brand value i (perceived likelihood that the brand represents value i),

e_i = the perceived attractiveness of value i to the consumer.

Expectancy-value theory thus helps us to understand how values have an influence on the choices we make, by influencing the attractiveness of a choice alternative. A number of studies demonstrated a values-behaviour relation. Bardi and Schwartz (2003), for instance, revealed substantial correlations between most values and their corresponding behaviour. For instance, a person who values achievement is more likely to engage in behaviour through which he can achieve something, but less likely to engage in universalist or benevolent behaviour such as helping others or protecting the environment. Feather (1995) used scenarios evidently connected to certain values to demonstrate the influence of values on behaviour. In one scenario, for instance, he confronted *self-direction* and *stimulation* values with *conformity* values, by presenting respondents with a situation in which a fictitious person during a weekend camp-out has to decide whether to explore a path leading from the camp on his or her own, or to stay in the camp with the group. Feather specified the choices in such a way that values were logically implied by the description of the choice alternative. Feather assumed, for instance, that exploring the path leading away from the camp was related to *self-direction* and *stimulation*. He didn't ask the respondent to what extent he believed that the choice was related to these values.

In the case of consumer choice, this approach is feasible where it comes to product categories closely tied to specific values, such as fair trade products or donating to charity. For instance, a study on fair trade consumption showed that this type of consumption is stimulated by universalism values (equality, unity with nature, protecting the environment), whereas power and achievement values correlate negatively with fair trade consumption (Doran, 2009). Other studies related personal values with leisure travel style (Madrigal, 1995), consumption of genetically modified food (Honkanen & Verplanken, 2004), or donating to charity (Maio & Olson, 1995). For most product categories, however, brands have the potential to activate a variety of values, and these brand values can be perceived differently, depending on the individual and the situation. For instance, a beer can represent social values when consumed in a pub with friends, but hedonic enjoyment (a moment for yourself) when consumed on the couch at home. The attractiveness of a brand then depends on the match between the perceived value propositions of the brand, for a certain individual in a certain context, with the value priorities of that individual in that context. This match can be examined with self-congruence theory (Sirgy, 1982). According to this theory, an assessment of the attractiveness of a choice alternative (e.g., a brand) can be made by matching characteristics of the alternative with characteristics of the individual. In the following overview, self-congruence theory is applied to value priorities.

Value congruence

Possessions can be considered a major contributor to and reflection of our identities: possessions, and thus the products and services we buy, can be regarded as an extended self (Belk, 1988; Fournier, 1998). This implies an interpretation of consumer behaviour as a means to create or support the consumer's identity. At least two motivating mechanisms have been identified that cause the need to construct our identity through our brand choices: the need for self-esteem, and the need for self-consistency (Sirgy, 1982). The self-esteem motive refers to the tendency to seek experiences that improve the opinion one has of oneself. The self-consistency motive denotes the tendency for an individual to behave consistently with his own self-perception. These motives lead to choices that support the consumer's personal identity, but they also motivate choices that help the consumer present himself to others (Edson Escalas & Bettman, 2005).

Choice behaviour, therefore, relates to the individual's self-concept: consumer behaviour is aimed at obtaining goods, which represent the same image (Kressmann *et al.*, 2006; Sirgy, 1982), the same personality (Aaker, Fournier, & Brasel, 2004) or the same values (Richins, 1994) as we see (or want to see) in ourselves. This has been labelled self-congruence, self-image congruence or image congruence (Sirgy, 1982; Kressmann *et al.*, 2006): the consumer tries to find a match between his self-image and the image of the brand. Self-congruence implies congruence between the associations that the consumer has with the brand, and the perception that the consumer has of himself (his self-concept).

A number of mathematical models have been developed to express self-congruence (Kressmann *et al.*, 2006; Sirgy, 1982; Sirgy, Grewal, Mangleburg, Park, Chon, Claiborne & Berkman, 1997). The basic form of these models is (Sirgy *et al.*, 1997):

$$\text{self-congruence} = \frac{\sum_{i=1}^{n}\left(BI_i - SI_i\right)}{n}$$

Where: BI_i = brand image aspect i,
         SI = self-image aspect i,
         n = number of image aspects.

Several studies propose or document a link between self-congruence and consumer behaviour. Examples include the influence of self-congruity on brand loyalty for cars (Kressmann *et al.*, 2006), and the proposed relation between self-congruity and shopping behaviour (Sirgy, Grewal & Mangleburg, 2000). Tourist travel behaviour was also found to be influenced by self-congruence (Beerli, Diaz Meneses & Moreno Gil, 2007; Sirgy & Su, 2000): the greater the agreement between a destination's image and one's self-concept, the greater the tendency for the tourist to visit that place.

The match between the values of the consumer and the perceived brand values is defined here as brand value congruence, or short value congruence. The concept of value congruence appeared in social psychology literature. For instance, a study by Gaunt (2006) showed that greater value congruence between partners leads to higher levels of marital satisfaction. In organizational behaviour literature, value congruence studies are used frequently: value congruence between organizational values and employee values, or between supervisor values and employee values, has been demonstrated to yield higher job satisfaction (e.g., Kristof-Brown, Zimmerman & Johnson, 2005; Meglino, Ravlin & Adkins, 1989). In marketing literature, so far, the concept of value congruence received little attention. Although the studies mentioned in Section 2.6 (Allen, Gupta & Monnier, 2008; Alsem, Wieringa & Hendriks, 2007; Lages & Fernandes, 2005; Limon, Kahle & Orth, 2009; Quester, Beverland &

Farrelly, 2006; Torelli *et al.*, 2012; Zhang & Bloemer, 2008, 2011) explore the fit between personal values and brand values, only the studies of Alsem *et al.* (2007) and Zhang and Bloemer (2008, 2011) explicitly refer to value congruence. For clothing stores and banks in the Netherlands, the studies of Zhang and Bloemer reported significant influence of value congruence on the quality of the consumer-brand relationship (affective commitment, trust and satisfaction) and on purchase intentions. They used Schwartz's value system to assess personal values and brand values. Proposition 2, however, pointed out that value activation is context-specific. For the evaluation of the effect of value congruence on consumer choice, the use of a value system activated toward the consumer choice context is preferred. To our knowledge, attempts to assess the impact of value congruence with a specific brand value system have not yet been reported.

Values play a central role in people's cognitive structure; they motivate people to choose, or to act. We previously showed that brands offer a value proposition (Proposition 3), indicating to the consumer how the brand can assist him in achieving his personal goals. According to the congruence principle, this depends on the match between the values proposed by the brand (the brand values) and the values central to the individual. Brands are more relevant to the consumer if there is a better match between the values represented by the brand and the values that are central to the consumer. This leads them to value-congruent choice behaviour.

> **Proposition 5:**
> **Brand attachment is stronger with a stronger match between the consumer's value system and the perceived brand value profile. This value congruence is more relevant when values are more central to the consumer.**

The relations expressed by Proposition 4 and 5 can be graphically represented with the brand value model (BVM) presented in Figure 2.3. The BVM illustrates that, in line with Proposition 4, brand values stimulate the intention to buy or use the brand, or to spread positive word-of mouth about it. The relation between brand values and buying intentions is mediated by the emotional attachment to the brand: favourable brand values result in a higher brand attachment, which, in turn, results in higher buying intentions. As was described in Section 2.7, four types of indicators can be used to measure brand attachment: brand affect, brand love, brand community and brand engagement. These indicators are included in Figure 2.3.

According to Proposition 5, the value congruence effect is expected to influence the relation between brand values and brand attachment. This is expressed by the dotted arrow in Figure 2.3.

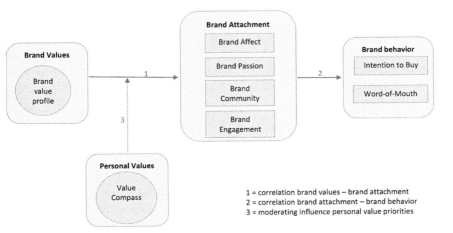

Figure 2.3 The brand value model

To summarize, the BVM includes a number of causally related constructs. The following four constructs are central to the model:

- Each brand is assumed to have a *brand value profile*. The brand value profile is the perceived value proposition of the brand, the combination of values the consumer expects to be embedded in the brand.
- Each consumer has a *Value Compass* motivating his actions and choices. The Value Compass is the value system that guides him in choosing between brands, or in the other choices he has to make as a consumer.
- *Brand attachment* represents the relation of the consumer with the brand.
- The intention to buy the brand and the intended word-of-mouth are used as indicators for *brand behaviour*, the behavioural intention toward the brand.

Three linkages connect these four constructs. First, there is a positive correlation between brand values and brand attachment: brands promising a higher value content are expected to generate a higher brand attachment. Next, a stronger attachment to a brand reflects a stronger perceived relationship with the brand, creating a higher willingness to buy the brand, or to spread positive word-of-mouth, as expressed by linkage 2. Finally, the third linkage symbolizes the effect of value congruence.

2.9 Brand values versus brand personality

Values and personality traits are concepts derived from psychology. Values refer to what people consider important; personality traits describe what people are like. Both psychologic concepts have been applied to brands: 'brands may take on personality traits and values similar to those of people' (Keller, 2008, p. 66). Since the publication of Aaker's brand personality framework (1997), brand personality has been a dominant brand concept in marketing literature. This section introduces the personality concept, and discusses the similarities and differences between personality and values, and how this influences the way they can be applied in a branding context.

Values and personality

The dominant approach in personality research is a trait approach, as was expressed in its most basic form by Guilford's definition of personality: personality is *'the individual's unique pattern of traits'* (Guilford, 1959, p. 5). A trait is defined here as *'any distinguishable, relatively enduring way in which one individual differs from others'* (p. 6). The core elements in personality theory include the following aspects (McCrae & Costa, 1996):

1   Basic tendencies.
2   Characteristic adaptations.
3   Self-concept.
4   Objective biography.
5   External influences.

Basic tendencies are the universal raw material of personality, unaffected by the environment. They include genetically determined elements such as physical characteristics (like length or eye colour) or physiological drives (e.g., need for food, need for oxygen or sexual drive). Personality traits are basic tendencies. *Characteristic adaptations* are acquired skills, habits, beliefs, attitudes, behaviours and relationships, which result from the interaction between individual and environment. They are the concrete manifestations of the basic tendencies: people react to their environment with thoughts, feelings and behaviours, which are consistent with their personality traits. Values, according to McCrae and Costa (1996), are considered characteristic adaptations. An individual's *self-concept* refers to the (implicit or explicit) views that an individual has of himself. This self-concept makes up the identity of a person. In marketing, a similar notion is used to describe the identity of a brand: the brand concept is the particular combination of attributes, benefits and marketing efforts used to translate these benefits into the brand's identity (Whan Park, Jaworski & MacInnis, 1986). The *objective biography* describes every significant thing a person did during his life. Finally, every person is subject to *external influences*, which help to shape the person. Characteristic adaptations (including values) are subject to these external influences.

There is a broad consensus in literature that personality traits can be classified according to five basic factors (Costa & McCrae, 1992; Goldberg, 1981), which are popularly referred to as the Big Five:

- *Openness*: appreciation for *art, emotion, adventure*, unusual ideas, *imagination, curiosity* and variety of experience.
- *Conscientiousness*: a tendency to show *self-discipline*, act *dutifully* and aim for *achievement*; planned rather than spontaneous behaviour.
- *Extraversion*: energy, positive emotions, *surgency* and the tendency to seek *stimulation* and the company of others.
- *Agreeableness*: a tendency to be *compassionate* and *cooperative* rather than *suspicious* and *antagonistic* toward others.
- *Neuroticism* (as opposed to *emotional stability*): a tendency to experience unpleasant emotions, such as *anger, anxiety, depression* or *vulnerability*.

The above description demonstrates that both personality traits and values are core elements of personality theory. Nonetheless, conceptual differences between values and personality traits support their separate treatment. People may explain behaviour by referring to traits or to values, but they refer to their values when they wish to justify choices or actions as legitimate or worthy in the attainment of a desirable goal: values serve as standards for judging the behaviour of the self and of others. Personality traits, on the other hand, describe a person and his or her capacities and abilities; they do not represent behavioural standards. A brief review of the conceptual differences and relations between personality traits and value priorities is given below. It is based on a comparison of the Five-Factor Model with Schwartz's value theory.

Origins

Personality traits are basic tendencies, enduring dispositions arising from genetically or physiologically determined elements. The origins of the personality traits in the Five-Factor Model have been traced to evolutionary adaptation to the environment. Following Turkheimer's (2000) first law of behaviour genetics (*All human behavioural traits are heritable*), variation in personality traits express viable evolutionary strategies to deal with the environment (Buss, 1996; Penke, Denissen & Miller, 2007). Values, on the other hand, have been learned by the individual (Olver & Mooradian, 2003). They reflect the strategies that people adopted to cope with biological needs and social or institutional demands (Schwartz & Bilsky, 1987; Schwartz, 2006). Individual differences in value priorities derive from each person's unique combination of biological endowments, in combination with the demands placed on the individual by his environment.

Content

Values refer to what people consider important. They are the guiding principles motivating action to pursue desirable goals. Traits, on the other hand, describe what people are like, rather than the intentions behind their behaviour (Roccas,

Sagiv, Schwartz & Knafo, 2002). The same term (e.g., ambition, honesty, efficiency) may refer either to a trait or a value, but the two references have different meanings. People who value a certain goal do not necessarily exhibit the corresponding trait; nor do those who exhibit a trait necessarily value the corresponding goal. For example, the trait *efficiency* refers to the frequency and intensity of efficient actions that an individual exhibits. The value *efficiency* refers to the importance that an individual attributes to being efficient. Not all individuals who consider efficiency as an important value have the ability to be efficient. In addition, people who are highly efficient do not automatically view efficiency as a core value to be pursued as a guiding principle in their lives. They happen to be efficient, but they do not necessarily consider efficiency important.

Structure

According to Schwartz's value theory, values are structured as a dynamic system of compatible and conflicting values. As was explained in Section 2.3, this system can be displayed as a circular structure. Values sharing compatible motivational goals correlate positively, and emerge in close proximity in this circular structure. Values expressing conflicting motivational goals correlate less positively, or even negatively and appear in opposing directions in this structure. The relations between personality traits in the Five-Factor Model, in contrast, are not specified. Personality traits were originally treated as independent factors (e.g., Goldberg, 1992), although some other studies point to interrelations among the factors (e.g., Hofstee, De Raad & Goldberg, 1992; John, Naumann & Soto, 2008) or the existence of higher order factors (Digman, 1997).

Comprehensiveness

The value system developed by Schwartz, as well as the Five-Factor Model, aim at comprehensive coverage. They do not seek to specify every single value or trait, but they claim to represent all basic factors that organize human traits, or all the guiding principles that motivate human behaviour.

Universality

An analysis of McCrae and Costa (1997) demonstrated that the structure of five basic factors of personality can be found in different cultures across the globe. Similarly, research in various cultures found supportive evidence for the cross-cultural validity of Schwartz's value theory (Schwartz, 1994; Schwartz, Melech, Lehmann, Burgess, Harris, Owens, 2001). Hence, the relative stability across cultural contexts is a common element of both psychological constructs (Roccas, Sagiv, Schwartz & Knafo, 2002).

Brand values and brand personality

The personality construct has been applied to a branding context. Brand personality refers to the set of human characteristics associated with a brand (Aaker, 1997). Aaker developed a brand personality framework in which she identified five brand personality dimensions. By using an extensive quantitative study, she revealed a brand personality scale consisting of 42 personality traits that can be categorized according to 15 facets. These facets, in turn, reflect the five dimensions of brand personality (see Figure 2.4).

Some brands score high on a particular factor. Harley Davidson or Marlboro, for instance, are profiled as typical *ruggedness* brands, while Revlon excels on *sophistication*. Other brands have strengths in more than one aspect.

Human and brand personality share a similar conceptualization (Aaker, 1997), but there is an essential difference. Living human beings have a personality. Even though brand personality refers to the personality of a brand, inanimate

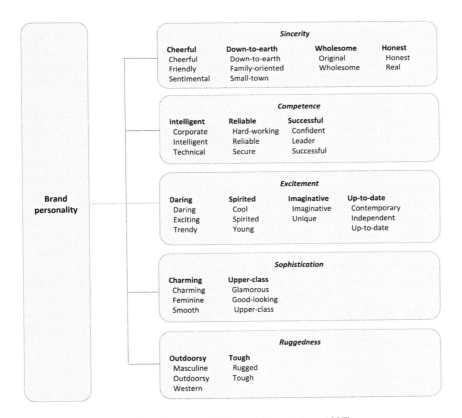

Figure 2.4 Brand personality framework (adapted from Aaker, 1997)

objects such as brands cannot be expected to have a proper personality, in the same way that brands cannot be expected to cherish certain values. Brand personality, therefore, relates to associations that people have with the brand. These perceptions of brand personality traits can be formed by any direct or indirect contact of the consumer with the brand.

Since Aaker's publication, the brand personality framework has received sizeable attention in marketing literature. Most recent studies on brand personality are based on Aaker's conceptualization of brand personality. In recent years, however, Aaker's scale has received criticism on several grounds (Austin, Siguaw & Mattila, 2003; Azoulay & Kapferer, 2003; Geuens, Weijters & De Wulf, 2009; Torelli *et al.*, 2012). The central focus of the criticism involves the problematic conceptual understanding of the personality construct in branding and the lack of universality of brand personality.

Characteristics of brands can be described by using analogies with human characteristics such as brand personality, brand values or brand relation. Although the word personality has a very specific meaning in psychology, its use in branding is rather loose (Azoulay & Kapferer, 2003). Aaker defined brand personality as '*the set of human characteristics associated with a brand*' (p. 347). Since inner values, physical traits, relationships or pictures of the typical user, are also human characteristics that can be associated with a brand, the risk of this more general definition is that empirically distinct brand constructs are included in a single brand personality construct (Azoulay & Kapferer, 2003).

Brand personality shows limited universality. A replication of the study in Japan and Spain showed that only three out of five dimensions apply in both countries. (Aaker, Benet-Martinez & Garolera, 2001). The ruggedness dimension is replaced in both Japan and Spain by a peacefulness dimension. In Spain, competence is replaced by a passion dimension. Lack of universality stimulated the development of country-specific brand personality instruments (Geuens, Weijters & De Wulf, 2009).

Concluding, it can be observed that, despite the relevance of values for branding, a systematic value system has not been incorporated into mainstream marketing literature. Instead, due to the general definition of brand personality, this *personality* construct is used occasionally as an indicator for *brand values*. Values and personality traits, however, are different concepts, each with their own characteristics. The conceptual differences between the two constructs therefore highlight the importance of investigating the benefits of applying a brand values construct to branding, as compared to the use of brand personality to characterize brands.

Proposition 6:
The brand values concept provides a meaningful alternative to the brand personality concept.

2.10 The value system as universal framework

One of the objections against the brand personality framework is its limited cross-cultural validity. If we wish to compare the use of brand values with brand personality, we need to take this cross-cultural aspect into consideration. Therefore, we devote attention here to a discussion on values as a human universal.

The question of the universality of psychological functions and processes reflects one of the most debated issues in cross-cultural psychology (Berry, Poortinga, Breugelmans, Chasiotis & Sam, 2011): to what extent are they common to humankind (universalism), and to what extent are they unique to specific cultural groups (relativism)? This question can also be raised with respect to values. Values were referred to previously, in Section 2.3, as reactions to three universal requirements (Schwartz & Bilsky, 1987): biological needs, social motives and institutional demands. But only our biological drives, being genetically determined, can be considered truly universal. Social and institutional demands are not identical across our planet. Hence, to what extent can we consider values a human universal? Different views are present. Authors like Triandis (1995), Markus and Kitayama (1991), and Hofstede (1980, 2011), emphasize differences between cultures. Some cultures, for instance, view the individual as an independent entity, with a unique configuration of internal attributes (e.g., abilities, traits or values). Such an environment might cultivate values that emphasize the person's individuality. In more collectivistic cultures, on the other hand, the contextual situation is emphasized, that is, the individual in relation to others. This stimulates the development of values emphasizing the interdependence of individuals. As opposed to the focus on cultural differences, Schwartz and Bilsky (1987), Schwartz (1992, 1994), Schwartz and Sagiv (1995), and more recently Fischer and Schwartz (2011), emphasize the cross-cultural similarities of the human value system.

Before elaborating on a cross-cultural comparison of value priorities, we first devote some attention to the influential study of Hofstede (1980, 2011). The importance of values in cross-cultural psychology was strongly influenced by this study. Hofstede defined culture as the '*collective programming of the mind that distinguishes the members of one group or category of people from others*' (Hofstede & Hofstede, 2005, p. 4) (Hofstede, 2011) thereby emphasizing the cultural differences between societies. Hofstede puts values at the core of culture. He categorizes societies based on five value orientations, to which he refers as dimensions of culture (Hofstede, 2011):

- *Power distance*, the extent to which the less powerful members of institutions and organizations within a society expect and accept that power is distributed unequally.
- *Individualism versus collectivism*, the extent to which a concern for oneself (everybody is expected to look after him- or herself) is valued in society, as opposed to a concern for the collectivity to which one belongs.

- *Masculinity versus femininity*, the extent to which masculine roles (e.g., performance, material success) or feminine roles (e.g., modesty, nurturance) are prevalent in a society.
- *Uncertainty avoidance*, the extent to which the members of a culture feel threatened by ambiguous or unknown situations.
- *Long-term versus short-term orientation*,[7] the extent to which a society values investing in the future versus values emphasizing the here and now.
- *Indulgence versus restraint*, related to the gratification versus control of basic human desires related to enjoying life.

In Hofstede's work, cultures are defined according to national boundaries. Each country is characterized by a score on each of the five dimensions. As an example, Figure 2.5 compares the cultural dimensions for Germany and the Netherlands, two neighbouring countries whose value profiles show many similarities. Both countries are individualistic, have low power distance, a moderate uncertainty avoidance (somewhat higher in Germany), and a predominantly short-term orientation (the Netherlands somewhat more long-term oriented). There is one striking difference between the two countries: Germany is a masculine country, whereas the Netherlands is strongly feminine. This can result in cultural differences such as a stronger emphasis on career, challenge and performance in Germany, and a stronger appraisal of leisure time, cooperative decision making and equality in the Netherlands.

Of all dimensions, individualism–collectivism is the most influential. The difference between individualism and collectivism lies in a primary concern for oneself, in contrast to a concern for the group(s) to which one belongs (Triandis, 1995). As was mentioned previously, individuality will be fostered in an individualistic culture. Consequences of individualism are, for example, priority of personal goals over group goals, an emphasis on exchange rather than on sharing and personal attitudes being more important for one's behaviour than social norms (Berry *et al.*, 2011).

The individualism–collectivism dimension, as well as the other dimensions identified by Hofstede, reflects societal values. Societal values are the solutions that different societies developed to regulate the human activities within a culture. This makes Hofstede's study a culture-level analysis. Classifying Germany as a postmodern masculine society says something about the prevailing values of the country; it does not, however, specify the value priorities of each German individual. Individuals and cultures are two different units of analysis (Berry *et al.*, 2011; Breugelmans, 2011; Van de Vijver & Leung, 1997). When cultural values are internalized, they become part of the psychological value structure of an individual (Breugelmans, 2011). This individual value structure is the focus of analysis in Schwartz's value theory. This value theory, therefore, is an individual-level analysis: the value system of compatible and conflicting value types was based on data collected from individuals. Similarly, when referring to the Value Compass, we emphasize the values motivating the behaviour of the individual consumer.

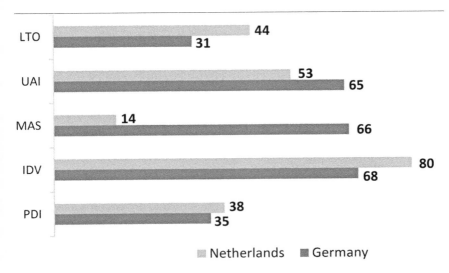

Figure 2.5 A comparison of Germany and the Netherlands according to Hofstede's cultural dimensions (based on data from Hofstede & Hofstede, 2005): PDI = power distance, IDV = individualism, MAS = masculinity, UAI = uncertainty avoidance, LTO = long term orientation

Culture-level and individual-level value dimensions are expected to be related (Schwartz, 1994b). Individual members of a society are socialized to internalize values that make them function within and conform to the values of the society of which they are members. For instance, in a culture where independence and freedom of thought are core values, individuals are taught to express their opinions. The average individual in such a society then can be expected to give a higher priority to independence and freedom values. Despite their inter-dependence, the culture-level and individual-level value dimensions are stat-istically independent (Schwartz, 1994b). For the analysis on the individual level, individual scores are used as a basis for analysis. On a culture level the country scores are the basis of analysis. An example of how this can lead to a difference between the individual and the cultural level is formed by the value items *humble* and *social power* (Fontaine & Fischer, 2011; Schwartz, 1994b). At the individual level these two items are not, or even negatively, correlated. Individuals who strive for social power typically do not value humility, and vice versa. In Schwartz's value system, these two value items are indicators of two conflicting value types: power and tradition, respectively. At the cultural level, however, the average scores on *social power* and *humble* are positively correlated: in cultures where hierarchy is important, both the importance of an unequal hierarchical power distribution, and the importance of respecting this power distribution (i.e., being humble) are instilled into their members.

The extent to which the cultural level and the individual level have a similar value structure, is expressed by their level of isomorphism. Even though the example with the value items *humble* and *social power* demonstrates a difference between the two levels, a recent multi-level analysis on data of Schwartz's value survey found a high level of isomorphism between the individual-level and the country-level, and high correlation between the levels (Fischer, Vauclair, Fontaine & Schwartz, 2010). This implies that differences between individuals and differences between countries on psychological values can be explained in terms of the same concepts or dimensions. This outcome is in line with the observation mentioned previously that the culture-level and individual-level value dimensions are conceptually related.

So far, our discussion demonstrated that value systems create a structure enabling the analysis or comparison of values. Hofstede's cultural dimensions, for instance, describe on a cultural level the structure by which societies can be compared. Although they are used to describe cultural differences, the cultural dimensions themselves are assumed to apply to different cultures. For instance, although some countries are more masculine than others, the concept of masculinity is expected to be relevant in every culture. On the individual level, Schwartz also provided evidence for the universal structure of his value system, by revealing the same value structure for individuals in different countries (Schwartz, 1992, 1994; Schwartz et al., 2001). As with Hofstede's cultural dimensions, universality of the structure of Schwartz's value system does not imply a universal rank ordering of value priorities. Value priorities are context specific: their relative importance in a certain culture depends on the demands placed on the individuals in that culture.

The possibility of differences in value priorities across societies does not imply that value priorities *have to* differ across societies. Cross-cultural comparisons of value priorities in Schwartz's value system showed a high correlation between the value hierarchies in different societies (Fischer & Schwartz, 2011; Schwartz & Bardi, 2001). Schwartz and Bardi referred to this similarity in value priorities as a pan-cultural baseline. They concluded that not only is the structure of the value system cross-culturally similar, but that also the average importance that people give to their values is similar across cultures.

Concluding, a value system is used as a structure to describe human values across different cultures, but some authors (e.g., Hofstede, 1980, 2011) emphasize cross-cultural differences, whereas others (Fischer & Schwartz, 2011; Schwartz & Bardi, 2001) emphasize cross-cultural similarities in value priority rankings. This conclusion leads us to the last proposition with respect to the Value Compass.

Proposition 7:
Compatibilities and conflicts between consumer values are similar across cultures. There are, however, cultural differences in the importance of consumer values.

2.11 Conclusion

Values are an important determinant of consumer behaviour, which can be illustrated with the widespread managerial use of brand values as descriptors of brand image. Consequently, insight in values, and how they influence behaviour, potentially provides a powerful tool in describing and understanding why and how consumers make the choices they make. This potential is increased by the progress made in the psychological field, which created additional understanding of the structure of the human value system, and the mechanism through which this value system influences behaviour. Marketing science, however, has not yet taken full advantage of the progress that was made in the understanding of the values concept.

For optimal application in the marketing domain, it is important to appreciate values within the dynamics of marketing. Consumer behaviour might activate different values than those relevant from a psychological point of view. So far, however, conceptualizations of values are borrowed from psychology, without adapting them to the marketing context. A specific challenge for marketing theory relates to the existence of brand values. Insight in the relation between brand values and consumer values offers further potential for understanding consumer behaviour. It will also help us understand how branding influences this behaviour. Additionally, it necessitates comprehension of the structure of the consumer's value system, as well as of the structure of the brand value system.

The purpose of this study is to develop a value system specific to consumer behaviour, and to create an understanding of how values motivate the consumer to become attached to brands. This purpose is guided by the following seven propositions:

1 Values are guiding principles. Values motivate people to make choices that improve their quality of life.
2 A consumer choice situation, being a specific choice context, activates a specific (sub)set of values. This set of values is structured as a dynamic value system of compatible and conflicting values.
3 The structure of the brand value system, the perceived value proposition of the brand, is similar to the structure of the consumer's value system.
4 Brand values stimulate the relationship between the consumer and the brand, by creating an emotional attachment to the brand. Brand attachment, in turn, results in an intention to buy or use the brand.
5 Brand attachment is stronger with a stronger match between the individual's value system and the perceived brand value profile. This value congruence is more relevant when values are more central to the individual.
6 The brand values concept provides a meaningful alternative to the brand personality concept.

7   Compatibilities and conflicts between consumer values are similar across cultures. There are, however, cultural differences in the importance of consumer values.

These propositions were derived in the review presented in this chapter, and provide the structure for the development and application of the Value Compass, as presented in the following chapters. The first two propositions guided the development of the Value Compass. The development process is presented in Part II. Part III focuses on the brand value model presented in Figure 2.3. The differences between brand values and brand personality are also investigated in this part. Part III is organized according to Propositions 3 to 6. Finally, the last part of this book investigates Proposition 7, by testing the cross-cultural validity of the Value Compass in a number of different countries.

Notes

1   Throughout this dissertation, values are expressed in italics.
2   Maslow did not make a sharp distinction between needs and values. In some instances he connects the individual's value system directly to his need structure, for instance: '*For the basically deprived man [on the lowest level of the needs hierarchy] the world is a dangerous place, a jungle (. . .). His value system is of necessity, like that of any jungle denizen, dominated and organized by the lower needs, especially the creature needs and the safety needs*' (Maslow, 1954, p. 178).
3   With respect to the strive for best possible living, there is a resemblance between the conceptualizations of needs and values. In Maslow's needs hierarchy (1954), a distinction is made between lower and higher needs. The highest need, self-actualisation, resembles best possible living: self-actualisation means living one's life according to one's full potential. Maslow's need hierarchy implies that lower needs need to be satisfied before the need of self-actualisation becomes relevant.
4   Inglehart (1997) uses a threshold of $6,000–$7,000 based on the 1990 dollar value, which equates to a 2014 dollar value of around $10,000.
5   Bhutan does not seem to qualify as the typical example of a country with prominent well-being values. Although it emphasizes Gross National Happiness, with an annual per capita GDP of $7,000 (www.CIA.gov, 2014) Bhutan is well below the observed threshold of $10,000.
6   The status of Proposition 1 is somewhat different than that of the other propositions in this book. Proposition 1 is derived from the literature to which we referred in Section 2.4, and can be considered a general frame of reference for the rest of this book. Propositions 2 to 7 are used to derive hypotheses which are tested throughout this book.
7   In his original work, Hofstede identified only the first four dimensions (Hofstede, 1980). The fifth and sixth dimension were added later (Hofstede, 2001, 2011; Hofstede & Hofstede, 2005).

References

Aaker, J. L. (1997). Dimensions of brand personality. *Journal of Marketing Research, 34*(8), 347–356.

Aaker, J. L., Benet-Martinez, V., & Garolera, J. (2001). Consumption symbols as carriers of culture: A study of Japanese and Spanish brand personality constucts. *Journal of Personality and Social Psychology, 81*(3), 492–508.

Aaker, J., Fournier, S. & Brasel, S. (2004). When good brands do bad. *Journal of Consumer Research, 31*(1), 1–16.

Aggarwal, P. & McGill, A. L. (2007). Is the car smiling at me? Schema congruity as a basis for evaluating anthropomorphized products. *Journal of Consumer Research, 34*(4), 468–479.

Ajzen, I. (1991). The theory of planned behavior. *Organizational Behavior and Human Decision Processes, 50*(2), 179–211.

Ajzen, I. & Fishbein, M. (2005). The influence of attitudes on behavior. In D. Dolores Albarracin, B. T. Johnson & M. P. Zanna, *The Handbook of Attitudes* (pp. 173–221). Mahwah, NJ: Lawrence Erlbaum Associates.

Allen, M. W., Gupta, R. & Monnier, A. (2008). The interactive effect of cultural symbols and human values on taste evaluation. *Journal of Consumer Research, 35* (8), 294–308.

Allport, G. W. (1961). *Pattern and Growth in Personality.* London, UK: Holt, Rinehart and Winston, Inc.

Allport, G. W. & Odbert, H. S. (1936). Trait-names: A psycho-lexical study. *Psychological Monographs, 47*(1), i.

Alsem, K. J., Wieringa, J. & Hendriks, M. (2007). The relation between values-based self-congruity and brand loyalty. *Proceedings of the 36th EMAC conference.* Reykjavik, Iceland: European Marketing Academy.

Aristoteles. (2009, original fourth century BC). *Nicomachean Ethics.* Translated D. Ross, Oxford, UK, Oxford University Press.

Arnold, M. J. & Reynolds, K. E. (2003). Hedonic shopping motivations. *Journal of Retailing, 79*(2), 77–95.

Arrian. (original 108 AD). *Discourses of Epictetus.* Retrieved 20 September 2011, from: www.archive.org/stream/discoursesofepic033057mbp/discoursesofepic033057mbp_djvu.txt

Austin, J. R., Siguaw, J. A. & Mattila, A. S. (2003). A re-examination of the generalizability of the Aaker brand personality measurement framework. *Journal of Strategic Management, 11*(2): 77–92.

Azoulay, A. & Kapferer, J.-N. (2003). Do brand personality scales really measure brand personality? *The Journal of Brand Management, 11*(2), 143–155.

Babin, B. J., Darden, W. R. & Griffin, M. (1994). Work and/or fun: Measuring hedonic and utilitarian shopping value. *Journal of Consumer Research, 20*(4), 644–655.

Bandyopadhyay, S. & Martell, M. (2007). Does attitudinal loyalty influence behavioral loyalty? A theoretical and empirical study. *Journal of Retailing and Consumer Services, 14*(1), 35–44.

Bardi, A. & Schwartz, S. H. (2003). Values and behavior: strength and structure of relations. *Personality and Social Psychology Bulletin, 29*(10): 1207–1220.

Batra, R. & Ahtola, O. T. (1990). Measuring the hedonic and utilitarian sources of consumer attitudes. *Marketing Letters, 2*(2), 159–170.

Beatty, S. E., Kahle, L. R., Homer, P. & Misra, S. (1985). Alternative measurement approaches to consumer values: The list of values and the Rokeach value survey. *Psychology & Marketing, 2*(3), 181–200.

Beerli, A., Díaz Meneses, G. & Moreno Gil, S. (2007). Self-congruity and destination choice. *Annals of Tourism Research, 34*(3), 571–587.

Belk, R. W. (1988). Possessions and the extended self. *Journal of Consumer Research, 15*(9), 139–168.

Berry, J. W., Poortinga, Y. H., Breugelmans, S. M., Chasiotis, A. & Sam, D. L. (2011). *Cross-Cultural Psychology: Research and Applications.* Cambridge, UK: Cambridge University Press.

Bowlby, J. (1979). *The making and breaking of affectional bonds.* London, UK: Tavistock.

Brakus, J. J., Bernd H. Schmitt, B. H. & Lia Zarantonello, L. (2009). Brand experience: What is it? How is it measured? Does it affect loyalty? *Journal of Marketing, 73*(5), 52–68.

Breugelmans, S. M. (2011). The relationship between individual and culture. In F. J. Van de Vijver, C. Athanasios & S. M. Breugelmans, *Fundamental questions in cross-cultural psychology* (pp. 135–162). New York, NY: Cambridge University Press.

Brunstein, J. C., Schultheiss, O. C. & Grassman, R. (1998). Personal goals and emotional well-being: The moderating role of motive dispositions. *Journal of Personality and Social Psychology, 75*(2), 494–508.

Bruun, H. H. (2007). *Science, Values and Politics in Max Weber's Methodology.* Aldershot, Hampshire, UK: Ashgate Publishing Limited.

Buss, D. M. (1996). Social adaptation and the five major factors of personality. In J. S. Wiggins, *The five-factor model of personality: Theoretical perspectives (pp. 180–207).* New York, NY: Guilford.

Carroll, B. A. & Ahuvia, A. C. (2006). Some antecedents and outcomes of brand love. *Marketing Letters, 17*(2), 79–89.

Chaudhuri, A. & Holbrook, M. D. (2001). The chain of effects from brand trust and brand affect to brand performance: The role of brand loyalty. *Journal of Marketing, 65* (4), 81–93.

Chitturi, R., Raghunathan, R. & Mahajan, V. (2007). Form versus function: How the intensities of specific emotions evoked in functional versus hedonic trade-offs mediate product preferences. *Journal of Marketing Research, 44*(4), 702–714.

Chitturi, R., Raghunathan, R. & Mahajan, V. (2008). Delight by design: The role of hedonic versus utilitarian benefits. *Journal of Marketing, 72*(3), 48–63.

CIA (2012). *The World Factbook.* Retrieved 22 January 2012, from www.cia.gov/library/publications/the-world-factbook/geos/bt.html

Costa, P. & McCrae, R. (1992). *Revised NEO Personality Inventory (NEOPI-R) and NEO Five-Factor Inventory (NEO-FFI) Professional Manual.* Odessa, FL: Psychological Assessment Resources.

Czellar, S. (2002). Consumer attitude toward brand extensions: An integrative model and research propositions. *International Journal of Research in Marketing, 20*(1), 97–115.

Deci, E. L. & Ryan, R. M. (2008). Hedonia, eudaimonia and well-being: An introduction. *Journal of Happiness Studies, 9*(1), 1–11.

Democritus (1999, original fifth–fourth century BC). Fragments. In C. Taylor, *The Atomists: Leucippus and Democritus: Fragments* (p. 23). Toronto, Canada: University of Toronto Press Incorporated.

Dhar, R. & Wertenbroch, K. (2000). Consumer choice between hedonic and utilitarian goods. *Journal of Marketing Research, 37*(1), 60–71.

Dick, A. S. & Basu, K. (1994). Customer loyalty: Toward an integrated conceptual framework. *Journal of the Academy of Marketing Science, 22*(2), 99–113.

Diener, E. (1995). A value-based index for measuring national quality of life. *Social Indicators Research, 36*(2), 107–127.

Diener, E. (2000). Subjective well-being: The science of happiness and a proposal for a national index. *American Psychologist, 55*(1), 34–43.

Diener, E. & Suh, E. (1997). Measuring quality of life: Economic, social, and subjective indicators. *Social Indicators Research, 40*(1–2), 189–216.

Diener, E., Suh, E. M., Lucas, R. E. & Smith, H. L. (1999). Subjective well-being: Three decades of progress. *Psychological Bulletin, 125*(2), 276–302.

Digman, J. M. (1997). Higher-order factors of the Big Five. *Journal of Personality and Social Psychology, 73*(6), 1246–1256.

Doran, C. J. (2009). The role of personal values in fair trade consumption. *Journal of Business Ethics, 84*(4), 549–563.

Edson Escalas, J. & Bettman, J. R. (2005). Self-construal, reference groups and brand meaning. *Journal of Consumer Research, 32*(3), 378–389.

Epicurus. (2005, original fourth–third century BC). Fragments. In N. Bakalis, *Handbook of Greek Philosophy: From Thales to the Stoics analysis and fragments* (p. 215). Victoria, BC, Canada: Trafford on Demand Publishing.

Feather, N. (1995). Values, valences and choice: The influence of values on the perceived attractiveness and choice of alternatives. *Journal of Personality and Social Psychology, 68*(6), 1135–1151.

Fischer, R. & Fontaine, J. R. (2011). Methods for investigating structural equivalence. In D. Matsumoto & F. J. Van de Vijver, *Cross-cultural research methods in psychology* (pp. 179–215). New York, NY: Cambridge University Press.

Fischer, R. & Schwartz, S. (2011). Whence differences in value priorities? Individual, cultural, or artifactual sources. *Journal of Cross-Cultural Psychology, 42*(7), 1127–1144.

Fischer, R., Vauclair, C.-M., Fontaine, J. R. & Schwartz, S. H. (2010). Are individual-level and country-level value structures different? Testing Hofstede's legacy with the Schwartz Value Survey. *Journal of Cross-Cultural Psychology, 41*(2), 135–151.

Fishbein, M. & Ajzen, I. (1975). *Belief, attitude, intention, and behavior: an introduction to theory and research*. Reading, MA: Addison-Wesley.

Fontaine, J. R. & Fischer, R. (2011). Data analytic approaches for investigating isomorphism. In D. Matsumoto & F. J. Van de Vijver, *Cross-cultural research methods in psychology* (pp. 273–298). New York, NY: Cambridge University Press.

Fournier, S. (1998). Consumers and their brands: Developing relationship theory in consumer research. *Journal of Consumer Research, 24*(4), 343–373.

Gaunt, R. (2006). Couple similarity and marital satisfaction: Are similar spouses happier? *Journal of Personality, 74*(5), 1401–1420.

Gaus, H., Jahn, S., Kiessling, T. & Drengner, J. (2010). How to measure brand values? *Advances in Consumer Research*, 697–698.

Geuens, M., Weijters, B. & De Wulf, K. (2009). A new measure of brand personality. *International Journal of Research in Marketing, 26*(2), 97–107.

Goldberg, L. (1981). Language and individual differences: The search for universals in personality lexicons. In L. Wheeler, *Review of Personality and Social Psychology* (pp. 141–165). Beverly Hills, CA: Sage.

Goldberg, L. R. (1992). The development of markers for the Big-Five factor structure. *Psychological Assessment, 4*(1), 26–42.

Grundlach, G. T., Achrol, R. S. & Mentzer, J. T. (1995). The structure of commitment in exchange. *Journal of Marketing, 59*(1), 78–92.

Guilford, J. P. (1959). *Personality*. New York, NY: McGraw-Hill.

Gutman, J. (1982). A means-end chain model based on consumer categorization processes. *Journal of Marketing, 46*(2): 60–72.

Guttman, L. (1968). A general non-metric technique for finding the smallest coordinate space for a configuration of points. *Psychometrica, 33*(4), 469–506.

Hirschman, E. C. & Holbrook, M. B. (1982). Hedonic consumption: Emerging concepts, methods, and propositions. *Journal of Marketing, 46*(3), 92–101.

Hofstede, G. (1980). *Culture's consequences: Comparing values, behaviors, institutions and organizations across nations*. Thousand Oaks, CA: Sage.

Hofstede, G. (2001). *Culture's consequences: Comparing values, behaviors, institutions, and organizations across nations* (2nd edition). Thousand Oaks, CA: Sage.

Hofstede, G. (2011). Dimensionalizing cultures: The Hofstede model in context. *Online Readings in Psychology and Culture, 2*(1). http://dx.doi.org/10.9707/2307–0919.1014.

Hofstede, G. & Bond, M. H. (1988). The Confucius Connection: From cultural roots to economic growth. *Organizational Dynamics, 16*(4), 4–21.

Hofstede, G. & Hofstede, G. (2005). *Cultures and organizations, software of the mind*. New York, NY: McGraw-Hill.

Hofstee, W. K., De Raad, B. & Goldberg, L. R. (1992). Integration of the Big Five and circumplex approaches to trait structure. *Journal of Personality and Social Psychology, 63*(1), 146–163.

Holbrook, M. B. & Hirschman, E. C. (1982). The experiential aspects of consumption: Consumer fantasies, feelings, and fun. *Journal of Consumer Research, 9*(2), 132–140.

Honkanen, P. & Verplanken, B. (2004). Understanding attitudes towards genetically modified food: the role of values and attitude strength. *Journal of Consumer Policy, 27*(4), 401–420.

Inglehart, R. F. (1997). *Modernization and postmodernization: Cultural, economic and political change in 43 countries*. Princeton NJ: Princeton University Press.

John, O. P., Naumann, L. P. & Soto, C. J. (2008). Paradigm shift to the integrative big five trait taxonomy. In O. P. John, R. W. Robins & L. A. Pervin, *Handbook of personality: Theory and research 3* (pp. 114–158). New York, NY: The Guilford Press.

Kahle, L. R. (1983). *Social values and social change: Adaptation to life in America*. New York, NY: Praeger.

Keller, K. L. (1993). Conceptualizing, measuring, and managing customer-based brand equity. *Journal of Marketing, 57*(1), 1–22.

Keller, K. L. (2003). Brand synthesis: The multidimensionality of brand knowledge. *Journal of Consumer Research, 29*(4), 595–600.

Keller, K. L. (2008). *Strategic brand management: Building, measuring, and managing brand equity* (3rd edition). Upper Saddle River, NJ: Prentice Hall.

Kluckhohn, C. (1951). Values and value orientations in the theory of action. In T. Parsons & E. A. Shils, *Toward a general theory of action*. Cambridge, MA: Harvard University Press.

Kluckhohn, F. R. & Strodtbeck, F. L. (1961). *Variations in Value Orientations*. Oxford, UK: Row, Peterson.

Kotler, P., Kartajaya, H. & Setiawan, I. (2010). *Marketing 3.0*. Hoboken, NJ: Jon Wiley & Sons, Inc.

Kressmann, F., Sirgy, M., Herrmann, A., Huber, F., Huber, S. & Lee, D.-J. (2006). Direct and indirect effects of self-image congruence on brand loyalty. *Journal of Business Research, 59*(9), 955–964.

Kristof-Brown, A. L., Zimmerman, R. D. & Johnson, E. C. (2005). Consequences of individuals' fit at work: A meta-analysis of person-job, person-organization, person-group and person-supervisor fit. *Personnel Psychology, 58*(2), 281–324.

Lages, L. F. & Fernandes, J. C. (2005). The SERVPVAL scale: A multi-item measurement instrument for measuring service personal values. *Journal of Business Research, 58*(11), 1562–1572.

Levy, S. (1990). Values and deeds. *Applied Psychology, 39*(4), 379–400.

Limon, Y., Kahle, L. R. & Orth, U. R. (2009). Package design as a communication vehicle in cross-cultural values shopping. *Journal of International Marketing, 17*(1), 30–57.

Lugnet (2012). Retrieved 16 December 2012, from International LEGO Users Group Network, global community of LEGO enthusiasts: www.lugnet.com

McAlexander, J. H., Schouten, J. W. & Koenig, H. F. (2002). Building brand community. *Journal of Marketing, 66*(1), 38–54.

McCrae, R. R. & Costa, P. T. (1996). Toward a new generation of personality theories: Theoretical contexts for the five-factor model. In J. Wiggins, *The five factor model of personality* (pp. 51–87). New York, NY: The Guilford Press.

McCrae, R. R. & Costa, P. T. (1997). Personality trait structure as a human universal. *American Psychologist, 52*(5), 509–516.

Madrigal, R. (1995). Personal values, traveler personality type, and leisure travel style. *Journal of Leisure Research, 27*(2), 125–142.

Maio, G. R. (2010). Mental representations of social values. *Advances in Experimental Social Psychology, 42,* 1–43.

Maio, G. R. & Olson, J. M. (1995). Relations between values, attitudes, and behavioral intentions: The moderating role of attitude function. *Journal of Experimental Social Psychology, 31*(3), 266–285.

Markus, H. R. & Kitayama, S. (1991). Culture and the self: Implications for cognition, emotion, and motivation. *Psychological Review, 98*(2), 224–253.

Maslow, A. H. (1954). *Motivation and Personality.* New York, NY: Harper & Row.

Meglino, B. M., Ravlin, E. C. & Adkins, C. L. (1989). A work values approach to corporate culture: A field test of the value congruence process and its relationship to individual outcomes. *Journal of Applied Psychology, 74*(3), 424–432.

Merz, M. A., He, Y. & Vargo, S. L. (2009). The evolving brand logic: A service-dominant logic perspective. *Journal of the Academy of Marketing Science, 37*(3),328–344.

Muniz, A. M. & O'Guinn, T. C. (2001). Brand community. *Journal of Consumer Research, 27*(4), 412–432.

Okada, E. M. (2005). Justification effects on consumer choice of hedonic and utilitarian goods. *Journal of Marketing Research, 42*(1), 43–53.

Olver, J. M. & Mooradian, T. A. (2003). Personality traits and personal values: A conceptual and empirical integration. *Personality and Individual Differences, 35*(1), 109–125.

Parsons, T. & Shils, E. A. (1951). *Toward a general theory of action: theoretical foundations for the social sciences.* Cambridge, MA: Harvard University Press.

Penke, L., Denissen, J. J. & Miller, G. F. (2007). The evolutionary genetics of personality. *European Journal of Personality,* 21(5), 549–587.

Pine, J. & Gilmore, J. H. (1999). *The Experience Economy: Work is Theatre & Every Business a Stage.* Boston, MA: Harvard Business Review Press.

Plato (2008, original circa 370 BC). *The Republic.* Translated R. Waterfield, Oxford, UK: Oxford University Press.

Quester, P., Beverland, M. & Farrelly, F. (2006). Brand-personal values fit and brand meanings: Exploring the role of individual values play in ongoing brand loyalty in extreme sports subcultures. In C. Pechmann & L. Price, *Advances in Consumer Research, 33: 21–27.* Duluth, MN: Association for Consumer Research.

Reichheld, F. F. (2003). The one number you need to grow. *Harvard Business Review, 81*(12), 46–55.

Richins, M. L. (1994). Special possessions and the expression of material values. *Journal of Consumer Research, 21*(3), 522–533.

Roccas, S., Sagiv, L., Schwartz, S. H. & Knafo, A. (2002). The Big Five personality factors and personal values. *Personality and Social Psychology Bulletin, 28*(6), 789–801.

Rohan, M. J. (2000). A rose by any name? The values construct. *Personality and Social Psychology Review, 4*(3), 255–277.

Rokeach, M. (1973). *The Nature of Human Values.* New York, NY: The Free Press.

Rokeach, M. (1979). *Understanding Human Values, Individual and Social.* New York, NY: The Free Press.

Schwartz, S. H. (1992). Universals in the content and structure of values: theoretical advances and empirical tests in 20 countries. In M. Zanna, *Advances in Experimental Social Psychology* *25*: 1–65. New York, NY: The Free Press.

Schwartz, S. H. (1994). Are there universal aspects in the structure and contents of human values? *Journal of Social Issues, 50*(4), 19–45.

Schwartz, S. H. (1994b). Beyond individualism/collectivism: New cultural dimensions of values. In U. Kim, H. C. Triandis, Ç. Kâgitçibasi, S.-C. Choi & G. Yoon, *Individualism and collectivism: theory, method, and applications* (pp. 85–122). Thousand Oaks, CA: Sage Publications.

Schwartz, S. H. (1996). Value priorities and behavior: Applying a theory of integrated value systems. In C. Seligman, J. M. Olson & M. P. Zanna, *The psychology of values: The Ontario symposium, volume 8* (pp. 1–24). Mahwah, NJ: Lawrence Erlbaum Associates, Inc.

Schwartz, S. H. (2006). Les valeurs de base de la personne: Théorie, mesures et applications. *Revue Française de Sociologie, 47*(4): 929–968.

Schwartz, S. H. & Bilsky, W. (1987). Toward a universal psychological structure of human values. *Journal of Personality and Social Psychology, 53*(3), 550–562.

Schwartz, S. H. & Sagiv, L. (1995). Identifying culture-specifics in the content and structure of values. *Journal of Cross-Cultural Psychology, 26*(1), 92–116.

Schwartz, S. H., Melech, G., Lehmann, A., Burgess, S., Harris, M. & Owens, V. (2001). Extending the cross-cultural validity of the theory of basic human values with a different method of measurement. *Journal of Cross-Cultural Psychology, 32*(5), 519–542.

Seligman, C. & Katz, A. N. (1996). The dynamics of value systems. In C. Seligman, J. M. Olson & M. P. Zanna, *The psychology of values: The Ontario symposium, 8* (pp. 53–76). New York, NY: Psychology Press.

Shimp, T. A. (2010). Integrated marketing communications in advertising and promotion (8th edition). China: Southwestern.

Sirgy, M. J. (1982). Self-concept in consumer behavior: A critical review. *Journal of Consumer Research, 9*(3), 287–300.

Sirgy, M. J. & Su, C. (2000). Destination image, self-congruity, and travel behavior: Toward an integrative model. *Journal of Travel Research, 38*(4), 340–352.

Sirgy, M. J., Grewal, D. & Mangleburg, T. (2000). Retail environment, self-congruity, and retail patronage: An integrative model and a research agenda. *Journal of Business Research, 49*(2), 127–138.

Sirgy, M. J., Grewal, D., Mangleburg, T. F., Park, J.-o., Chon, K.-S., Claiborne, C., Johar, J. S. & Berkman, H. (1997). Assessing the predictive validity of two methods of measuring self-image congruence. *Journal of the Academy of Marketing Science, 25*(3), 229–241.

Spates, J. L. (1983). The sociology of values. *Annual Review of Sociology*, 9, 27–49.

Sprott, D., Sandor, C. & Spangenberg, E. (2009). The importance of a general measure of brand engagement on market behavior: Development and validation of a scale. *Journal of Marketing Research, 46*(2), 92–104.

The Chinese Culture Connection. (1987). Chinese values and the search for culture-free dimensions of culture. *Journal of Cross-Cultural Psychology, 18*(2), 143–164.

Thomson, M., MacInnis, D. J. & Whan Park, C. (2005). The ties that bind: Measuring the strength of consumers' emotional attachments to brands. *Journal of Consumer Psychology, 15*(1), 77–91.

Torelli, C. J., Özsomer, A., Carvalho, S. W., Keh, H. T. & Maehle, N. (2008). A measure of brand values: cross-cultural implications for brand preferences. *Advances in Consumer Research Conference*. San Francisco, CA.

Torelli, C. J., Özsomer, A., Carvalho, S. W., Keh, H. T. & Maehle, N. (2012). Brand concepts as representations of human values: Do cultural congruity and compatibility between values matter? *Journal of Marketing, 76*(7), 92–108.

Triandis, H. C. (1995). *Individualism & Collectivism.* Boulder, CO: Westmore.

Turkheimer, E. (2000). Three laws of behavior genetics and what they mean. *Current Directions in Psychological Science, 9*(5),160–164.

United Nations (2011). *Happiness: towards a holistic approach to development.* Retrieved 25 August 2011, from Resolutions adopted by the General Assembly at its 65th session: www.un.org/ga/search/view_doc.asp?symbol=A/RES/65/309&Lang=E

Valette-Florence, P. (1986). Les démarches de styles de vie: concepts, champs d'investigation et problèmes actuels. *Recherche et applications en marketing, 1*(1), 93–110.

Van de Vijver, F. J. & Leung, K. (1997). *Methods and data-analysis for cross-cultural research.* Newbury Park, CA: Sage.

Vargo, S. L. & Lusch, R. F. (2004). Evolving to a new dominant logic for marketing. *Journal of Marketing, 68*(1), 1–17.

Vargo, S. L. & Lusch, R. F. (2008). Service-dominant logic: Continuing the evolution. *Journal of the Academy of Marketing Science, 36*(1), 1–10.

Verplanken, B. & Holland, R. W. (2002). Motivated decision making: Effects of activation and self-centrality of values on choices and behavior. *Journal of Personality and Social Psychology, 82*(3), 434–447.

Verplanken, B., Trafimow, D., Khusid, I., Holland, R. W. & Steentjes, G. M. (2009). Different selves, different values: Effects of self-construals on value activation and use. *European Journal of Social Psychology, 39*(6), 909–919.

Vinson, D. E., Scott, J. E. & Lamont, L. M. (1977). The role of personal values in marketing and consumer behavior. *Journal of Marketing, 41*(2), 44–50.

Voss, K. E., Spangenberg, E. R. & Grohmann, B. (2003). Measuring the hedonic and utilitarian dimensions of consumer attitude. *Journal of Marketing Research, 40*(3), 310–320.

Waterman, A. S. (1993). Two conceptions of happiness: Contrasts of personal expressiveness (eudaimonia) and hedonic enjoyment. *Journal of Personality and Social Psychology, 64*(4), 678–691.

Weber, M. (1949, original 1904). *The methodology of the social sciences.* Translation, Edward A. Shils and Henry A. Finch, New York, NY: The Free Press.

Whan Park, C., Jaworski, B. J. & MacInnis, D. J. (1986). Strategic brand concept-image management. *Journal of Marketing, 50*(4), 135–145.

Wilkie, W. L. & Pessemier, E. A. (1973). Issues in marketing's use of multi-attribute attitude models. *Journal of Marketing Research, 10*(4), 428–441.

Yoo, B. & Donthu, N. (2001). Developing and validating a multidimensional consumer-brand equity scale. *Journal of Business Research, 52*(1), 1–14.

Zhang, J. & Bloemer, J. M. (2008). The impact of value congruence on consumer-service brand relationships. *Journal of Service Research, 11*(2), 161–178.

Zhang, J. & Bloemer, J. M. (2011). Impact of value congruence on affective commitment: Examining the moderating effects. *Journal of Service Management, 22*(2), 160–182.

Part II

Values and the consumer

Chapter 3

Development of the Value Compass

3.1 Introduction

In the preceding literature review, the importance of values within the dynamics of marketing was highlighted. We found that, despite the relevance of values for branding, a consumer-oriented value system has not yet been incorporated into mainstream marketing literature. Instead, conceptualizations of values are borrowed from psychology, without adapting them to the marketing context. The general purpose of this research is to create an understanding of how values motivate consumer behaviour. This was phrased in the introductory chapter as follows:

> The development of a value system that can be universally applied to assess the effect of brand values and personal values on consumer choice.

Part II is devoted to the development of this value system. It contains two chapters. Chapter 3 discusses the development process. Chapter 4 presents the outcomes: the description of the Value Compass and the value types of which it is composed. The following questions will be addressed in Part II:

- Which values are relevant for consumer choice?
- To what extent can these values be organized into a meaningful value system?
- To what extent is the Value Compass, and the values it contains, compatible with existing value typologies?

In answering these questions, we follow the conclusions put forth by the propositions in the previous chapter. Proposition 1 and 2 specifically apply to the issues addressed by these questions.

Values are guiding principles. Values motivate people to make choices that improve their quality of life (Proposition 1).

Values as guiding principle in life implies that values guide choice behaviour, in any kind of setting that an individual encounters in life. Within marketing, the focus is on a specific type of choice: the choices that consumers make in order to satisfy their needs. Branding, for instance, involves an effort to influence consumers in such a way that they prefer or choose the brand under consideration. Consequently, a prerequisite of successful branding is knowledge of the consumer decision-making process. According to Proposition 1, consumer behaviour, like any other behaviour, is guided by values. Hence, successful branding necessitates insight in the value structure of the consumer.

A consumer choice situation, being a specific choice context, activates a specific (sub)set of values. This set of values is structured as a dynamic value system of compatible and conflicting values (Proposition 2).

The literature review in the previous chapter described the historic development of the value concept. In that overview, we could see that Schwartz's value theory (1992) emerged as the leading contemporary view on values. Schwartz conceptualized values as guiding principles in an individual's life. The review also highlighted that values only affect behaviour if they are activated by the situation or the information a person is confronted with (Verplanken & Holland, 2002). For instance, the value *family life* has the potential of influencing a purchase decision concerning furniture, but only if the buyer believes there is a relation between the type and style of furniture and the quality of his family life.

This chapter is devoted to the development of the Value Compass, the value system that describes the values that motivate consumer choice. The consumer values in this value system were selected from a comprehensive set of values developed by De Raad and Van Oudenhoven (2008). They used the lexical approach[1] to create a list of value-relevant terms, which they asserted to represent a complete overview of value-related items in the Dutch language. When creating this overview, they used a computerized database of the Dutch language. This database was primarily built on Van Dale's *Comprehensive Dictionary of Contemporary Dutch* (Pijnenburg & Sterkenburg, 1984), containing 130,778 words. For tracking down and identifying all value descriptors from this lexicon, De Raad and Van Oudenhoven (2008) used a broad definition of values: a value was defined as '*a relatively enduring characteristic of individuals that reflects what is important to them and that guides them in their behaviors and their decisions*' (p. 86). By using this definition, the list of 130,778 words was reduced in a number of stages, until a list of 671 potential value items resulted. To avoid omission of relevant value descriptors, De Raad and Van Oudenhoven included the value items from the Rokeach Value Survey and the value items from the Schwartz Value Survey in their list of 671 value items. The values of the Value Compass were selected out of this list. The selection process and the subsequent development of the Value Compass were guided by a stepwise approach, involving the following stages.

1   Value activation: selection of values with relevance for consumer choice.
2   Reduction of this set of consumer values to a more manageable set of items.
3   Identification of interrelations between consumer values.
4   Visual representation of these interrelations.
5   Organization of consumer values into value types.
6   Assessment of the value types of the Value Compass.
7   Assessment of the overall structure of the Value Compass.

Each stage of the development process is detailed in Section 3.2. Section 3.3 summarizes the outcomes.

3.2 The development of the Value Compass

Stage I

Activation of values to a brand choice context

The Value Compass focuses on value items applicable to consumer behaviour. Not all values are expected to have the same relevance for consumer behaviour. For instance, it is easily imaginable that '*elegantie*' *(elegance)*, one of the 671 value items of De Raad and Van Oudenhoven (2008), is relevant for consumer behaviour, when choosing which dress to wear, or when buying interior design products. But this set of 671 value items also contains values such as '*zelfbehoud*' *(self-preservation)* or '*geletterdheid*' *(literacy)*, values that might have more limited relevance for consumer behaviour. Therefore, the applicability of each of the 671 value items of De Raad and Van Oudenhoven for a branding context had to be evaluated.

A jury of 25 people scrutinized each of the 671 value descriptors on their applicability in a branding context. The jury consisted of people from different age categories and socio-cultural backgrounds, and contained an equal proportion of males and females. Since the list of 671 value items was provided in Dutch, all members were fluent in the Dutch language. The jury judged each value item with respect to its potential relevance for a brand choice context: based on personal judgement, the jury members had to mark each value item with a 'yes' (i.e., the value is applicable for consumer behaviour) or a 'no' (the value is not applicable for consumer behaviour).

To avoid the removal of potentially useful value items, the initial selection criterion was not very stringent. Values were retained if 40 per cent or more of the jury members, that is at least 10 jury members, were able to attribute the value to a brand. The selection process resulted in a list with 190 value items, which were approved by 10 or more jury members.

International application of the Value Compass, to be examined in Chapter 8, necessitates a list of value descriptors available in the English language. Since the original list of De Raad and Van Oudenhoven (2008) was published in Dutch, the value items were converted into English through a translation – back-translation procedure (Van de Vijver & Leung, 1997). All 190 brand value descriptors approved by the jury were translated into English, then back-translated into Dutch. A comparison was made between the original value item and the back-translated meaning: the original and the back-translated item had to be the same, or to have a considerable overlap in meaning and interpretation. The meaning of the Dutch value descriptors and the translated English meaning were compared with the *Oxford Dictionary of English* (2005), in combination with synonym systems available on the internet. The translation procedure resulted in a list of 190 English brand value descriptors. This list can be found in the appendix.

Result of Stage 1

Jury judgement reduced the list of 671 potential value items into a set of 190 value items that potentially can be applied in a brand choice context.

Stage 2

Reduction of the set of value items: assessment by a student sample

The next phase in the reduction process involved further assessment of the remaining list of 190 value descriptors. These items were submitted in a survey, in which respondents had to rate the relevance of each value item in a consumer choice context: '*How important is this value for you when you have to make a choice between products or services?*'. Ratings were provided on a 5-point scale ranging from *very unimportant* to *very important*. Box 3.1 motivates the choice for using ratings in this study, as opposed to ranking the values.

The database of the Hanze University of Applied Science Groningen was used to randomly select students. The Hanze University is a university in the city of Groningen, a city located in the North of the Netherlands. The selected respondents received an email, followed by two reminders, with a request to fill out the survey online. Respondents could access the online survey by clicking on a link in the email. Surveymonkey[2] was used to create the survey and to collect the responses. Due to the length of the questionnaire, there is the potential of an order effect when rating the 190 value items. Therefore, the sample was randomized: each respondent received a differently ordered list of the 190 value items. The survey was available to a sample of 6,744 students, from 13 February until 1 March 2010. A total of 1,821 students (27 per cent) responded. Only the results of respondents filling out more than 50 per cent of the survey were used. This left a total of 740 respondents.

The survey results created an importance rating for each of the 190 value descriptors. This rating was used to further reduce the number of value items.

Box 3.1 Ranking versus rating

Treating values in terms of value priorities suggests that values can be rank-ordered by importance: more important values receive a higher priority in a choice setting than less important values. This implies that a ranking procedure can be used to determine value priorities. Ranking was used by Rokeach (1973) and Inglehart (1997). In the studies of Schwartz (1992, 1994), however, a rating procedure is used to determine the importance of values. An important reason for using ratings is that ranking poses practical problems with longer lists of values. For respondents, rating values on a Likert-type rating scale is an easier and less time-consuming task than ranking values in order of importance; it would be a daunting task to rank 190 values in order of importance.

A comparison between ranking and rating measures in brand image associations showed that both types of measurement generally create highly correlated results, except when evaluating less important items (Driesener & Romaniuk, 2006). Asking respondents to assign unique rankings created artificial differences between brands in the lower rankings, since ranking forces a choice, even when there is none. Rating, on the other hand, does not force respondents to discriminate among equally important values or to compare directly values they may experience as incomparable. Finally, a rating procedure may also be conceptually closer to actual choice behaviour (Schwartz, 1994). Ranking requires respondents to express sharp, definitive preferences between every pair of values. However, the process of weighing and combining value priorities is usually not so precise and self-conscious: people are typically only loosely aware of more subtle differences in priorities.

Considering that ranking and rating produce highly correlated results, but taking into account that rating is easier for the respondent and potentially closer to actual choice behaviour, we preferred to ask the respondents to rate the importance of values.

Elimination of unimportant value items

In the jury assessment in Stage 1, value items were retained when approved by at least 40 per cent of the jury members. But even if potentially applicable, some of the retained value items can still be relatively unimportant for brand-related value judgements. We eliminated unimportant value items by using a combination of criteria:

- In the values approved in Stage 1, a stricter criterion is used for the evaluation of the items: value items approved by less than 50 per cent of the jury members are considered candidates for elimination.

- In the survey, the importance of the value items is measured on a 5-point scale. Value items rating lower than an average of 3.5 are considered less important for a brand choice situation.[3]

Value items were eliminated if they are less important according to both criteria: an average importance rating of lower than 3.5 in the survey AND approved by less than 50 per cent of the jury members. As a result of this elimination procedure 38 value descriptors were removed.

Elimination of synonyms

Of the remaining 162 value items, correlations between items were investigated. Value items showing a strong correlation in the survey are perceived in a more or less similar way by the respondents. As an example, consider *individualism* and *individuality,* two potentially related values out of the list of 162 value items. If these two value items are highly correlated, then we can assume that people do not differentiate between these value items and see both words as being synonyms. As a rule of thumb, we consider word pairs with a correlation coefficient above 0.70 as being highly correlated (Hair, Black, Babin, Anderson & Tatham, 2006), hence, synonymous. In these word pairs, the item in the word pair with the lowest average importance rating was eliminated.

Three word pairs were found to have a correlation coefficient higher than 0.70:

- Being environmentally friendly and being environmentally conscious.
- Individuality and individualism.
- Self-confidence and self-assurance.

The second item of each of these word pairs had the lowest average importance rating, and was eliminated. A total of 159 brand value descriptors remained.

Elimination of ambiguous value items

Some words have multiple meanings, and in addition words mean different things to different people. For instance, one of the values in the list is *being idealistic about the future.* The word *ideal* has two different connotations.[4] For some people *ideal* refers to something desirable, as in the idealistic goal of bringing an end to poverty in the world. For others, however, this value emphasizes a more negative connotation of having fairytale-like, somewhat unrealistic expectations about the future: idealistic as opposed to realistic.

It is important to remove value items with an unclear, multiple or otherwise ambiguous meaning. In order to do so, the structure of the item set was investigated by applying principal components analysis (PCA). The primary purpose of this analysis is to examine the underlying structure among a set of value items. With PCA, related value items are grouped in components representing dimensions within the data (Hair *et al.*, 2006). The factor loading of the items specifies the correlation of the item with the dimension in which it is placed. Items have a cross-loading when they have high factor loadings on two or more different dimensions. This implies an unclear dimensionality of the item, hence, an indication of an unclear meaning of the item. A rule-of-thumb specifies that items with a factor loading of at least 0.40 are acceptable, with cross-loadings not higher than 0.30 (Hair *et al.*, 2006). An additional indicator for the quality of an item is its communality. The communality of an item is the variance of the item, which is accounted for by all the factors in the analysis. A rule-of-thumb specifies that at least 50 per cent of the variance of each item must be taken into account. This implies that only variables with communalities higher than 0.50 should be included in the analysis (Hair *et al.*, 2006).

An unrestricted PCA, with varimax rotation, was executed to assess the value items. Items were eliminated by using the criteria mentioned above:

- Factor loading of the item should be higher than 0.40.
- Highest cross-loading of the item should be lower than 0.30.
- Communality of the item is higher than 0.50.

In order to avoid losing potentially useful items, a conservative elimination approach was used. Value items were rejected if they failed to meet at least two elimination criteria. Elimination criteria were applied more strictly for value items with lower jury approval or with a lower average importance rating. In case of doubt, the item was retained. After eliminating ambiguous value items, a set of 117 value items relevant to brand choice remained.

Result of Stage 2

Assessment of the importance of value items in a survey, in combination with jury assessment, was used in a number of elimination procedures. The set of 190 value items was reduced to a set of 117 value items relevant to brand choice.

Stage 3

Relations between consumer values: examination with PCA

So far, a list of value items was produced with relevance for consumer behaviour. But, according to Proposition 2, values are more than a list of unrelated items: some values (e.g., *beauty* and *goodlooking*) represent a more similar motivation, whereas other values (e.g., *beauty* and *safety*) seem less related. This implies that values can be organized according to the (dis)similarities in underlying motivations. The objective of this stage in the development of the Value Compass is to explore whether the set of 117 value items can be organized in groups representing similar motivations.

To structure the value items, principal components analyses (PCA) with varimax rotation was used. A number of factor solutions were examined. First, a forced two-factor solution in PCA divided the set of 117 value items in two groups. This forced two-factor solution accounted for 34.7 per cent of the variance in the dataset. The results of the two-factor solution resemble the utilitarian-hedonic dimension central to consumer behaviour literature, a dimension that distinguishes between choices motivated by instrumental buying reasons (e.g., the functional or practical aspects of a product), as opposed to behaviour driven by hedonic gratification (e.g., pleasure or amusement) or stimulation derived from experiencing a brand (for further information we refer to Section 2.6). The two-factor solution of the Value Compass confirms the importance of this utilitarian-hedonic dimension:

- The first factor of the two-factor solution represents hedonic motivations. It is characterized by a mix of inner-directed experiences (e.g., *fun, enjoying life, pleasure*) and other-directed sensations (e.g., *friendship, caring, romance*).
- The second factor is of utilitarian nature. It comprises instrumental values, including values such as *functionality, precision* and *professionalism*. This utilitarian factor also comprises values emphasizing achievement and values aimed at making a difference with others or obtaining prestige (e.g., *being successful, status, good-looking, power*).

Both factors represent a mix of inner-directed and other-directed values. This distinction corresponds with a division that can be found in marketing literature, the division between inner-directed utilitarian and experiential motivations, and other-directed symbolic motivations (Whan Park *et al.*, 1986). This categorization of motivations was described in Section 2.6.

In the next step, three- and four-factor solutions were computed. The distinction between inner-directed and other-directed motivations was confirmed by these solutions. In the four-factor solution (explained variance 41.9 per cent), besides the utilitarian and hedonic values, the two types of other-directed motivations were distinguished: one factor with values emphasizing the importance of care, friendship, and love, and another factor emphasizing performance and making a difference with others. This latter factor includes values such as *status, being successful* and *power*.

Other-directed motivations involve the relation that the individual wants to have with others. A number of these motives were identified in motivation theory (McClelland, 1987). Motivation theory distinguishes between the motivation to achieve or to perform better than others (achievement motive and power motive), and the motivation to establish or maintain a relationship with others (affiliation motive). The distinction between values promoting personal interests and values emphasizing the well-being and interests of others (social outcomes) also corresponds with one of the two dimensions underlying Schwartz's value system, the self-enhancement versus self-transcendence dimension (Schwartz, 1992). The division in self-centered and other-directed motivations can also be found in the individualism-collectivism continuum central to cross-cultural psychology (Hofstede, 1980, 2011; Triandis, 1995).

Summarized, PCA organizes the values of the Value Compass in four factors that show similarities to motivational constructs discussed in literature. The first two factors of the Value Compass resemble *the utilitarian-hedonic continuum* predicted by consumer behaviour theory.

- The first factor represents hedonic pleasure (e.g., *fun, enjoying life, pleasure, excitement*). The values in this factor correspond with the hedonic dimension as defined by Batra and Ahtola (1990) and Hirschman and Holbrook (1982), and the experiential motivations from the classification of Whan Park *et al.* (1986).
- The second factor is of utilitarian nature, and contains values such as *expertise, functionality* and *precision*. This factor corresponds with the utilitarian dimension in consumer behaviour literature.

The values in the third and fourth factor motivate choice behaviour through which the individual can express how he wishes to relate to others. These factors resemble the distinction in social and individual outcomes central to psychology and cross-cultural theory: a motivational continuum reflecting the importance of *the care for others versus the promotion of self-interests.*

- The third factor represents the concern to establish and maintain relationships with others, and to take care of others. It consists of values such as *caring for someone, friendship, intimacy, safety* and *harmony,* as well as future-oriented values (e.g., *providing for a better world, being environment-friendly*).
- The fourth factor represents the promotion of personal interests, values concerned with making a difference with others. This factor includes values such as *status, power* and *beauty.* It is noteworthy to observe that *beauty* is part of this factor: by making oneself beautiful (e.g., with fashionable clothes), one can express a difference with others.

Within the factor *care for others,* a distinctive group of values emerges related to a feeling of responsibility for the future. It includes values such as *being environment-friendly* and *providing for a better world.* These values promote the importance of a higher future quality of life, and seem to correspond with the cultural dimension long-term orientation (Hofstede, 2011). A PCA with five-factor solution was performed to verify whether these values can be grouped together. The five-factor solution (explained variance 44.4 per cent) indeed revealed future-related value items as a separate factor. Further analyses with additional factors yielded no conclusive results. An overview of the value groups of the Value Compass, and the values characterizing each group, is presented in Table 3.1.

The internal consistency of the five value factors was inspected with Cronbach's alpha, over all items in each factor, and with corrected item-to-total correlations. The lower limit for a reliability test based on Cronbach's alpha is 0.70 (Hair *et al.*, 2006). The five factors show a high reliability coefficient, ranging from 0.83 to 0.95 (Table 3.1), but a note of prudence is necessary. Cronbach's alpha increases with the number of items. In this analysis, the number of value items per factor is relatively high: five items for *care for the future* to 33 items for *care for others*. Consequently, a high Cronbach's alpha can be expected. Additional information is provided by the corrected item-to-total correlations. Correlations vary from 0.380 (*spirituality*) to 0.693 (*status*). With the exception of two items (*craftsmanship* and *spirituality*), item-to-total correlations are higher than 0.40.

The five factors explain 44.4 per cent of the variation in the dataset. This still leaves 55.6 per cent of variation unaccounted for. This, in combination with the large number of items in each factor, points toward the necessity of further interpretation of the factor structure. As a further step in this analysis, we will look in Stage 4 at the spatial configuration of items.

Result of Stage 3

The values of the Value Compass are organized in a structure consisting of five value groups: promotion of self-interests, care for others, care for the future, the hedonic value group and the utilitarian value group.

Stage 4

The structure of the Value Compass: creation of a value space with MDS

Multidimensional scaling (MDS) is a scaling technique that gives a visual representation of relations between items (Borg & Groenen, 2005; Fischer & Fontaine, 2011; Guttman, 1968). Schwartz (1992) used this technique to identify the structure of his value system.[5] In the multidimensional space produced by MDS, the distances between points represent the associations between items. The greater the conceptual similarity between any two items, the closer their locations should be in the multidimensional value space. For instance, consider the values *pleasure* and *enjoying life*. Some respondents might consider *pleasure* an important value. If these respondents also, on average, consider *enjoying life* important, then this is a sign that *pleasure* and *enjoying life* are correlated. These two related value items then appear in close proximity to each other in a value space. Similarities and dissimilarities between value items are derived from the correlations between the importance ratings of the value items in the survey.

An MDS-solution can be interpreted visually by means of a so-called regional interpretation of the multidimensional space (Fischer & Fontaine, 2011; Van de Vijver & Leung, 1997). Similar items, items that belong conceptually together, can be found in the same region in the multidimensional space; values in conceptual opposition to each other (e.g., hedonic values and utilitarian values) are predicted to appear in opposing regions (Schwartz, 1994b). The regions in a value space emerge from a common origin. Beginning in this origin, partition lines can be drawn to group the value items belonging to the same region (e.g., value group) and to separate the regions from each other. The exact position of each line is a more or less arbitrary decision about where one set of value items ends and another begins.

MDS was used here to graphically represent the value groups uncovered in the previous stage. The 117 value items of the Value Compass were submitted to an MDS procedure similar to the one described by Schwartz (1992). The resulting value space is shown in Figure 3.1. A number of observations can be made. As expected, more similar values are located closer to each other. We can also see that the value items representing a value group occupy a distinct region in the value space. These regions were separated by drawing partition lines.

The value space reflects the structure of motivations predicted by the factor analysis: opposing types of motivations can be found in opposing positions in the value space. The Y-axis corresponds with the distinction between utilitarian and hedonic values. When moving up along the Y-axis, we see that values represent an increasing utilitarian motivation for consumer behaviour, and a decreasing hedonic motivation. The X-axis corresponds with the extent to which the consumer wishes to pursue his own interests: *promotion of self-interests versus care for others*. When moving to the right on this horizontal axis, the pursuit of self-interest becomes more important, and the concern for others less important.

In a value space, the presence of empty areas suggests that significant areas of the motivational continuum are missing (Schwartz, 1994). The value space in Figure 3.1 shows no such empty spaces, suggesting that the values of the Value Compass provide comprehensive coverage. On the other hand, we cannot discern sharp distinctions between adjacent value groups. Values that belong to different groups but share similar motivational concerns are located close to each other in the value space. For instance, even though *innovation* and *being successful* belong to different value groups, they appear in close proximity. Both value items share an achievement motivation, the need to do something better, although the object of achievement is somewhat different in these two value items. *Innovation* has a more functional achievement orientation. An individual favours innovative brands because the values progress. *Being successful* refers to

Table 3.1 The five groups of values of the Value Compass (corrected item-to-total correlation of each item is mentioned between brackets)

Hedonic versus utilitarian values 'Fun ↔ Function'		Promotion of self-interests versus care for others 'Me ↔ Us'		
Fun: hedonic values (α = 0.942)	Function: utilitarian values (α = 0.931)	Promotion of self-interests: values aimed at making a difference with others (α = 0.899)	Care for others: affiliation-oriented values (α = 0.945)	Care for the future: increasing the future quality of life (α = 0.825)
adventure (0.538)	accessibility (0.541)	beauty (0.611)	being humane (0.579)	environmental protection (0.692)
ambition (0.531)	accuracy (0.557)	being successful (0.636)	carefulness (0.509)	being environment-friendly (0.671)
being active (0.566)	authenticity (0.456)	cosmopolitan (0.556)	caring (0.667)	improving society (0.445)
being sportive (0.454)	certainty (0.528)	elegance (0.608)	cheerfulness (0.575)	providing for a better world (0.646)
being unique (0.494)	clarity (0.575)	good-looking (0.663)	confidentiality (0.512)	recycling (0.650)
comfortable life (0.479)	common sense (0.494)	high performance (0.512)	cosiness (0.535)	
courage (0.542)	convenience (0.474)	indulgence (0.438)	feeling of security (0.525)	
curiosity (0.500)	cost efficiency (0.479)	leadership (0.528)	femininity (0.485)	
enjoying life (0.649)	craftsmanship (0.391)	masculinity (0.510)	family life (0.537)	
enjoying things (0.623)	creativity (0.448)	perfection (0.536)	friendliness (0.669)	
enjoyment (0.626)	customer orientation (0.567)	power (0.570)	friendship (0.664)	
enthusiasm (0.633)	delivering quality (0.542)	reputation (0.565)	good manners (0.546)	
excitement (0.664)	efficiency (0.590)	sense of beauty (0.653)	harmony (0.659)	
fitness (0.445)	experience (0.532)	status (0.693)	health (0.693)	
flexibility (0.573)	expertise (0.578)	style (0.623)	honesty (0.580)	
fun (0.659)	functionality (0.583)		hospitality (0.609)	
guts (0.563)	innovation (0.584)		hygiene (0.576)	
imagination (0.481)	intellect (0.606)		intimacy (0.603)	
independence(0.571)	knowledge (0.583)		keeping a promise (0.528)	

individuality (0.512)
inspiration (0.608)
optimism (0.616)
passion (0.609)
physical exercise (0.505)
pleasure (0.637)
quality of life (0.604)
self-confidence (0.636)
sense of humor (0.614)
sensuality (0.617)
spontaneity (0.612)
to laugh (0.648)
varied life (0.590)
vitality (0.652)
wealth (0.486)
well-being (0.635)
wisdom (0.513)

originality (0.563)
precision (0.604)
professionalism (0.612)
progress (0.599)
punctuality (0.525)
reliability (0.586)
smart solutions (0.600)
sustainability (0.541)
usefulness (0.555)

loyalty (0.576)
nature (0.482)
openness (0.552)
peace (0.643)
protection (0.556)
respect (0.572)
romance (0.580)
sincerity (0.493)
safety (0.589)
solidarity (0.594)
spirituality (0.380)
tolerance (0.546)
trust (0.625)
truth (0.618)

a more personal desire to achieve, including an element of comparison with others: '*I choose successful brands because I want to show to others that I am successful*'. Hence, *innovation* belongs to the utilitarian value group, and *being successful* to the self-oriented value group.

The value space illustrates that the Value Compass is organized as a circular structure of adjacent value groups compatible with each other, and opposing value groups conflicting with each other. This structure of compatible and conflicting motivations is similar to the structure of Schwartz's value system described in Chapter 2. Schwartz identified two central dimensions organizing his value system: Openness to change versus Conservatism, and Self-enhancement versus Self-transcendence. The latter dimension bears a substantive similarity with the distinction between *Promotion of self-interests* and *Care for others* in the Value Compass. Self-transcendence resembles *care for others*; it constitutes of values emphasizing the acceptance of others as equals and concern for their welfare. The values motivating the pursuit of self-interest can be partly retraced in Schwartz's value dimension self-enhancement, particularly in his value types achievement and power. The more aesthetic aspect in this value group (*beauty, elegance, style),* however, is not represented by any of Schwartz's value types.

The other dimension of the Value Compass, *Fun versus Function*, is absent in Schwartz's value system, even though the hedonic ('*Fun*') values in the Value Compass show overlap with Schwartz's value types hedonism and stimulation. The presence of utilitarian values is the most striking difference between the Value Compass (activated toward consumer choice) and Schwartz's value system (applied to life in general). Apparently, utilitarian values are of more limited relevance when assessing life in general, but their importance increases for consumer behaviour. Schwartz does include the utilitarian value items capable and intelligent in his value system, but he relates them to the value type achievement, where they emphasize personal success.

Within most of the value groups, we can distinguish considerable variability in meaning between value items. For instance, the items *beauty* and *leadership* have quite a different meaning in everyday life, but in the Value Compass they both belong to the same value group. Another example is formed by the values representing *care for others / care for the future*. This group occupies a large area in the value space. It seems to fall apart in at least three separate dimensions. There is a subgroup with a focus on *safety* and *honesty*, which seems to correspond with the value types security (the safety aspect) and benevolence (the honesty aspect) in Schwartz's value system. Another subgroup emphasizes personal relations, including values such as *friendship, family life, caring for someone* and *romance*. The third subgroup, focusing on care for the future, already emerged as the fifth factor in the PCA. Variability in meaning indicates the potential of further subdivision of value groups. This potential is explored in the following stage of the study.

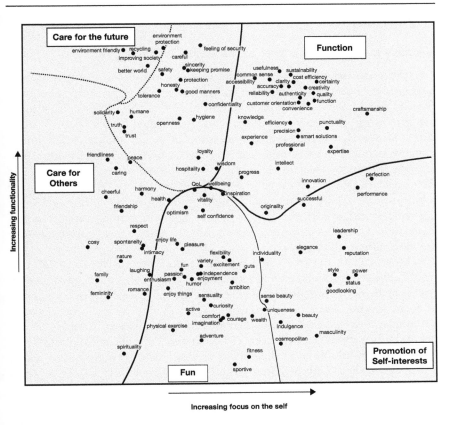

Figure 3.1 The Value Compass: organization of consumer values in a value space

Finally, we want to point out that *well-being* and *quality of life* (*QoL*) centre around the origin of the value space, implying that these two values are intrinsic to the other values of the Value Compass. This is in line with Proposition 1: *values motivate people to make choices that improve their quality of life*. The value space provides visual support for the proposition that quality of life can be enhanced by pursuing any of the values of the Value Compass.

Result of Stage 4

The values in the Value Compass can be placed in a two-dimensional value space. This value space represents a motivational continuum. More similar values are located in closer proximity. The more distant values are positioned in the value space, the more conflicting they are.

Stage 5

Identification of the value types of the Value Compass

The previous analysis showed that the values in the Value Compass can be organized in a circular structure organized along two dimensions: *Fun versus Function* and *Promotion of Self-Interests versus Care for Others*. In this value space, five groups of values were identified, each represented by a number of value items. However, variability in the meaning of items indicates multidimensionality within at least some of these groups. This suggests the existence of separate constructs, separate value types, within these five value groups. The factor analysis performed in Stage 3 confirms this suggestion: the five-factor solution based on which the value groups were formed, explained 44.4 per cent of the variance in the dataset. Hence, 55.6 per cent of variance is still unaccounted for. The purpose of the assessment in Stage 5 is to further analyse the variability in the dataset.

Within each of the five value groups, exploratory analysis with PCA in combination with a visual interpretation of the value space, was used to identify conceptually distinct motivational types. Additionally, we organized a number of focus groups. Each focus group consisted of five to eight respondents. Respondents were randomly chosen out of the employee database of the Hanze University of Applied Sciences Groningen. All value items of the Value Compass were submitted to these focus groups. Each focus group was asked, independent of the other focus groups, to cluster items into value types representing meaningful consumer choice motivations.

This exploratory assessment, combining statistical analysis and the qualitative focus group assessment, indeed indicated the existence of additional value types. Table 3.2 provides the overview of the value types revealed by the exploratory assessment.[6] Below, we briefly present these value types.

Within the values representing hedonic motivations, two distinct value types were identified. In addition to a cluster of values stressing the importance of *pleasure* and *enjoyment*, another cluster of value items was revealed that motivates *stimulation* or sensation-seeking behaviour. The utilitarian value group also hosts two distinct value types. One set of values stresses the importance of *functionality*, choice behaviour in which the instrumentality of the preferred choice is more appreciated than its intrinsic (pleasure) value. A related group of values emphasizes *achievement*, a motivation to improve performance. This value type includes values such as *innovation, progress* or *smart solutions*.

The self-centred values stress the importance of making a difference with others. Two clusters of values were distinguished here. Values such as *beauty* or *elegance* motivate to make a difference by appearance. Another set of value items is prestige-oriented, motivating brand choices aimed at showing *success* or *status*. This latter set of values seems closely related to Schwartz's value type power (Schwartz, 1992).

We found the most complex structure in the group of values motivating care for others. Besides the values stressing *social responsibility / care for the future*, which were already identified in Stage 3, four additional motivational types were uncovered: *safety, honesty, care* and *intimacy*. Safety values (e.g., *feeling of security, protection*) emphasize the importance of having and providing personal security. The importance of trusting someone's intentions is embodied by values such as *honesty* and *loyalty*. Finally, it is possible to differentiate between values emphasizing caring for and taking care of others (e.g., *family life, friendship, respect*), and values stressing the importance of having an intimate relation (e.g., *romance, sensuality, intimacy*).

For each value type, we can expect that some value items are more representative of the motivational goal expressed by the value type than others: we already observed that values in a value space represent a motivational continuum in which values spatially located near partition lines might be less typical for their value type than values located in the centre of the regions. The example of the value items *being successful* and *innovation* in the description of Stage 4 provided a good illustration. In the same vein, Schwartz *et al.* (2001) expected and reported a relatively low internal reliability for the value types in his value system, with Cronbach's alpha measures of the internal consistency ranging from 0.45 to 0.79. A test of the internal consistency of the value types of the Value Compass, however, showed a fairly high internal consistency, by showing alphas between 0.767 (*social responsibility*) and 0.933 (*enjoying life*) (Table 3.2). These results largely surpass the results reported by Schwartz *et al.* A possible explanation is the difference in scope of both value systems: Schwartz's value system presents motivations for life in general, whereas the Value Compass has the specific focus on consumer behaviour.

Selection of marker values: content validity and focus group assessment

The previous discussion showed that any value type invokes a combination of connotations, expressed by the value items that are used to represent the value type. The meaning of a value type gradually blends with the meaning attached to adjacent value types in the motivational continuum.

To describe each value type, we identified a set of marker values, a manageable set of three to four value items whose meaning best represents the motivational goal of the value type. To accomplish this aim, we assessed the content validity of each value item, the degree of correspondence of the meaning of the item with the meaning attached to the value type it represents. In this assessment, the content validity of each value item was determined by, again, a combination of qualitative and quantitative assessment. In the qualitative assessment, the value items were submitted to the focus groups described previously. Each focus group evaluated, for each value item, the extent to which the meaning of the value item matches with the meaning of its value type. This resulted in a list of value items providing a good match with their value type. Next, out of this list, the focus groups had to define a set of value items

Table 3.2 The value types of the Value Compass, with marker values printed in bold (the internal consistency -Cronbach's α- of each value type is mentioned within parentheses)[7]

Care for others: affiliation-oriented values				Care for the future: increasing the future quality of life
Care & affection (α = 0.890)	Intimacy (α = 0.794)	Honesty (α = 0.872)	Safety (α = 0.782)	Social responsibility (α = 0.767)
being humane	**cosiness**	good manners	carefulness	environmental protection
caring for someone	femininity	**honesty**	confidentiality	**being environment-friendly**
cheerfulness	**intimacy**	hospitality	**feeling of security**	**providing for a better world**
family life	**romance**	**keeping a promise**	hygiene	**recycling**
friendliness	**sensuality**	**loyalty**	**protection**	improving society
friendship	spirituality	openness	**safety**	
harmony		sincerity		
health		tolerance		
nature		trust		
peace		truth		
respect				
solidarity				

Fun: Hedonic values	Promotion of self-interests: Values aimed at making a difference with others			Function: Utilitarian values	
Enjoying life (α = 0.933)	*Stimulation* (α = 0.806)	*Prestige* (α = 0.816)	*Beauty* (α = 0.842)	*Functionality* (α = 0.904)	*Achievement* (α = 0.814)
ambition	**adventure**	high performance	**beauty**	accessibility	expertise
being unique	**being active**	**leadership**	cosmopolitan	accuracy	**innovation**
a comfortable life	**being sportive**	perfection	**elegance**	authenticity	**intellect**
curiosity	**courage**	**power**	**good-looking**	certainty	originality
enjoying life	fitness	reputation	masculinity	clarity	professionalism
enjoying things	guts	**status**	**sense of beauty**	common sense	**progress**
enjoyment	individuality	**being successful**	style	convenience	**smart solutions**
enthusiasm	physical exercise			cost efficiency	
excitement				craftsmanship	
flexibility				creativity	
fun				customer orientation	
imagination				delivering quality	
independence				**efficiency**	
indulgence				experience	
inspiration				**functionality**	
optimism				knowledge	
passion				**precision**	
pleasure				punctuality	
self-confidence				**reliability**	
sense of humor				sustainability	
spontaneity				usefulness	
to laugh					
varied life					
vitality					
wealth					
wisdom					

providing a well-balanced description of the value type. This subjective evaluation of the focus groups was combined with a statistical assessment of factor loadings. For this assessment, the factor loading of each value item on its value type (i.e., the correlation of the item with its value type) was established with the help of confirmatory factor analysis (CFA, see Box 3.2 for additional information). Value items selected by the focus groups and with a high factor loading, that is, a factor loading of at least 0.50, were assumed to have a high content validity. These values were assigned as marker items. The resulting marker values are printed in bold in Table 3.2.

Result of Stage 5

Exploratory analysis of the Value Compass identified 11 value types: care and affection for close others, intimacy, safety, honesty, social responsibility, enjoying life, stimulation, prestige, beauty, functionality and achievement. Each value type is represented by three to four marker values.

Box 3.2   Confirmatory Factor Analysis

Confirmatory Factor Analysis (CFA) is a statistical technique through which a hypothesized model can be validated by comparing the theoretical structure of the model with the observed structure in the actual data (Fischer & Fontaine, 2011; Hair et al., 2006). CFA is theory-driven: the researcher has to specify in advance which factors exist within an existing set of items, and which items are used as indicators for which factor. The statistics in CFA then show how well the specified factors match the actual data. CFA is used, for instance, in cross-cultural research to test structural equivalence of models across cultures. In a cross-cultural study, Schwartz and Boehnke (2004) confirmed the structure of the Schwartz Value System with a CFA approach. CFA can be executed with statistical software such as AMOS and LISREL.

A model (e.g., the Value Compass) in CFA consists of a number of interrelated constructs (e.g., value types). Each construct is represented by a number of items (e.g., value items); these items are measured empirically (e.g., submitted in a survey to a group of respondents). CFA produces two types of indicators (Hair et al., 2006):

1 Evidence of construct validity provides confidence that items (e.g., value items) used in a test actually represent a construct (e.g., value type) in the model.
2 Indicators of goodness-of-fit assess the structure of the hypothesized model. In technical terms, goodness-of-fit indicators show how well a specified model (e.g., a value system) reproduces the covariance matrix of the indicator items.

Construct validity

Construct validity is the extent to which a set of measured items (e.g., value items) reflect the construct (e.g., the value type) those items are designed to measure (Hair et al., 2006). Construct validity can be assessed by examining convergent and discriminant validity.

The **convergent validity** indicates the degree of shared variance of the items representing a construct. Items which are used for a specific construct should share a high proportion of variance with this construct. The following indicators are relevant:

- Factor loading (λ): An item should have a high loading on the construct it represents. A rule of thumb is that $\lambda \geq 0.5$, ideally $\lambda \geq 0.7$, represents high factor loading. This indicator corresponds with the item-to-total correlation used in exploratory techniques.
- Construct reliability (CR): the internal consistency of the value type. Cronbach's alpha is a commonly applied reliability measure. A slightly different indicator, frequently used in combination with CFA, is construct reliability (CR). CR takes into account the error variance associated with each item (σ). It is calculated by:

$$CR = \frac{\left(\sum_{i=1}^{n} \lambda_i\right)^2}{\left(\sum_{i=1}^{n} \lambda_i\right)^2 + \left(\sum_{i=1}^{n} \delta_i\right)}.$$

A CR of 0.7 or higher suggests good reliability.

The **discriminant validity** is the extent to which the constructs in a model are distinct from each other. The discriminant validity between two value types can be calculated as:

$$\text{Discriminant validity}_{\text{of constr.1 comp. w. constr.2}} = \frac{\text{variance extracted}_{\text{constr.1}}}{\text{squared correlation coefficient}_{\text{constr.1\&2}}}$$

The variance extracted (VE) by a construct is the average percentage of variance extracted by the construct from the set of items representing the construct. It is calculated as the total of all squared standardized factor loadings divided by the number of items:

$$VE = \frac{\sum_{i=1}^{n} \lambda_i^2}{n}.$$

A value type shows discriminant validity if

$$\frac{\text{variance extracted}}{\text{squared correlation coefficient}} > 1 \text{ (Hair et al., 2006)}$$

Goodness-of-fit

With goodness-of-fit (GOF) measures a theoretical model can be compared to reality, as represented by the data. The closer the model is to the actual data, the better the fit of the model. GOF is assessed by a combination of fit indicators (Hair et al., 2006). The following indicators are frequently used:

- The fundamental measure of fit is **chi-square ($\chi 2$).** A small (insignificant) χ^2 value indicates a good match between the theoretical structure and the observed results, hence, a good fit. This would be the case with higher p-values (larger than 0.05)[8]. Unfortunately, the χ^2 value is also influenced by the sample size and the number of variables. Consequently, especially with a large sample size or a large number of variables, χ^2 is not a reliable indicator.
- **Comparative Fit Index (CFI)** is an index assessing to what extent the model fits better as compared to a model assuming no correlation between the constructs. CFI ranges between 0 and 1. In models with larger sample size (sample size higher than 250), a CFI $\geq$ 0.92 indicates a good fit, and a CFI $\leq$ 0.90 is an indication of a poor fit.
- **Root Mean Square Error of Approximation (RMSEA)** assesses the residual covariance: it gives an indication of the amount of variability in the actual data not explained by the model. An RMSEA $\leq$ 0.08 is an indication of a good fit, RMSEA $\geq$ 0.10 indicates a poor fit.

Stage 6

Assessment of the value types of the Value Compass in a second survey round

In the previous sections, the value types of the Value Compass were identified by using exploratory techniques. The uncovered value types appeared to represent distinct motivations.

In addition to this exploratory analysis, we felt the importance of corroborating these results with confirmatory evidence. To collect this evidence, we used the results of a second survey. This additional survey was submitted to a new sample of students of the Hanze University of Applied Sciences Groningen. The design of this test was similar to the study described in

Table 3.3 The construct validity of the value types in the Value Compass

Value type	Marker values	Convergent validity		Discriminant validity with adjacent value types
		α	CR	
Enjoying life	Enjoying life, excitement, fun, pleasure	0.775	0.776	With Stimulation: 2.51 With Affection: 1.19
Stimulation	Adventure, being active, being sportive, courage	0.748	0.754	With Enjoying life: 2.35 With Beauty: 8.65
Beauty	Beauty, elegance, good-looking, sense of beauty	0.853	0.848	With Stimulation: 11.65 With Prestige: 2.14
Prestige	Being successful, leadership, power, status	0.769	0.786	With Beauty: 1.78 With Achievement: 1.86
Achievement	Innovation, intellect, progress, smart solutions	0.720	0.726	With Prestige: 1.52 With Functionality: 0.96
Functionality	Efficiency, functionality, precision, reliability	0.676	0.678	With Achievement: 0.88 With Safety: 1.36
Safety	Feeling of security, protection, safety	0.817	0.825	With Functionality: 2.32 With Honesty: 2.05
Honesty	Honesty, keeping a promise, loyalty	0.803	0.810	With Safety: 1.96 With Affection: 1.76
Social responsibility	Environment-friendly, providing for a better world, recycling	0.859	0.860	With Honesty: 4.21 With Affection: 1.72
Care & affection	Caring for someone, family life, friendship, harmony	0.755	0.754	With Honesty: 1.30 With Intimacy: 0.94
Intimacy	Cosiness, intimacy, romance, sensuality	0.767	0.767	With Affection: 0.98 With Enjoying life: 1.33

Stage 2. Similar to this previous study, the respondents had to rate the relevance of each value item in a branding context on a 5-point Likert scale. Only this time, they focused on the marker items of the value types of the Value Compass: the respondents had to assess the (randomized) set of the 41 marker values derived in the previous stage. These marker items were administered through an online survey to a student sample of 1,468 students. Respondents received an email, with a request to fill out the survey. The survey could be accessed by clicking on the link in the email. The survey was available from 22 March until 6 April 2010. A total of 318 students filled out the value list in this questionnaire. Since the list of values was a lot shorter than the list administered in the survey described in Stage 2, virtually all respondents who started the survey also completed the survey.

The results of this second survey were used to confirm the structure of the Value Compass as was uncovered in the earlier stages. In the analysis of the second dataset, the value items were forced into the value type structure proposed by the exploratory analysis in Stage 5 (see Table 3.2). The content of these 'forced' value types then was validated through an analysis of their construct validity, performed with confirmatory factor analysis (CFA). Construct validity of a value type is the extent to which the value items actually reflect the value type they are supposed to measure. It can be assessed by examining the factor loadings of the value items on their value type (convergent validity) and of the divergence of the value type with other value types (discriminant validity; see Box 3.2). In the test of discriminant validity, we focused on those value types that are most closely related, that is, on neigh-bouring value types. If it can be demonstrated that the most related value types are distinct from each other, then certainly the less compatible value types also show discriminant validity.

Table 3.3 presents the outcomes. Results confirm the existence of the value types as revealed in the previous stages, with the marker values representing these value types. All value types show acceptable internal consistencies, presenting evidence of their convergent validity. Most value types are also clearly distinct from neighbouring value types in the Value Compass. Two pairs of value types, however, are less evidently differentiated from each other, showing discriminant validity smaller than 1.0. The two functional value types *achievement* and *functionality* intermix to some extent. A similar observation can be made for *intimacy* and *care and affection*.

Result of Stage 6

The test of construct validity confirms the existence of nine to 11 value types, which are clearly distinct from each other. Each of these value types can be represented by three to four marker values. Table 3.4 presents an overview of these value types and their marker values.

Table 3.4 Value Compass: the value types and their marker values

Care & affection	Intimacy	Honesty	Safety	Social responsibility
caring for someone	cosiness	honesty	feeling of security	being environment-friendly
family life	intimacy	keeping a promise	protection	providing for a better world
friendship	romance	loyalty	safety	recycling
harmony	sensuality			

Enjoying life	Stimulation	Prestige	Beauty	Functionality	Achievement
enjoying life	adventure	leadership	beauty	efficiency	innovation
excitement	being active	power	elegance	functionality	intellect
fun	being sportive	status	good-looking	precision	progress
pleasure	courage	being successful	sense of beauty	reliability	smart solutions

Stage 7

Confirmation of the structure of the Value Compass: goodness-of-fit test with CFA

Stage 6 confirmed the existence of nine to 11 consumer value types, each represented by the marker values listed in Table 3.4. Construct validity of the separate value types, however, does not imply that these value types, and the interrelations between these value types, form a good representation of the circumplex structure of the Value Compass. The purpose of stage 7 is to validate whether the structure of the Value Compass can actually be represented by these value types. CFA provides a number of statistics that can be used to examine this goodness-of-fit (see Box 3.2).

Four models were tested. The first model is the Value Compass with the 11 value types. The value types *intimacy* and *care and affection* are combined in the second model. In the third model, the value types *achievement* and *functionality* are combined (and *intimacy* and *care and affection* are treated separately). Finally, in the fourth model, both combinations are used (hence, assuming nine value types). The test results are presented in Table 3.5.

The results of the goodness-of-fit test confirm the structure of the Value Compass. The values that guide consumer behaviour can be organized in a model consisting of the 11 value types revealed in the previous stages. Even

Table 3.5 Validity of the structure of the Value Compass

Model	Hypothesis	χ^2	Df	RMSEA	CFI	Decision[1]
A	Value Compass consists of 11 factors	1709.2	724	0.067	0.948	
B	Value Compass consists of 10 factors (*intimacy* and *care & affection* combined)	1787.4	734	0.069	0.945	
C	Value Compass consists of 10 factors (*achievement* and *functionality* combined)	1753.8	743	0.068	0.946	
D	Value Compass consists of 9 factors (*achievement* and *functionality* together, *intimacy* and *care & affection* together)	1922.9	743	0.073	0.938	
–	Model A has a better fit than model B	$\Delta\chi^2 = 78.2$	$\Delta df = 10$	$\chi^2_{critical} = 18.31$		Supported
–	Model A has a better fit than model C	$\Delta\chi^2 = 44.6$	$\Delta df = 10$	$\chi^2_{critical} = 18.31$		Supported
–	Model A has a better fit than model D	$\Delta\chi^2 = 213.7$	$\Delta df = 19$	$\chi^2_{critical} = 30.14$		Supported

1 A model has good fit with RMSEA $\leq$ 0.08, and CFI $\geq$ 0.92. Consequently, the models A, B, C, and D all are acceptable models. A model has a significant better fit than a comparable model if the decrease in χ^2 is bigger than the critical χ^2, taking the decrease in degrees of freedom into account ($p = 0.05$)

though all models provide adequate fit (based on the criteria RMSEA ≤ 0.08 and CFI ≥ 0.92), a model with 11 value types provides a better fit than a model with nine or 10 value types.

Result of Stage 7

The Value Compass consists of 11 interrelated value types. These value types are interrelated in the form of a circular value system organized along two dimensions. This system can be presented visually in the form of a value space.

3.3 Conclusion

Consumer behaviour is motivated by values. These values are more than a list of unrelated items. In this chapter, we demonstrated that consumer behaviour is motivated by a specific set of values, and that these values are interrelated: some values represent more similar motivations, whereas other values are less related.

This chapter presented the development of the Value Compass, the value system representing the values that motivate consumer behaviour. From a comprehensive list of value items, a jury selected those value items that are relevant for consumer behaviour. Subsequently, in a step-by-step development process involving a number of survey rounds, these selected value items were used to uncover the structure of the Value Compass. With the help of exploratory and confirmatory factor analyses, related value items were grouped into value types, each representing a distinct motivation for consumer behaviour. In total, the Value Compass was found to comprise 11 value types. By using multidimensional scaling, it was demonstrated that these value types, and the consumer values they represent, can be organized according to a circular structure that can be visualized in the form of a value space. In this value space, values with more similar motivational goals can be found in close proximity, whereas values representing more dissimilar or conflicting motivations have a more distant position from each other. The value types in the value space were found to be organized along two dimensions, resembling value orientations found in psychology and benefit dimensions found in marketing literature. The first dimension, representing values motivating the pursuit of self-interest as opposed to values motivating to care for and give attention to others, resembles the dimension self-enhancement versus self-transcendence in Schwartz's value system (Schwartz, 1992). The second dimension distinguishes between hedonic (pleasure-oriented) values and utilitarian (functionality-oriented) values, a distinction central to consumer behaviour.

In this chapter, we revealed the values that consumers use when they evaluate brands or make other consumer choice decisions, and we demonstrated how these values are related to each other. Each of these value types will be more extensively described in the next chapter.

Notes

1   The lexical hypothesis postulates that those individual differences that are most salient and socially relevant in people's lives will eventually become encoded into their language. The more important such a difference, the more likely it becomes expressed as a single word (John, Angleitner & Ostendorf, 2006). For instance, by using the lexical approach, Allport and Odbert (1936) developed a list of nearly 18,000 personality trait items based on a review of all entries of *Webster's New International Dictionary*. The trait list of this influential study served as input for the personality trait inventory of Costa and McCrae (1992), and, as mentioned in Section 2.2, for Rokeach's value survey (1973).

2   Surveymonkey is a tool that can be used to publish surveys online. This tool can be accessed through *www.surveymonkey.com*

3   In the Likert scale, a rating of 3 implies a neutral score. A rating of 1 or 2 implies that the value is considered (very) unimportant, a rating of 4 or 5 means (very) important. With a mean rating of 3.5, the criterion is stringent enough to exclude items with a neutral impact on brand choice, but not so stringent that only important items are included.

4   *The Oxford Dictionary of English* (2005) lists the following for ideal: 1. satisfying one's conception of what is perfect, most suitable; 2. existing only in the imagination.

5   Schwartz uses the term SSA (Smallest Space Analysis) whenever he describes his methodology (e.g., 1992, 2006). To connect to formal use of terminology (Borg & Groenen, 2005; Hair *et al.*, 2006), we use the term multidimensional scaling (MDS) to describe this technique.

6   As explained in Stage 4, *well-being* and *quality of life*, being at the origin of the value space, can not be attributed to any of the value types. Consequently, they are not categorized among any of the value types mentioned in Table 3.2.

7   The assessment indicated that the value types *sensuality* and *indulgence* tend to belong to another value group (attention for others and fun respectively), as compared to the results of the PCA analysis in Stage 3. In Table 3.2, the switch of these two items to another value group has been taken into account.

8   Generally, in cross-tabulations, researchers are looking for a significant χ^2 ($p < 0.05$), indicating a significant difference between variables. In CFA, however, the researcher is looking for a confirmation that there is *no* (significant) difference between the observed and the theoretical structure. In other words, the researcher is looking for an insignificant χ^2 ($p > 0.05$).

References

Allport, G. W. & Odbert, H. S. (1936). Trait-names: A psycho-lexical study. *Psychological Monographs, 47*(1).

Batra, R. & Ahtola, O. T. (1990). Measuring the hedonic and utilitarian sources of consumer attitudes. *Marketing Letters, 2*(2), 159–170.

Borg, I. & Groenen, P. J. (2005). *Modern multidimensional scaling: Theory and applications.* New York, NY: Springer.

Costa, P. & McCrae, R. (1992). *Revised NEO Personality Inventory (NEOPI-R) and NEO Five-Factor Inventory (NEO-FFI) Professional Manual.* Odessa, FL: Psychological Assessment Resources.

De Raad, B. & Van Oudenhoven, J. P. (2008). Factors of values in the Dutch language and their relationship to factors of personality. *European Journal of Personality, 22*(2), 81–108.

Fischer, R. & Fontaine, J. R. (2011). Methods for investigating structural equivalence. In D. Matsumoto & F. J. Van de Vijver, *Cross-cultural research methods in psychology* (pp. 179–215). New York, NY: Cambridge University Press.

Guttman, L. (1968). A general non-metric technique for finding the smallest coordinate space for a configuration of points. *Psychometrica, 33*(4), 469–506.

Hair, J. H., Black, W. C., Babin, B. J., Anderson, R. E. & Tatham, R. L. (2006). *Multivariate Data Analysis* (6th edition). Upper Saddle River, NJ: Pearson Prentice Hall.

Hirschman, E. C. & Holbrook, M. B. (1982). Hedonic consumption: Emerging concepts, methods, and propositions. *Journal of Marketing, 46*(3), 92–101.

Hofstede, G. (1980). *Culture's consequences: Comparing values, behaviors, institutions and organizations across nations.* Thousand Oaks, CA: Sage.

Hofstede, G. (2011). Dimensionalizing cultures: The Hofstede model in context. *Online Readings in Psychology and Culture, 2*(1). http://dx.doi.org/10.9707/2307–0919.1014.

John, O. P., Angleitner, A. & Ostendorf, F. (2006). The lexical approach to personality: A historical review of trait taxonomic research. *European Journal of Personality, 2*(3), 171–203.

McClelland, D. C. (1987). *Human motivation.* Cambridge, UK: Cambridge University Press.

Pearsall, J. & Hanks, P. (2005). *Oxford Dictionary of English* (2nd edition). London, UK: Oxford University Press.

Rokeach, M. (1973). *The nature of human values.* New York, NY: The Free Press.

Schwartz, S. H. (1992). Universals in the content and structure of values: theoretical advances and empirical tests in 20 countries. In M. Zanna, *Advances in experimental social psychology (Vol. 25, pp 1–65).* New York, NY: The Free Press.

Schwartz, S. H. (1994). Are there universal aspects in the structure and contents of human values? *Journal of Social Issues, 50*(4), 19–45.

Schwartz, S. H. (1994b). Beyond individualism/collectivism: New cultural dimensions of values. In U. Kim, H. C. Triandis, Ç. Kâgitçibasi, S.-C. Choi & G. Yoon, *Individualism and collectivism: theory, method, and applications* (pp. 85–122). Thousand Oaks, CA: Sage Publications.

Schwartz, S. H. (2006). Les valeurs de base de la personne: Théorie, mesures et applications. *Revue Française de Sociologie, 47*(4): 929–968.

Triandis, H. C. (1995). *Individualism & collectivism.* Boulder, CO: Westmore.

Van de Vijver, F. J. & Leung, K. (1997). *Methods and data-analysis for cross-cultural research.* Newbury Park, CA: Sage.

Verplanken, B. & Holland, R. W. (2002). Motivated decision making: Effects of activation and self-centrality of values on choices and behavior. *Journal of Personality and Social Psychology, 82*(3), 434–447.

Whan Park, C., Jaworski, B. J. & MacInnis, D. J. (1986). Strategic brand concept-image management. *Journal of Marketing, 50*(4), 135–145.

Chapter 4

Description of the Value Compass

4.1 Introduction

Consumer behaviour involves making choices. Consumers have to decide, often on a daily basis, which brands to buy. These brands are instrumental for consumers: by consuming they attempt to satisfy their needs. Consumers are expected to choose those brands that match best with what they would like to have, to feel, to be, or to experience. Brands help consumers in realizing what they feel important. As a consequence, brand choice can be considered to be guided by consumer values, as was argued in the previous chapters. We saw that the values guiding brand choice are organized as a coherent system of values, each providing a different motivation to improve the quality of life. Some of these values reinforce each other, while other values have a conflicting impact on choice behaviour. This value system, the Value Compass, is organized as a circular structure organized along two central dimensions:

- *Fun versus Function.* This dimension represents values motivating people to improve their quality of life by making hedonic choices, as opposed to values motivating people to improve their quality of life by making utilitarian (functional) choices.
- *Promotion of Self-Interests versus Care for Others.* This dimension represents values motivating people to promote their own personal interests, to make a difference with others, as opposed to values motivating choices aimed at living in harmony with others, caring for others and taking care of others. Among the care-oriented values, a distinction can be made between, on the one hand, caring for and taking care of close others, and on the other hand, sustainability-oriented values, promoting a sense of responsibility for the future.

The Value Compass is schematically represented in Figure 4.1. Within this value system, different types of values can be identified. This chapter is devoted to a presentation of these value types. Hedonic and utilitarian values are presented in Section 4.2, the value types of the second dimension are described in Section

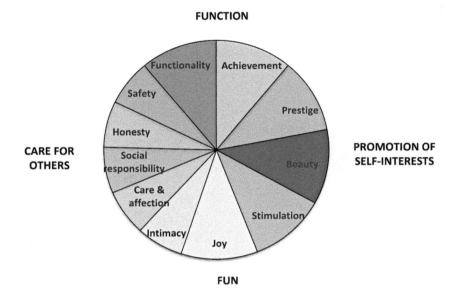

Figure 4.1 Schematic presentation of the Value Compass

4.3. Section 4.4 contains a comparison of the Value Compass with Schwartz's Value System. Finally, Section 4.5 presents the relative importance of consumer values in a sample of Dutch consumers.

4.2 Fun versus function

The first central dimension underlying the Value Compass opposes hedonic values such as *joy, sensation,* or *excitement,* to functional values expressing *intellect, efficiency* or *functionality.* Hedonic values stimulate behaviour with an intrinsic value, behaviour aimed at enjoying and experiencing something for its own sake. Utilitarian values stimulate choices motivated by the instrumental value or usefulness of the brand.

4.2.1 Fun: hedonic values

Hedonism focuses on the intrinsic value of pleasure. Hedonism was already propagated by Epicurus as a central motivation in life: '*Pleasure is our first and kindred good. It is the starting-point of every choice and of every aversion*' (Letter to Menoeceus, 128–129). Consumer behaviour motivated by hedonic values results in choices aimed at the experience of joy or stimulation. Two value types are distinguished: *enjoying life* and *stimulation.*

Enjoying life

The motivational goal of this value type is **To have pleasure and to enjoy life**. This value type includes values such as *enjoying life, fun, pleasure, passion, varied life* and *excitement*. The focus on individual pleasure emphasizes the individualistic aspect of this value type. This individualistic aspect is also illustrated by the inclusion of *independence* as one of the values of this value type.

The value type *enjoying life* shows an overlap with Schwartz's value type hedonism, which also includes the values of pleasure and enjoying life. The key characteristic of *enjoying life* is the focus on the enjoyable emotions that result from consumption; the pleasure, amusement or joy derived from consuming a brand. The active search for these experiences, the search for arousal, is represented by the following value type: *stimulation*.

Stimulation

The motivational goal of *stimulation* is **The experience of stimulating sensations.** It includes values such as *adventure, courage, being active* and *being sportive*. The goal of sensation-seeking behaviour is the increase of stimulation. Sensation seeking has been defined as '*the seeking of varied, novel, complex, and intense sensations and experiences, and the willingness to take physical, social, legal, and financial risks for the sake of such experience*' (Zuckerman, 1994, p. 27). The importance of sensations for consumer behaviour has been boosted by the publication of *The Experience Economy* (Pine and Gilmore) in 1999. Pine and Gilmore argued that businesses must orchestrate memorable events for their customers, and that the experience of being part of such an event becomes the product.

The value types *enjoying life* and *stimulation* are related. The value type *stimulation* symbolizes the active search for stimulating experiences, to some extent even thrill-seeking behaviour, whereas the values in value type *enjoying life* emphasize pleasure itself, the joy, passion or excitement resulting from experiences. The hedonic values are connected to the other-directed values (*care for others*) by the value type *intimacy*. *Intimacy* symbolizes both a caring, intimate relation as well as the motivation to enjoy (together with) the other.

4.2.2 Function: utilitarian values

Utilitarian values embody competence, the ability to do something successfully or efficiently. In the psychological literature, the concept of competence has been related to self-efficacy, the individual's confidence in his ability to solve a problem or accomplish a task (Bandura, 1986). Bandura made a distinction between outcome expectations – the belief that certain behaviours will lead to certain outcomes (e.g., studying results in high grades) – and efficacy expectations – the belief that one can effectively perform the behaviours necessary to produce the outcome (e.g., believing that one has the capability to study). Effective performance has been specified as a motivational goal in its own right, evolving from the need to deal effectively with the environment (White, 1959; Yarrow, McQuiston, MacTurk, McCarthy, Klein & Vietze, 1983). Competence is also considered a basic human need in self-determination theory. This theory maintains that an understanding of human motivation requires a consideration of innate psychological needs for competence, autonomy and relatedness. In this theory, the need for competence is the desire to have an effect on the environment as well as to achieve desired outcomes (Deci & Ryan, 2000). In management literature, the competence concept has received central attention since the publication of *The core competence of the corporation* (Prahalad & Hamel, 1990). Core competences are the company's collective knowledge, and have to be identified and stimulated in order to create competitive advantage.

The Value Compass distinguishes between successful performance – value type *achievement* – and efficient performance – value type *functionality*. Both value types refer to a utilitarian motivation, a motivation in which the instrumental benefits of consumer choice are valued. In Schwartz's value system, this utilitarian aspect is absent. Schwartz relates competence to the value type achievement, but he does not include functionality in his value system.

Functionality

The motivational goal of *functionality* is **Performance according to specifications.** This value type represents values like *efficiency, common sense, functionality* and *reliability*. The focus is on usefulness or utility: the value is not derived from doing a task for its own sake, but to reach some other desired end state (Wigfield & Eccles, 2000). In the Value Compass, utilitarian values oppose hedonic values. Consumers high in *functionality* favour choices where the instrumentality of their preferred choice is more important than its intrinsic (pleasure) value. For instance, when buying a car they won't consider the fun of driving, but rather the efficiency and reliability the car provides in arriving at a certain destination.

Functionality has a focus on reliable, efficient performance: being able to obtain the desired outcomes, preferably with using fewer resources than alternative options. In comparison with *achievement* values, the emphasis is on efficacy, the ability that a certain course of action produces a certain outcome. *Achievement* has a progress orientation, with the emphasis on improving the abilities.

Achievement

The motivational goal of *achievement* is **Higher performance by improving competence**. It stimulates choice behaviour where progress is an important motivation, representing values such as *smart solutions, progress, innovation, intellect* and *expertise*. Improving competence implies an innovative aspect: doing something better often implies doing it differently from before. McClelland (1987) linked achievement with the search for stimulation: people want to achieve because they need variety and stimulation.

Achievement is a utilitarian value type, neighbouring the value type *prestige* in the value space. Both value types emphasize performance. But the point of reference for *achievement* is higher performance as compared to previous performance, whereas a choice motivated by *prestige* focuses on better performance of oneself as compared with the performance of others. This forms a difference with Schwartz's value type achievement. In his value type achievement, he includes the aspect of comparison with others, by including values such as successful and influential.

4.3 Promotion of self-interests versus care for others

The way individuals want to relate to others is an important motivation: consumer choice is influenced by how consumers wish to be perceived by others, or how they wish to have an influence on others. This is expressed by the second dimension underlying the Value Compass: *the promotion of self-interest versus care for others*.

An important element in this dimension is social comparison. Social comparison theory states that people have a drive to evaluate their opinions and abilities in comparison with other people (Festinger, 1954). A number of motivational processes guiding social comparison have been identified, including both vertical and lateral comparison (Suls, Martin & Wheeler, 2002; Taylor, Wayment & Carrillo, 1996). Vertical comparison involves comparison with dissimilar others, including both upward and downward comparison. Downward comparison means comparing yourself with people who are worse off. Upward comparison, with superior role models, can provide hope and inspiration. Both upward and downward comparison satisfies self-enhancement, the need to maintain a positive sense of self. Values in the Value Compass motivating the pursuit of self-interest represent this self-enhancement motive. Lateral comparison is aimed at affiliation: the need to affiliate with others similar to oneself. Assimilation is stimulated by the belief that one could obtain the same status as the other, by psychological closeness, or by sharing opinions or abilities with the other. The affiliation motivation is represented by values promoting the care for others.

On a cultural level, the social patterns of individualism and collectivism (Hofstede, 1980, 2011; Triandis, 1995) seem related to these values. In individualistic societies, the interests of the individual prevail over the interests of the group, which seems to relate to the pursuit of self-interest in the Value Compass. Collectivistic societies emphasize the interdependence relation with the group. This seems to coincide with values emphasizing the relations with others. Schwartz (1992) identified two basic dimensions underlying his value system. One of these dimensions opposes values promoting personal interests (individual outcomes) with values emphasizing the well-being and interests of others (social outcomes): self-enhancement versus self-transcendence. This dimension corresponds with the dimension *promotion of self-interests* versus *care for others* in the Value Compass.

4.3.1 The pursuit of self-interest

Choice behaviour can be motivated by values promoting the importance of making a difference with others: the pursuit of one's own interests or one's relative success and dominance over others. There are different ways to make a difference, ranging from status, leadership and performance to beauty and elegance. Two value types guide social comparison in consumer behaviour: the desire to have a more prestigious or more powerful position than others and the desire to be more attractive than others.

Prestige

People have the need for self-respect, or self-esteem, and the need to receive respect or esteem from others (Maslow, 1954). These needs involve a desire for reputation, prestige, status, fame, appreciation or dominance. They are represented in the Value Compass by the value type *prestige*. In the psychological domain, these values were related to the power motive (e.g., Schwartz, 1992). The power motive is the motive to have impact, control or influence over another person, group or the world at large (McClelland, 1987; Winter, 1973). On a cultural level, Hofstede defines power distance as '*the extent to which the less powerful members of institutions and organizations within a country expect and accept that power is distributed unequally*' (Hofstede, 2011). In countries with high power distance, people accept the power and status of a superior.

The motivational goal of the value type *prestige* is defined as **Attainment of social status and prestige, and impress, influence or control over people**. This goal is similar to the motivational goal of the value type power in Schwartz (1992). The values in this value type (e.g., *power, status, leadership*) emphasize the importance of power or social status. Consumer behaviour motivated by *prestige* values can make a person choose brands that make it possible to influence or control someone else. A prestige motivation can also lead to conspicuous consumption: the desire to signal wealth or respect by buying brands that express prestige or status (Bagwell & Bentheim, 1996; Han, Nunes & Drèze, 2010; Vigneron & Johnson, 1999). Conspicuous consumption has been referred to as the 'Veblen-effects' (Bagwell & Bernheim, 1996). As Veblen puts it: '*In order to gain and to hold the esteem of men, wealth must be put in evidence, for esteem is awarded only on evidence*' (Veblen, 1899, p. 24). Owning prestigious possessions was shown to correlate with the power motive (Winter, 1973).

As mentioned previously, the value types *prestige* and *achievement* are related to each other. *Prestige* motivates to perform better than others, whereas *achievement* emphasizes the improvement of the performance in itself. But the distinction is gradual. *Prestige* is connected to the value type *achievement* by values such as *being successful* and *high performance*. These values relate to both the need for power (to perform better, or to be more successful than somebody else) as well as to the need for achievement (the intrinsic motivation to improve and demonstrate competence). For instance, an individual can value success, because success creates prestige and respect, and consequently the opportunity to receive respect from others (*prestige*). But he can also be motivated by an internal drive to improve performance (*achievement*).

Beauty

The motivational goal of this value type is **Expression of a unique appearance**. This value type represents values associated with physical beauty (*beauty, good-looking*), as well as values emphasizing the aesthetic aspects of appearance or behaviour (*style, elegance*). Consumer choice behaviour motivated by this value type is aimed at symbolic consumption. The consumer chooses brands that help him to create a certain desired appearance: he wants to look good, elegant, stylish or attractive, in order to support his self-concept, to impress others or even to be admired by others.

4.3.2 The care for others

The values in this group express the need for affiliation: the tendency to receive gratification from harmonious relationships (Murray, 1938). Affiliation embodies the importance of interdependence with others: family members, friends, co-workers or other members of the same country or society (Markus & Kitayama, 1991). Individuals rating high on these values increase their quality of life through their relations with others. Consumer behaviour then will be guided by considering the quality of life of others, as well as by showing or confirming membership of the group to which one belongs. Schwartz (1992) refers to these values as self-transcendence values: values emphasizing the concern for the welfare and interests of others. This group of values contains five value types: *care & affection, intimacy, safety, honesty* and *social responsibility*.

Care & Affection

This value type incorporates the concern for the well-being of others, and to establish or maintain friendly relations with them. The motivational goal of this value type is **Care for the quality of life of close others.** This value type includes values such as *care, friendship, respect, friendliness* and *family life*. These values resemble the need for love, affection and belongingness identified by

Maslow (1954), and Schwartz's value type benevolence, which he defined as the concern for the welfare of close others in everyday interaction. Consumer behaviour guided by this value type focuses on satisfying the needs of others (e.g., buying presents), or on the importance of living in friendship and harmony with others (e.g., home improvement for a more comfortable family life).

The value *health* is included in Schwartz's value type security. In the Value Compass it seems to match more with care-related values. This provides an indication that this value type not only refers to harmonious relations with others, but also to a state of inner harmony. Inner harmony is the motivational goal of spirituality, a value type that was hypothesized by Schwartz (1992) but did not materialize as a separate value type in his cross-cultural studies. In the Value Compass, *spirituality* is included in the value type *intimacy*.

Intimacy

The previous value type, *care & affection*, is concerned with the well-being of close others. The value type *intimacy* reflects a specific form of caring for others. The motivational goal for the value type *intimacy* is **The creation of an intimate relation with a significant other**. The values in this value type (*romance, sensuality, intimacy, cosiness*) emphasize close personal relations. Intimacy is focused on the pleasure and the warm, happy feelings one gets out of a relation with beloved others, which includes a romantic love relation or the relation between parent and child. The aspect of pleasure related to an intimate relation links this value type to the hedonic value types *enjoying life* and *stimulation*. In his publication 'Lovemarks', Roberts (2005) claims that the intimacy-related values *intimacy, sensuality* and *mystery*, are essential drivers of brand loyalty because they create love and respect for a brand.

Safety

The motivational goal of this value type is: **a feeling of (physical and emotional) security, free from anxiety.** The value type includes values such as *safety, protection* and *feeling of security*. The values in this value type resemble Maslow's safety needs (Maslow, 1954). Our value type *safety* is defined in a more restricted sense than Schwartz's value type security, which also includes harmony and stability in relationships. It is the most instrumental of the value types expressing care for others; in the value space it neighbours the value type *functionality*.

Safety is aimed at reducing uncertainty. The reduction of uncertainty is a primary motivation in human behaviour. People can be characterized by their uncertainty orientation (Sorrentino & Short, 1986). Certainty-oriented people will value safety and security, whereas someone oriented toward uncertainty will '*search for meaning, attempting to make sense out of his environment, and will seek out new or novel situations*' (Sorrentino & Short, 1986, p. 382). We can expect that certainty-oriented consumers show lower ratings on values belonging to the value type *stimulation*, and relatively higher ratings for the value type *safety*. Uncertainty orientation has also been related to achievement motivation (Sorrentino & Short, 1986): an achievement motivation makes a person to engage actively in behaviour with uncertain outcomes. The conflicting motivations of *stimulation* and *achievement* on the one hand and *safety* on the other hand are visible in the opposing positions they occupy in the value space of the Value Compass. On a cultural level, a distinction can be made between cultures high in uncertainty avoidance and low in uncertainty avoidance (Hofstede & Hofstede, 2005). Uncertainty avoidance is defined here as '*the extent to which the members of a culture feel threatened by ambiguous or unknown situations*' (p. 167). In cultures where safety values are more important, the motivation for anxiety reduction is expected to be relatively strong.

Honesty

The motivational goal of this value type is **A feeling of confidence, being able to trust the other's intentions**. The value type includes values such as *honesty, keeping a promise, loyalty* and *trust*.

Schwartz's value type benevolence includes the value types *care & affection* and *honesty* of the Value Compass. However, the analysis of discriminant validity in Section 3.2 showed that *care & affection* and *honesty* can be treated as separate value types, representing distinct motivational goals. In consumer behaviour, the value type *honesty* can provide for several motivations, for instance, a tendency to prefer honest products (e.g., produced in a sustainable way, not abusing scarce resources), a tendency to prefer honest suppliers (e.g., trustworthy, being committed), or a tendency toward loyal buying behaviour (e.g., a person being loyal or committed to a specific brand due to past positive experience).

Social responsibility

The Value Compass distinguishes between values focusing on the here and now, as opposed to values aiming at the future quality of life. The motivational goal of *care for the future*, or *social responsibility*, is **A sense of responsibility for the quality of life of future generations**. This value type includes values such as *environmental-friendliness* and *providing for a better world*.

Schwartz (1992) made a distinction between benevolence and universalism. Universalism closely resembles the value type *social responsibility*, but Schwartz does not explicitly include the time dimension in his definition of universalism. In Schwartz's value system, there is no distinction between providing for the current and for the future quality of life. In his work on cultural dimensions, Hofstede does include a future-oriented cultural dimension (Hofstede, 2011).

This dimension, labelled by Hofstede as '*long-term versus short-term orientation*', represents a time element similar to the distinction between providing for a future quality of life and a current quality of life in the Value Compass. Hofstede points out that values typical for long-term orientation are strong in East Asian cultures, due to Confucianist influences.

Care for the future is also linked to the concept of sustainability. The Brundtland Commission of the United Nations defined sustainable development as '*development that meets the needs of the present without compromising the ability of future generations to meet their own needs*' (1987, p. 43). Sustainable development can particularly flourish in a context where people cherish the values included in the value type *social responsibility*.

4.4 Concluding remarks on the differences between the Value Compass and Schwartz's value system

Schwartz (1992) defined values as guiding motivations for life in general. He conceptualized his value system as a circular structure of dynamic relations among 10 value types. In this circular structure, conflicting values are in opposing directions from the centre, and complementary values are adjacent to one another. Schwartz's value system is organized along two bipolar dimensions: self-enhancement versus self-transcendence, and openness values versus conservation values.

The Value Compass was developed to provide guidance for a more specific setting: values are activated toward brand choice. In the previous chapter, we found that the Value Compass, like Schwartz's value system, is organized as a value system with a circular structure. The Value Compass was found to consist of 11 value types, organized along two bipolar dimensions: *Promotion of self-interest versus Care for others*, and *Fun versus Function*. The first dimension resembles the dimension self-enhancement versus self-transcendence of Schwartz's value system. The second dimension, *Fun versus Function*, is connected to the utilitarian-hedonic distinction found in consumer behaviour literature, but does not relate to Schwartz's value system.

Table 4.1 compares the values of the Value Compass with corresponding values in Schwartz's value system. The comparison illustrates that the activation toward consumer behaviour created a context in which additional motivations appeared. This is particularly true for utilitarian values, and for the value types *beauty* and *intimacy*. On the other hand, some of the value types of Schwartz's value system seem to be irrelevant to consumer behaviour. This is particularly true for tradition and conformity, two value types representing the conservation of the status quo, and respect for the past and for traditions. Apparently, these values do not have a useful application to consumer behaviour in a western society such as the Netherlands.

Table 4.1 Comparison of the Value Compass with Schwartz's value system (SVS)

Value type in Value Compass	Corresponding value type in the SVS	Further explanation
Enjoying life	Hedonism	Enjoying life and hedonism share a similar motivation.
Stimulation	Stimulation	Similar.
Intimacy	–	Not represented in the SVS.
Care & affection	Benevolence	Benevolence is defined by Schwartz as 'the concern for the welfare of close others in everyday interaction' (p. 11). This also reflects the general idea behind the value type care & affection of the Value Compass, although Schwartz uses other marker values for benevolence. Benevolence seems to have a broader interpretation.
Honesty	Benevolence	Schwartz's benevolence includes honesty and loyalty.
Safety	Security	Safety and security share a similar motivation.
Soc. responsibility	Universalism	The motivational goal of universalism is defined by Schwartz as 'understanding, appreciation, tolerance, and protection for the welfare of all people and for nature' (p. 12).
–	Tradition, conformity	Tradition and conformity seem to lose relevance when values are activated toward consumer choice processes. They are not present in the Value Compass.
Functionality	–	Utilitarian values (i.e., functionality) are relevant for consumer behaviour, but Schwartz does not identify utilitarian value types. Functionality does have an overlap with Schwartz's type self-direction. Although some marker values of self-direction (independence and curiosity) are included in the value type enjoying life of the Value Compass, the motivational goal of self-direction ('independent thought and action [. . .] derived from organismic needs for control and mastery' (Schwartz, 1992, p. 5) seems more closely related to the utilitarian need for competence, as expressed by the value type functionality of the Value Compass.
Achievement	Achievement	The utilitarian value type achievement of the Value Compass resembles the value type achievement of the SVS, defined by Schwartz as 'personal success through demonstrating competence according to social standards' (p. 8).
Prestige	Achievement, power	The value type prestige shares elements with Schwartz's value types achievement and power.
Beauty	–	Not represented in the SVS.

In the literature review in Chapter 2, we mentioned that Rokeach (1973) distinguished between terminal and instrumental values. Schwartz (1992) did not find this distinction. In line with Schwartz's observations, the Value Compass does not distinguish between instrumental and end values either. The Value Compass, however, does recognize a special position for *quality of life* and *well-being*. In the analysis in Chapter 2, both items appeared in the centre of the value space. These items are positively correlated with all other values and are considered an outcome of the successful pursuit of any other value. A similar observation was made by Schwartz (1994) concerning the related value *happiness*.[1]

4.5 Value profile for the Netherlands

Individual values are partly a result of a background shared with other individuals in society, and partly represent individual differences (Hofstede, 1980, 2011; Schwartz, 1994b; Schwartz & Bardi, 2001) reflecting individuals' unique needs, temperaments and experiences (Schwartz & Bardi, 2001). The shared background of a group of individuals can be related to evolutionary-biological aspects of human nature, and to cultural or institutional demands (Schwartz & Bilsky, 1987). When creating a value profile for a consumer target group, or for a country or society as a whole, then the average value rating for each value type reflects the shared background in this population. A variety in responses around this mean are operationalized by the standard deviation: a higher standard deviation reflects larger individual differences within the population.

The value profile

Table 4.2 presents the value profile of the Netherlands, based on data collected in the second student survey in Chapter 3. The value profile was derived from the average ratings for each of the value types of the Value Compass, over all individuals in the test. For instance, for the value type *honesty*, first an individual honesty score was calculated. This individual score is a weighted average of the respondent's ratings on the three value items *honesty, loyalty* and *keeping a promise*. Weights were derived based on the loadings of each item in this test on its value type. For instance, individual ratings of honesty = 3, keeping a promise = 4 and loyalty = 3, result in the following individual rating for the value type honesty:

$$\frac{(0.64 \times \text{honesty}) + (0.86 \times \text{keeping a promise}) + (0.79 \times \text{loyalty})}{0.64 + 0.86 + 0.79}$$

$$= \frac{(0.64 \times 3) + (0.86 \times 4) + (0.79 \times 3)}{0.64 + 0.86 + 0.79}$$

$$= 3.38^2$$

Next, the sample mean for honesty was derived from averaging the results of all the individuals in the test. This resulted in a mean rating of 4.026. In the value profile in Table 4.2, values are ranked by importance. This profile was labelled the value profile of the Netherlands, even though, essentially, it is the value profile of the Dutch student sample. The mean value ratings reflect the shared background of the individuals in the Dutch student sample. For instance, the value type *honesty* is the most important value guiding brand choice, with a mean of 4.026. Individual variation around this mean reflects unique personality and experience. To continue with the individual ratings for *honesty* in the example mentioned above: *honesty* is a less important motivation for this hypothetical consumer than for the average consumer in the sample. As a consequence, this individual could be relatively less sensitive to appeals for brand loyalty. The extent of the individual variation can be derived from the standard deviation results listed in the table. A higher standard deviation implies bigger individual differences in the population.

Table 4.2 shows that not all value types are equally important. Honesty, functionality and hedonic considerations are the relatively important motivations for brand choice. The differences in standard deviation in Table 4.2 illustrate that, for some value types, the individual differences are bigger than for other value types. In particular, values emphasizing care for the future (e.g., values stimulating environmentally-friendly consumer behaviour) are subject to relatively large individual differences. Individual variation in value priorities can be related to life's circumstances. People adapt their values to the situation they are faced with. Value priorities have been shown to be related to, among others, life cycle, level of education, age, gender and income level (Inglehart, 1997; Schwartz, 2006).

Table 4.2 Value profile of the Netherlands

Value type	Mean	Std. Deviation	n	95% Conf. Interval
Honesty	4.026	.859	302	[3.929, 4.123]
Functionality	3.897	.680	304	[3.820, 3.974]
Enjoying life	3.895	.680	311	[3.819, 3.971]
Safety	3.729	.824	296	[3.635, 3.823]
Achievement	3.681	.693	263	[3.597, 3.765]
Care & affection	3.610	.780	299	[3.521, 3.699]
Beauty	3.520	.849	280	[3.420, 3.620]
Social responsibility	3.301	.946	301	[3.194, 3.408]
Stimulation	3.278	.773	305	[3.191, 3.365]
Prestige	3.248	.878	296	[3.148, 3.348]
Intimacy	3.212	.768	281	[3.122, 3.302]

4.6 Conclusion

The Value Compass consists of 11 value types, each offering a distinct motivation for consumer behaviour. The structure of the Value Compass resembles the structure of value systems that are used in psychology to explain the motivational structure of individuals. But the specific focus on consumer choice activated a number of other values, which do not appear in value systems with a more psychological orientation. More specifically, the Value Compass demonstrates that consumer behaviour specifically activates a choice between conflicting hedonic and instrumental motivations, a value dimension that is not represented in Schwartz's value system. Other differences involve the presence of the value types *intimacy* and *beauty*, and the absence of tradition and conformity values in the Value Compass.

The Value Compass is related to a specific behavioural context: consumer behaviour. The next chapters will investigate to what extent this specific activation of values toward consumer behaviour also creates a closer link with, and thus an explanation for, this type of behaviour.

Notes

1   In the development process of the Value Compass, the value *happiness* was filtered out in Stage 2, because of the multidimensional meaning of this word.
2   The factor loadings in this equation were derived from the CFA analysis executed on the results of the second student survey. Factor loadings for all other value items are available upon request from the author.

References

Bagwell, L. S. & Bentheim, D. B. (1996). Veblen effects in a theory of conspicuous consumption. *The American Economic Review, 86*(3), 349–373.

Bandura, A. (1986). *Social foundations of thought & action: A social cognitive theory*. Upper Saddle River, NJ: Prentice Hall.

Deci, E. L. & Ryan, R. M. (2008). Hedonia, eudaimonia and well-being: An introduction. *Journal of Happiness Studies, 9*(1), 1–11.

Epicurus. (2005, original fourth–third century BC). Fragments. In N. Bakalis, *Handbook of Greek philosophy: From Thales to the Stoics analysis and fragments* (p. 215). Victoria, BC, Canada: Trafford on Demand Publishing.

Festinger, L. (1954). A theory of social comparison processes. *Human Relations, 7*(2), 117–140.

Han, Y. J., Nunes, J. C. & Drèze, X. (2010). Signaling status with luxury goods: The role of brand prominence. *Journal of Marketing, 74*(4), 349–373.

Hofstede, G. (1980). *Culture's consequences: Comparing values, behaviors, institutions and organizations across nations*. Thousand Oaks, CA: Sage.

Hofstede, G. (2011). Dimensionalizing cultures: The Hofstede model in context. *Online Readings in Psychology and Culture, 2*(1). http://dx.doi.org/10.9707/2307-0919.1014.

Hofstede, G. & Hofstede, G. (2005). *Cultures and organizations, software of the mind*. New York, NY: McGraw-Hill.

Inglehart, R. F. (1997). *Modernization and postmodernization: Cultural, economic and political change in 43 countries.* Princeton, NJ: Princeton University Press.

McClelland, D. C. (1987). *Human motivation.* Cambridge, UK: Cambridge University Press.

Markus, H. R. & Kitayama, S. (1991). Culture and the self: Implications for cognition, emotion, and motivation. *Psychological Review, 98*(2), 224–253.

Maslow, A. H. (1954). *Motivation and personality.* New York, NY: Harper & Row.

Murray, H. A. (1938). *Explorations in personality.* New York, NY: Oxford University Press.

Pine, J. & Gilmore, J. H. (1999). *The experience economy: Work is theatre & every business a stage.* Boston, MA: Harvard Business Review Press.

Prahalad, C. & Hamel, G. (1990). *The core competence of the corporation.* Boston, MA: Springer.

Roberts, K. (2005). *Lovemarks: The future beyond brands.* New York, NY: PowerHouse Books.

Rokeach, M. (1973). *The nature of human values.* New York, NY: The Free Press.

Schwartz, S. H. (1992). Universals in the content and structure of values: theoretical advances and empirical tests in 20 countries. In M. Zanna, *Advances in experimental social psychology, 25, 1–65).* New York, NY: The Free Press.

Schwartz, S. H. (1994). Are there universal aspects in the structure and contents of human values? *Journal of Social Issues, 50*(4), 19–45.

Schwartz, S. H. (1994b). Beyond individualism/collectivism: New cultural dimensions of values. In U. Kim, H. C. Triandis, Ç. Kâgitçibasi, S.-C. Choi & G. Yoon, *Individualism and collectivism: theory, method, and applications* (pp. 85–122). Thousand Oaks, CA: Sage Publications.

Schwartz, S. H. (2006). Les valeurs de base de la personne: Théorie, mesures et applications. *Revue Française de Sociologie, 47*(4): 929–968.

Schwartz, S. H. & Bardi, A. (2001). Value hierarchie across cultures: Taking a similarities perspective. *Journal of Cross-Cultural Psychology, 32*(5), 268–290.

Schwartz, S. H. & Bilsky, W. (1987). Toward a universal psychological structure of human values. *Journal of Personality and Social Psychology, 53*(3), 550–562.

Sorrentino, R. M. & Short, J.-A. C. (1986). Uncertainty orientation, motivation and cognition. In R. M. Sorrentino & E. T. Higgins, *Handbook of motivation and cognition, volume 1: Foundations of social behavior* (pp. 379–403). New York, NY: Guilford Press.

Suls, J., Martin, R. & Wheeler, L. (2002). Social Comparison: Why, with whom, and with what Effect? *Current Directions in Psychological Science, 11*(5), 159–163.

Taylor, S. E., Wayment, H. A. & Carrillo, M. (1996). Social comparison, self-regulation and motivation. In R. M. Sorrentino, & E. Tory Higgins, *Handbook of motivation & cognition, volume 3: The interpersonal context* (pp. 3–28). New York, NY: The Guilford Press.

Triandis, H. C. (1995). *Individualism & collectivism.* Boulder, CO: Westmore.

Veblen, T. (1994, original 1899). *The theory of the leisure class: An economic study of institutions.* London, UK: Unwin Books. Republished New York, NY: Dover Publications.

Vigneron, F. & Johnson, L. W. (1999). A review and a conceptual framework of prestige-seeking consumer behavior. *Academy of Marketing Science Review, 1*(1), 1–15.

White, R. W. (1959). Motivation reconsidered: The concept of competence. *Psychological Review, 66*(5), 297–333.

Wigfield, A. & Eccles, J. S. (2000). Expectancy-value theory of achievement motivation. *Contemporary Educational Psychology, 25*(1), 68–81.

Winter, D. G. (1973). *The power motive.* New York, NY: The Free Press.

World Commission on Environment and Development (1987). *Our common future*. Oxford, UK: Oxford University Press.

Yarrow, L., McQuiston, S., MacTurk, R., McCarthy, M., Klein, R. & Vietze, P. (1983). Assessment of mastery motivation during the first year of life: Contemporaneous and cross-age relationships. *Developmental Psychology, 19*(2), 159–171.

Zuckerman, M. (1994). *Behavioral expressions and biosocial bases of sensation seeking*. New York, NY: Cambridge University Press.

Part III

Values and branding

Chapter 5

Brand values and brand choice

5.1 Introduction

Values guide people's behaviour, thereby motivating them to make choices. In our study, we proposed that consumer behaviour is also guided by values. Consumer values were found to be organized in a coherent system in which they are related to each other. In this value system, the Value Compass, some values are compatible with each other, and we can expect them to reinforce consumer choice. Other values have a conflicting influence on consumer choice.

Part II presented the development of the Value Compass. The purpose of Part III is to demonstrate the impact of values on consumer choice. This is in line with the second objective of this dissertation: '*The assessment of the effect of values on consumer choice*'. This objective implies that we need to assess the extent of this effect, and the mechanisms through which this effect takes place. In other words, we need to answer the following questions:

- How do brand values influence consumer behaviour?
- How important is the influence of brand values on consumer behaviour?
- How, and to what extent, does a match between brand values and personal values reinforce consumer behaviour?

In Chapter 2, we proposed the brand value model (BVM), which is reproduced below.

The BVM relates values to consumer behaviour. The constructs and relations hypothesized by this model were derived in Chapter 2. In the current and the next chapter we test these relations. Section 5.2 describes the test design; the results can be found in the subsequent sections. These results are structured according to the linkages proposed by the model:

1 The correlation between brand values and brand attachment.
2 The mediating effect of brand attachment on the relation between brand values and brand behaviour.
3 The moderating effect of value congruence.

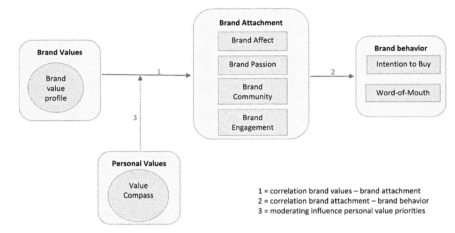

Figure 5.1 Brand Value Model: the impact of values on brand choice

The correlation between brand values and brand attachment

The brand value profile is the perceived value proposition of the brand, i.e., the combination of values the consumer expects to find in the brand. Our Proposition 4 states that '*brand values stimulate the relationship between the consumer and the brand, by creating an emotional attachment to the brand*'. Consequently, we expect that a consumer who perceives more favourable values in a certain brand, will become more attached to this brand. This relationship between brand values and brand attachment, expressed by the first linkage in Figure 5.1, is explored in Section 5.5.1. However, before this relation can be explored, we need to investigate the structure of the brand attachment construct and the structure of the brand value profile. These structures are investigated in Sections 5.3 and 5.4, respectively.

Brand attachment mediates the influence of brand values on brand behaviour

The BVM predicts a positive correlation between brand attachment and brand behaviour: a stronger attachment to the brand results in a higher intention to buy the brand or a higher probability that the consumer engages in positive word-of-mouth about the brand (linkage 2). Essentially, linkage 2 proposes that the effect of brand values on brand behaviour is mediated by brand attachment. Brands with a higher value content are expected to generate a higher brand attachment, which is expected to result in a higher willingness to buy the brand, or to spread positive word-of-mouth. This mediation effect is explored in Section 5.5.2.

A match between brand values and personal values stimulates
brand attachment

We can expect that consumers feel stronger brand attachment if the brand proposes values that are more central to the consumer (Proposition 5). In other words, a stronger brand attachment is expected if there is a match between the Value Compass of the consumer and the value profile of the brand. This is expressed by the third linkage in the BVM. The effect of this match between consumer values and brand values, referred to as value congruence, is explored in Chapter 6.

5.2 Method

Sample

The tests of the BVM were based on data derived from a single, extensive questionnaire, which was distributed among students of the Hanze University of Applied Sciences Groningen, The Netherlands, between 12 September 2010 and 30 September 2010.[1] These students were randomly drawn from the student database of the university.

Design

Selected respondents received an email on 12 September 2010, with a request to fill out the survey. This email was followed by two reminders (respectively one week and two weeks after they received the first mail). The survey was available online, respondents could access the survey by clicking on the link they could find in the email. Surveymonkey was used to publish the survey online and to collect the responses. To ensure a culturally homogeneous sample, only questionnaires filled out by Dutch respondents were used. To avoid gender differences influencing the outcomes, the sample was weighted by gender so as to represent a sample consisting of 50 per cent males and 50 per cent females.

The survey consisted of three parts, in which the following variables were submitted: personal values, brand values, brand attachment and brand behaviour. First, respondents had to evaluate their own value priorities. Next, respondents were presented three to four brands, and they had to indicate to what extent certain values could be applied to these brands. The values of the Value Compass were used for the evaluation of personal value priorities and brand values. Respondents also had to give their overall evaluation of these brands by answering questions related to their brand attachment and their behavioural intention (intention to buy or use the brand, or intention to spread positive word-of-mouth). Below, we give a more detailed description of each of the submitted variables.

Personal values

Respondents were asked to rate their own value priorities. The respondents received the same instruction as in the survey used for the development of the Value Compass: they had to rate the relevance of each value item in a consumer choice context, by answering the question *'How important is this value for you when you have to make a choice between products or services?'*. Ratings were provided on a 5-point scale ranging from *very unimportant* to *very important*. The ratings for the value items then were used to construct value types.

In the survey, respondents had to evaluate their own value priorities as well as the brand values for each of the brands they were presented with. This resulted in a long questionnaire. A pretest of the survey showed that this would lead to a high degree of boredom with the respondents, resulting in a low response. Consequently, for the purpose of this test, a shortened version of the Value Compass was developed. A shorter list of value items, or marker values, was used for this version. In addition, the closely related value types *achievement* and *functionality*, as well as the value types *care & affection* and *intimacy* were combined.

We can only use an adapted version of the Value Compass if it provides adequate fit, as compared to the original version. Confirmatory Factor Analysis (CFA) was used to estimate factor loadings of the marker values of the adapted version, and then to test its goodness-of-fit. The test showed that the shortened version of the Value Compass provides adequate fit (goodness-of-fit test with CFA, $\chi 2$ = 900.2 with df = 194, CFI = 0.965, $RMSEA$ = 0.069[2]). Consequently, this short version was used in the tests of the BVM. The loadings of the marker values on their value types, as computed in the CFA, were used to construct the value types of the short version of the Value Compass: for each respondent, the average rating for a value type was computed from his weighted average rating of the items representing the value type, with weights derived from their factor loadings. The sample mean per value type then is the mean rating across all respondents. This procedure was explained in more detail in Section 4.5.

Table 5.1 presents the descriptives used for the value types of the short version of the Value Compass, based on the sample results. This table also presents the marker values that were used for each value type. From the table we can see that, despite differences in the marker values representing the value types, the order of value priorities in the short version of the Value Compass is largely similar to the order of value priorities in the original version, as was presented in Table 4.2.

Brand values

After evaluating their own value priorities, a number of brands were presented to the respondents. All selected brands are consumer brands with a global presence, expected to be well-known to the respondents of the survey. In total

Table 5.1 Descriptives for the short version of the Value Compass

Value type	Mean	Std. deviation	n	95% conf. interval
Honesty (marker item: honesty)	4.109	1.020	943	[4.039, 4.179]
Safety (marker item: safety)	3.880	1.051	963	[3.808, 3.952]
Enjoying life (enjoying life, excitement, fun)	3.875	.853	928	[3.816, 3.933]
Functionality (expertise, functionality, smart solutions)	3.771	.726	919	[3.722, 3.821]
Affection (caring for someone, family life, friendliness)	3.670	.879	933	[3.610, 3.730]
Social responsibility (env. friendly, providing better world, recycling)	3.325	.925	953	[3.262, 3.389]
Beauty (beauty, elegance, style)	3.303	.878	951	[3.242, 3.363]
Stimulation (adventure, being active, being sportive)	3.271	.818	948	[3.215, 3.327]
Prestige (power, status, being successful)	3.134	.878	949	[3.074, 3.194]

16 brands were included in the survey. To give a broader coverage of consumer brands, the brands were selected out of a number of different product categories:

- Cars: Audi, BMW, Toyota, Volkswagen and Volvo.
- Fast moving consumer goods: Coca Cola and Heineken.
- Entertainment and lifestyle: Discovery, Disney, IKEA and Starbucks.
- ICT: Apple, Nokia and Sony Ericsson.
- Social media: Facebook and Twitter.

Each respondent had to evaluate three or four brands. The selection of brands was randomized across respondents. To avoid within-subject interaction effects, only the first brand evaluated by the respondent was used in the tests of the BVM.[3] Following Proposition 3, the value profile of a brand is expected to consist of brand values similar to the consumer values in the Value Compass. Therefore, respondents evaluated the value profiles of these brands with the same value items as they had used to evaluate their own value priorities. They had to indicate to which extent they thought that each value was proposed by the brand: '*A brand can represent certain values. Could you indicate to what extent the following brands represent these values (for instance, 'Audi represents strength')?*' Ratings were obtained on a 5-point Likert scale ranging from *totally disagree* to *totally agree*. The results were used as input for the test of the structure of brand value profiles, which is presented in Section 5.4.

Brand attachment

Brand attachment was determined for each brand in the survey. Brand attachment was measured by a scale, which consists of a number of items representing the four dimensions proposed in Chapter 2: brand affect, brand love, brand community and brand engagement. Table 5.2 provides a specification of the items of the brand attachment scale, including the references to the sources from which the items were taken. Ratings for the items were obtained on a 5-point Likert scale, ranging from *totally disagree* to *totally agree*. Each dimension is calculated as a weighted average of the item ratings, with weights derived from the factor loadings of the items. The validation of the proposed structure of the brand attachment construct, including specification of the factor loadings, is presented in the following section.

Brand behaviour

Brand behaviour is operationalized by the intention to (re)purchase the brand, and the intention to provide positive word-of-mouth. These constructs were operationalized by a number of items, presented in Table 5.2. Ratings for each of these items were obtained on a 5-point Likert scale, ranging from *totally disagree* to *totally agree*.

Response

A total of 1,678 Dutch students responded to the mail, and opened the online survey by clicking on the link that was provided to them. Not all of these students actually started filling out the survey: for about half of them, participation did not involve more than reading the welcome page of the online survey. Only the students who completed the personal value priorities were counted as respondents. This resulted in 850 respondents. The whole survey was completed by 310 students: 36.5 per cent. The large drop-out ratio in the survey was probably due to the length of the questionnaire.

Organization of results

The survey results were used to test the BVM. These tests are presented in this and the following chapter. We start with the analysis of the constructs used

Table 5.2 Operationalization of brand attachment and brand behaviour

Dimension of brand attachment	Corresponding items	Source
Brand affect	I like [brand X]	Wilkie & Pessemier (1973)
Brand passion	I love [brand X] I am passionate about [brand X]	Brand love scale of Carroll & Ahuvia (2006)
Brand community	I identify with people who use [brand X] I feel a connection with other [brand X] users	adapted from Keller (2008) community integration scale of McAlexander et al. (2002)
Brand engagement	I often feel a personal connection between [brand X] and myself I have a special bond with [brand X]	BESC-scale of Sprott et al. (2009)
Dimension of brand behaviour	Corresponding items	Source
Buying intention	I will buy / use [brand X] the next time I buy/use [this product] I intend to keep buying [brand X]	Chaudhuri & Holbrook (2001)
Word-of-mouth	I talk in a positive way about [brand X] to my friends	Carroll & Ahuvia (2006)

in the BVM: the brand attachment construct is examined in Section 5.3 and the structure of the brand value profile in Section 5.4. Section 5.5 examines the relationships between these constructs: the relation between brand values and brand attachment (linkage 1 in Figure 5.1) is tested in Section 5.5.1, and the mediating effect of brand attachment in the relation between brand values and behaviour (linkage 2) in Section 5.5.2. The analysis of the influence of value congruence on brand attachment (linkage 3) is described in Chapter 6.

5.3 Brand attachment

5.3.1 The structure of the brand attachment construct

According to the BVM, the presence of brand values is expected to strengthen the relation between the consumer and the brand. Brand attachment, the emotional attachment of the consumer to a brand, is used in this model as an indicator for this relation. The literature review suggested that brand attachment can be represented by four dimensions: brand affect, brand passion, brand community and brand engagement. Each of these dimensions was operationalized in the BVM with one (for brand affect) or two items (see Table 5.2).

Before we can test the structure and the relations implied by the BVM, it is necessary to validate the structure of the brand attachment construct as proposed here. The analysis of the structure of the brand attachment construct is based on the data obtained from the survey described in the previous section.

Analysis of the structure of the brand attachment construct

METHOD OF ANALYSIS

A principal components analysis, using varimax rotation, was used to assess the underlying structure of the brand attachment construct. Confirmatory factor analysis (CFA) was used to verify the goodness-of-fit of the hypothesized structure.

RESULTS

The principal components analysis revealed the predicted structure of the four attachment dimensions. We observed a high factor loading of the items on the factors on which they were supposed to load.

The goodness-of-fit of the structure of the brand attachment construct was verified with CFA. Figure 5.2 shows the resulting path diagram. This path diagram represents brand attachment and its four dimensions (brand affect, brand love, brand community and brand engagement). It also shows the extent to which these dimensions are represented by the scale items used in the survey. For instance, brand love is represented by the two items 'I love the brand' and 'I am passionate about the brand'. As we can recall from Box 3.3, items are assumed to give a good representation of a concept if the factor loading (λ) is greater than or equal to 0.7. In the path diagram, we can see that the two items representing brand love have high factor loadings

Table 5.3 Brand attachment dimensions revealed by principal components analysis with varimax rotation (bold numbers indicate the factor on which each item predominantly loads)

Item	Brand affect	Brand passion	Brand community	Brand engagement
I like [brand]	**0.91**	0.34	0.20	0.15
I love [brand]	0.35	**0.76**	0.27	0.40
I am passionate about [brand]	0.40	**0.74**	0.36	0.31
I identify with people who use [brand]	0.24	0.32	**0.82**	0.35
I feel a connection with other [brand] users	0.19	0.24	**0.75**	0.52
I feel a personal connection between [brand] and me	0.13	0.29	0.42	**0.81**
I have a special bond with [brand]	0.18	0.31	0.33	**0.84**

of 0.93 and 0.91, respectively. The error (δ), the extent to which the brand love construct does not explain the variance in the measured item, is low: δ = 0.13 for 'I love', and δ = 0.16 for 'I am passionate'. With the high factor loading and the low error term, the construct reliability of the brand love construct is considerably higher than the norm value of 0.7 (see Box 3.3 for further background information):

$$\text{Construct reliability}_{\text{brand love}} = \frac{\left(\sum_{i=1}^{n} \lambda_i\right)^2}{\left(\sum_{i=1}^{n} \lambda_i\right)^2 + \left(\sum_{i=1}^{n} \delta_i\right)^2} = 0.92 \ .$$

The construct reliability of brand community (CR = 0.92) and brand engagement (CR = 0.94) is equally high.[4] We can conclude that the items used in the survey give a good representation of the dimension they are supposed to represent.

The indicators at the bottom of the diagram measure the goodness-of-fit of the model: the extent to which the brand attachment construct is represented by its four dimensions: brand affect, brand love, brand community and brand engagement. A CFI > 0.92 and a RMSEA < 0.08 are indicators of a good fit. The model provides a good fit (CFI = 0.99), but the RMSEA is relatively high. This is an indication of variability in the actual data that is not explained by the model. Here, the RMSEA > 0.08 seems to provide an indication of the conceptual difference between brand affect and the other three dimensions of brand attachment. This can be seen from the covariances expressed at the right-hand side of the path diagram.

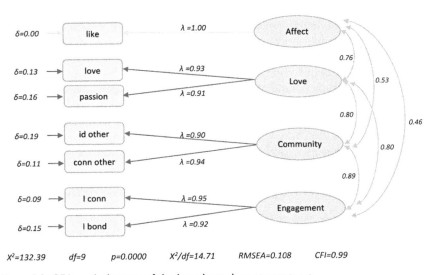

Figure 5.2 CFA: path diagram of the brand attachment construct

The interconstruct correlation between brand love, brand community and brand engagement is high. Particularly the high correlation between brand community and brand engagement (corr. = 0.89) was to be expected: both constructs represent a connection between the consumer and the brand (see Section 2.7). But brand affect shows a lower correlation with brand love (corr. = 0.76), and particularly with the brand connection dimensions (corr. = 0.53 with community and corr. = 0.46 with engagement).

Brand attachment is the emotional attachment of an individual with a brand. It expresses the relationship that an individual feels with a brand. The analysis confirms that brand attachment is represented by the four dimensions predicted by theory: brand affect, brand love, brand community and brand engagement.

The results indicate a difference between brand affect and the other three brand attachment dimensions (brand love, brand community and brand engagement). Affect defines a more general evaluation of the brand, hence conceptually closer to an indication of the overall attitude toward the brand. The item used to measure brand affect, '*I like* . . .', has been referred to as an indicator for attitude (Holbrook & Hirschman, 1982; Wilkie & Pessemier, 1973). We conclude that brand affect represents a relatively weak attachment to the brand, whereas the other three dimensions are indicators for a stronger emotional response of the individual with the brand. The difference we found between these constructs is in line with the earlier observation that a strong emotional attachment results in a rich set of affectively laden schemas that link the brand to the self, whereas a favourable attitude alone does not necessarily link the brand to the self (Thomson, MacInnis & Whan Park, 2005).

The central purpose of this study is concerned with (brand) values, not with the creation of a brand attachment construct. Further exploration of the conceptual differences between indicators of weaker brand attachment (e.g., brand affect) and indicators of stronger brand attachment (e.g., brand love, brand community and brand engagement) merits attention, but it is beyond the purpose of this study. Brand attachment as used here presents a reasonable fit with the variability observed in the underlying items, and incorporates a good deal of the conceptual richness connected with the attachment construct. Therefore, brand attachment will be used as as indicator of the relation the consumer experiences with the brand.

5.3.2 Brand attachment and brand behaviour: descriptives

Table 5.4 presents the descriptives of the brand attachment and brand behaviour dimensions, over all individuals in the test. Ratings were derived from the items representing the dimensions, with weights derived from the factor loadings of each item. For instance, for *brand passion*, first an individual rating was obtained for the items *I love [this brand]*, and *I am passionate about [this brand]*. Suppose the individual rates *I love [this brand]* = 3 and *I am passionate about [this brand]* = 4, then we get the following individual rating for brand passion:

$$\frac{\left(0.93\times\text{I love}\right)+\left(0.91\times\text{I am passionate}\right)}{0.93+0.91}=\frac{\left(0.93\times3\right)+\left(0.91\times4\right)}{0.93+0.91}=3.49$$

The individual's brand attachment was calculated as the (weighted) average of the four brand attachment dimensions.[5]

Table 5.4 presents the sample means for each construct. These were calculated by averaging all individual results, over all brands in the test. For instance, the sample mean for brand passion of 2.433 is the average of all individual ratings for brand passion. The table demonstrates that the average brand affect is higher than the average brand passion. Apparently, it is easier for a brand to be liked than to be loved. The creation of engaged customers, and customers who feel connected with other users of the brand, seems to be even more difficult to realize. These results show that a stronger form of brand attachment, i.e., a stronger relation with the brand, is more difficult to attain.

Table 5.4 Brand attachment and brand behaviour in numbers

Brand attachment (BAtt)	Mean	Std. deviation	n	95% conf. interval
Brand affect	3.459	1.280	353	[3.320, 3.598]
Brand passion	2.433	1.199	346	[2.303, 2.563]
Brand community	2.057	1.131	343	[1.934, 2.180]
Brand engagement	1.809	1.065	345	[1.693, 1.924]
Brand attachment (overall)	2.231	1.014	325	[2.127, 2.336]

Brand behaviour	Mean	Std. deviation	n	95% conf. interval
Behavioural intention (BI)	2.523	1.337	328	[2.238, 2.667]
Word-of-mouth (WoM)	2.931	1.347	346	[2.788, 3.073]

Brand attachment leads to brand behaviour: regression model	t-value (p < 0.001)	F-ratio	R^2
BI = 0.200 + 1.033 × BAtt[1]	t (308) = 22.47;	F(1,308) = 504.91	0.620
WoM = 0.792 + 0.959 × BAtt	t (323) = 18.65;	F(1,323) = 348.10	0.517

In Section 5.5, the impact of brand values on brand attachment will be assessed, with the brand attachment construct validated in this section. But before doing so, it is necessary to validate the structure of the perceived value profile of a brand. This is presented in the next section.

5.4 The brand value profile

The structure of the brand value system, the perceived value proposition of the brand, is similar to the structure of the consumer's value system (Proposition 3).

5.4.1 The structure of the brand value profile

Each consumer has a Value Compass guiding his behaviour as a consumer. In Chapter 3, we proposed that the values in the Value Compass are organized as a circular structure of compatible and conflicting value types. This value system is organized along two central dimensions: *fun versus function*, and *promotion of self-interests versus care for others*.

Proposition 3 was derived in Section 2.6. According to this proposition, consumers perceive the value proposition of a brand as having the same structure as their own Value Compass. For example, suppose a consumer considers a travel agency because of the wild water rafting trips or backpack holidays it offers. He might expect this travel agency to be strong in providing fun and stimulation, but opposing values such as offering safety, efficiency or convenience might be less relevant for the image of the travel agency. And probably this consumer is not interested in the latter values, if he is looking for fun and excitement: we expect that the consumer, consciously or subconsciously, will be looking for a match between his own value priorities and the value profile of the travel agency. The potential of this match between the value priorities of the consumer and the value profile of a brand will be discussed later. Now, it is relevant to make the observation that, following Proposition 3, the consumer is expected to interpret the value profile of the travel agency as a coherent structure of compatible and conflicting brand values, organized according to a structure identical to his own Value Compass. Consequently, Proposition 3 leads us to the following hypothesis:

$H_{5.1}$: **The structure of a brand value profile is equal to the structure of the Value Compass.**

Test of Hypothesis 5.1

METHOD

The study of the structure of the brand value profile is based on the data resulting from the survey described in Section 5.2. Below, we describe the analysis and the outcomes of the study.

ANALYSIS

The hypothesis assumes equality between the structure of the Value Compass (the personal value system) and the brand value profile (the brand value system). Confirmatory factor analysis (CFA) provides an instrument to test equality between structural models: multigroup structural equation modelling (Hair et al., 2006). This type of modelling was used to test the assumption that the structure of the Value Compass is equal to the structure of the brand value profile. Framed in terms of CFA: the Value Compass and the brand value profile have equal structure if the CFA model in which the structure of the relationships between value types is constrained to be equal in both systems fits as well as the CFA model in which the structure is allowed to be different between the two systems (Hair et al., 2006). The statistical software package Lisrel was used to analyse the CFA models.

For comparing the equality of two models, a stepwise procedure can be used (Hair et al., 2006). First, we defined the factors (value types) of the Value Compass and the brand value profile. For the Value Compass, personal value items were assigned to their value types as specified in Table 5.1. The brand value items were then forced into the same structure, by creating brand value types identical to the personal value types of the Value Compass. Example: the personal value type prestige consists of the personal value items being successful, status and power. Consequently, we defined the brand value type prestige as being represented by the brand values being successful, status and power. As a result, a brand value profile was created consisting of exactly the same value types as the Value Compass. After proposing a factor structure for the two value systems, CFA was used to test whether this factor structure creates a good fit with the actual survey results. Thus, we tested if the Value Compass has a good fit when it is organized as a value system consisting of eight value types, a test similar to the goodness-of-fit test mentioned in Section 5.2.[6] This test was labelled Subhypothesis A1. We also tested whether the brand value profile can be organized as a value system with the

Table 5.5 Testing the equality of structure of the Value Compass and the brand value profile

Model	(Sub)hypothesis	χ^2	df	RMSEA	CFI	Decision
A1	Value Compass (PV system) consists of eight factors	952.9	202	0.070	0.963	
A2	Brand value profile (BV system) consists of eight factors	1210.8	202	0.082	0.979	
B	Eight factors exist for both systems (PV and BV)	2155.4	404	0.076	0.974	Supported
C	The two systems' factor loadings are equal	2196.2	419	0.075	0.974	Supported
D	There are equal factor loadings for both systems **AND** the errors are equal for both systems	2285.4	442	0.075	0.973	Supported
E	There are equal factor loadings for both systems **AND** the errors are equal for both systems **AND** the systems have equal factor variances and covariances	2581.2	478	0.077	0.970	Supported

same eight value types (Subhypothesis A2). Support for subhypothesis A1 and A2 validates the structure of the Value Compass and the brand value profile, but it does not confirm that these structures are equal. For supportive evidence that these two structures are actually equal, a number of subsequent tests need to be executed (Hair et al., 2006):

1   *Test whether both systems can be represented by the same eight factors (subhypothesis B: the combination of hypothesis A1 and A2).*
2   *Test of equality of factor loadings for both systems (subhypothesis C).*
3   *Test of equality of factor structures and error variances (subhypothesis D).*
4   *Test of equality of factor structures, measurement errors and interrelations between factors (subhypothesis E).*

Each subsequent subhypothesis puts stricter constraints on system equality. If each subhypothesis is supported, then we have confirmation for the (overarching) hypothesis 5.1.

RESULTS

The test results for each subhypothesis are presented in Table 5.5. For support or rejection, the same criteria were used as mentioned in Text Box 3.3 (RMSEA $\leq$ 0.08 with CFI $\geq$ 0.92).
    The tests show that each hypothesis is supported. Equality of the PV system and the BV system is confirmed.[7]

The results of the analysis confirm the hypothesis. The structure of the consumer's value system (the Value Compass) is equal to the structure of the perceived value proposition of the brand (the brand value profile). This implies that both the consumer's value system and the brand value profile can be described with the same value types, related to each other in the same circular structure of compatible and conflicting value types. In both systems, this circular structure is organized along the two dimensions *fun versus function* and *promotion of self-interests versus care for others*.

The evidence of the equality between these two systems is important. It implies that not only human values, but also values attributed to objects (i.e., non-human entities), here brands, can be represented by a similar structure of compatible and conflicting value types. When assessing the effect of brand values on choice behaviour, we can apply the same value types and the same structure to the brand value profile as to the consumer's Value Compass. In the next subsection, we illustrate this with a number of examples.

5.4.2 *Illustration of the use of brand value profiles*

Values help to give meaning to a brand (Gutman, 1982), and these brand values form an important aspect of the brand image (Keller, 2008). Now that we have provided evidence for the structure of the brand value profile, we can use this structure to analyse brand image. In this section, we included a number of examples of the use of brand value profiles. We used examples with brands that were included in the survey. In Example 1, we take a closer look at the value profiles of two brands (Toyota and Disney). Example 2 presents a comparison of two value types (*social responsibility* and *prestige*) across a number of brands. The last example shows how competitors can be compared based on their value profiles. We make a comparison between three car brands: Audi, Toyota and Volvo.[8]

For the construction of the brand value profiles, we used the results of the survey described in Section 5.2. The score for each brand value type was estimated as the weighted average score of the brand value items by which it is represented, similar to the procedure followed to construct personal value types: weights were derived from the factor loadings of the marker values, as explained in the method section of this chapter. We demonstrated in the previous section that the structure of the brand value profile is identical to the structure of the consumer's value system. Consequently, when estimating a brand value type, we can apply the same weights and factor loadings to its marker values as those estimated for the corresponding personal value type.

Example 1: two examples of brand value profiles

In Figure 5.3, two brand value profiles are shown: the brand value profile of Disney and the brand value profile of Toyota. The average brand value ratings (average BV) in this figure are calculated as the unweighted average of the separate value types. This average level of brand values represents the overall strength of a brand. Stronger brands manage to create a richer set of associations, consequently, a higher level of associated brand values.

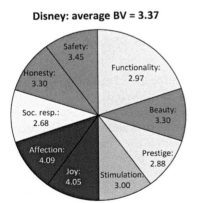
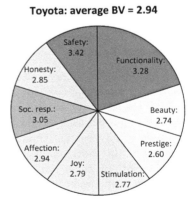

Figure 5.3 Brand value profiles of Disney and Toyota

Disney

For Disney, the average score on the nine brand value types together is 3.37. Two brand values stick out in the value profile of Disney: *joy* and *care & affection*. Disney apparently incorporates the possibility of enjoying time together with friends and family. There is an emphasis on the 'now': with Disney one can enjoy now. We can also see that the brand is not perceived as to emphasize a better future quality of life (rating for *social responsibility* is low).

Toyota

Toyota is a functional, safe car: the brand has the highest scores in *safety* and *functionality*. The brand is also seen as relatively sustainable (high *social responsibility*). Toyota is not characterized as a fun, aesthetically appealing (beautiful), or prestigious brand. If we compare the value profile of Toyota with Disney, then we see that the overall perceived brand strength of Toyota (mean brand value rating 2.94) is lower than Disney's brand strength (rating 3.37). Disney managed to realize a richer set of associations with the brand name, resulting in a higher overall brand value rating.

Example 2: comparison of brands on brand values

Brands can be compared on their brand values. Figure 5.4 illustrates this.

In the comparison with respect to *social responsibility*, IKEA, Toyota and to a lesser extent Starbucks have a relatively high rating. Apple, Coca Cola and Heineken are not characterized as socially responsible brands.

For the same set of brands we also compared their *prestige* values. Apple, Starbucks and particularly Audi are considered as brands offering prestige. Toyota, the second most sustainable brand, appears to be the least prestigious brand.

Example 3: comparison of brand value profiles of Audi, Volvo and Toyota

This example illustrates an alternative way of comparing brand value profiles. Figure 5.5 presents a comparison of a number of car brands.

Audi is a relatively strong brand: the brand rates high on most brand values. Audi distinguishes itself as a functional and prestigious brand with an important aesthetic value (*beauty*). Audi is also a brand with a high hedonic value (*joy, stimulation*). In short, Audi provides functionality, pleasure and status. The brand's score on these values is clearly higher than the other two brands that are being compared. In terms of *care & affection* (e.g., care for the fellow passengers), the value profiles of the three brands are more similar. Volvo is seen as a safe car. Compared with Toyota, Volvo is also more prestigious. Toyota distinguishes as the brand with the strongest social responsibility.

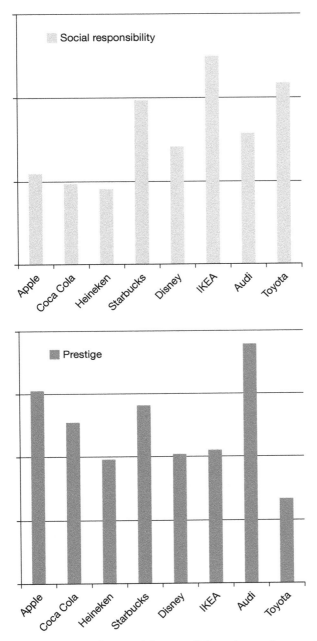

Figure 5.4 Comparison of brands on social responsibility values and on prestige values

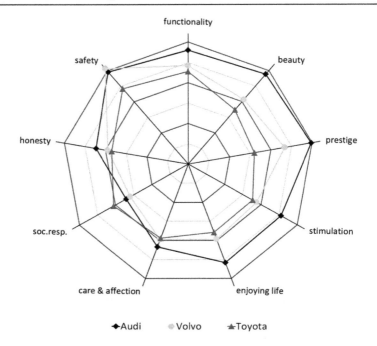

Figure 5.5 Comparison of brand value profiles of car brands

5.5 The relation between brand values, brand attachment and behaviour

Brand values stimulate the relationship between the consumer and the brand by creating an emotional attachment to the brand. Brand attachment, in turn, results in an intention to buy or use the brand (Proposition 4).

The relation between brand values and brand attachment, as proposed by linkage 1 of the BVM (Figure 5.1), is explored in Subsection 5.5.1. In Subsection 5.5.2, the focus is on the mediating influence of brand attachment on the intention to buy or use the brand.

5.5.1 The influence of brand values on brand attachment

Brand values are the perceived value proposition of the brand. Brand values can be considered behavioural beliefs: by buying or using a brand, the individual beliefs to obtain the values (e.g., *safety, prestige, pleasure*) proposed by the brand. According to Proposition 4, consumers are expected to look for brands that propose values that are relevant for them. A stronger brand, that is a brand with higher value content, is more relevant to the consumer; consumers are expected to be more attached to those brands. Therefore:

H $_{5.2}$: Brand values correlate positively with brand attachment

Test of Hypothesis 5.2

METHOD

The results of the survey described in Section 5.2 were used to explore the relation between brand values and brand attachment. Here, we describe the analysis and the outcomes.

ANALYSIS

A multiple regression analysis was executed on the results of the survey. Brand attachment was used as the dependent variable, and the nine brand value types as independent variables:

$$BAtt = b_0 + \sum_{i=1}^{9} \left(b_i \times BV_i \right),$$

where: BAtt = Brand Attachment,
* BV_i = Brand Value for value type i*

The brand attachment construct was derived in Section 5.3. Each of the brand value types is a weighted average of its marker values, with weights derived from the factor loadings, as specified in Section 5.2.

RESULTS

The multiple regression shows a moderately strong and significant influence of all brand value types together on brand attachment: F (9, 265) = 12.726, p < 0.001). The regression analysis yields adequate explained variance: (adjusted) R^2 = 0.278, which means that 27.8 per cent of the variance in brand attachment is explained by brand values.

We observed some multicollinearity between value types: variance inflation factor (VIF) ranges between 2.05 and 2.95. This implies that each value type shares a part of its variance with the other value types in the model. This is not surprising, considering the circular structure of the value model: the value system explicitly assumes interrelations between value types. The observed level of multicollinearity is below the threshold level of VIF = 10 (Hair et al., 2006). However, it is possible that the observed multicollinearity influences results. Therefore, we examined the direct correlations of the independent variables with the dependent variable (Hair et al., 2006): a series of simple regression analyses was executed, with each BV_i as *independent and BAtt as dependent variable. In these simple regressions, each of the nine brand value types was shown to give a positive correlation with brand attachment, tested significantly with p < 0.001.*

The results of the analysis demonstrate that the presence of brand values correlates positively with brand attachment. A brand with a higher value content, in other words, a stronger brand, is more relevant to consumers: the presence of relevant brand values makes people feel more attached to the brand. This holds true for all the value types in a brand value profile: if a brand manages to improve its perceived value proposition on any of the values of its value profile, without decreasing the value proposition on the other brand values, then this increases brand attachment.

We have to emphasize that the perceived value proposition of a brand is individual, and differs from consumer to consumer. Table 5.6 illustrates this with two examples. We can see that despite the relatively low level of social responsibility values attributed to the Disney brand (see Example 1 in the previous section), there are also consumers who do consider Disney to be a responsible brand. Consumers who consider Disney a responsible brand (the high social responsibility quartile) feel a higher emotional attachment with the Disney brand than consumers who do not see Disney as a responsible brand (the quartile of consumers who gives the lowest rating to their perception of Disney's social responsibility values). The second example shows the extent to which the brand Heineken is perceived to provide joy. These examples illustrate that differences in the perceived value proposition of a brand exist between consumers, and that these differences correlate with a difference in their attachment to the brand.

Table 5.6 Illustration of differences in perceived brand values between consumers

Disney: *Perceived social responsibility & brand attachment*	*Average BV social responsibility*	*Average BAtt*
low responsibility quartile (n = 24)	1.550	1.739
high responsibility quartile (n = 24)	3.874	3.400
Heineken: *Perceived joy value & brand attachment*	*Average BV joy*	*Average BAtt*
low joy quartile (n = 21)	2.253	1.541
high joy quartile (n = 20)	4.815	3.050

5.5.2 The mediating influence of brand attachment on brand behaviour

As implied by Proposition 4, brand values have a positive influence on brand attachment: '*Brand values stimulate the relationship between the consumer and the brand, by creating an emotional attachment to the brand*'. This was demonstrated in the previous section. Proposition 4 then continues with referring to the relation between brand attachment and behavioural intention: '*Brand attachment, in turn, results in an intention to buy or use the brand*'. This suggests mediation: brand attachment is expected to mediate the relation between brand values and brand behaviour.

Mediation occurs when the effect of a stimulus on behaviour is mediated by other variables (Baron & Kenny, 1986): there is not a direct relation between the independent variable and the dependent variable, but the independent variable influences a mediator variable, which in turn has an impact on the dependent variable. This implies for our study that the perceived presence of certain brand values (independent variables) creates an emotional attachment to the brand (mediator), which in turn is expected to increase the intention to buy or use the brand, or to spread word-of-mouth (dependent variable). The following example illustrates this mediator effect. Suppose an individual believes that driving a BMW offers a certain prestige to the driver. The prestige value of the BMW makes it an attractive brand to this individual. This person likes the brand, might become passionate about BMW because of its prestige value, might identify with other BMW-drivers or might even develop the feeling that he has a personal bond with BMW. The stronger the emotional attachment to BMW, the higher the intention to buy the BMW.[9] This leads to the following hypothesis:

H$_{5.3}$: The influence of brand values on brand behaviour is mediated by brand attachment

Test of Hypothesis 5.3

METHOD

The mediator effect of brand attachment on the relation between brand values and brand behaviour was analysed with the data obtained in the survey described in Section 5.2. Below, we describe this analysis.

ANALYSIS

A direct relation between brand values (BV) and brand behaviour (BI) can be schematically represented as:

$$BV \rightarrow BI$$

In a mediation model, the relation between brand values and brand behaviour is indirect; brand values (the independent variable) influence the dependent variable brand behaviour through the mediator variable brand attachment (BAtt):

$$BV \rightarrow BAtt \rightarrow BI$$

For the clarity of this analysis, the mediator effect of brand attachment was not tested for each brand value (BV_i) separately. Instead, the average brand value rating (BV) was used as representing the nine value types. As explained in Section 5.4.2, BV can be interpreted as an indicator of the strength of a brand.

Regression analysis should satisfy the assumptions of linearity, homoscedasticity and normality. A preliminary analysis, however, showed non-normality in the model. A transformation procedure was executed, in which the variable BAtt (brand attachment) was transformed in its natural logarithm. This type of data transformation can correct violations of the assumptions, without affecting the correlations in the model (Hair et al., 2006). The transformed model satisfied the above-mentioned assumptions, and consequently was used to test the mediator effect. Below, we report results based on the log-transformed variable BAtt, defined as: $BAtt^\star = ln(BAtt)$. In order to keep the interpretation of results intuitively more appealing, we continue to refer in the text to the effect of brand attachment (and not to the effect of the natural logarithm of brand attachment).

The following regression equations were used:

1   *Direct relation:* $BI = b_0 + b_1 \times BV$

2   *Indirect (mediated) relation:* $BI = b_0 + b_1 \times BV + b_2 \times BAtt^\star$

where: $BAtt^\star$ = *(log-transformed) Brand Attachment,*

   BV = *Compound Brand Value Construct;*

$$BV = \frac{\sum_{i=1}^{9} BV_i}{9},$$

BI = *Behavioural Intention.*

A significant mediation effect is present if the effect of BV (the independent variable) on BI (the outcome variable) is less in the second equation than in the first. Perfect mediation holds if the independent variable (BV) has no significant effect on the outcome variable (BI) in the second equation (Baron & Kenny, 1986).

The mediation effect was tested for the two items representing brand behaviour: BI and WoM (word-of-mouth). In order to assess the mediator effect on WoM, BI as outcome variable was replaced by WoM as outcome variable. The significance of the mediation was tested with the Sobel test, a test designed to test the significance of a mediator effect (Baron & Kenny, 1986; Preacher & Leonardelli, 2008).

RESULTS

The results confirm the hypothesis. The influence of brand values (BV) on behavioural intention (BI) is mediated by brand attachment (BAtt★). Mediation is perfect: brand values have no effect when the mediator effect of brand attachment is taken into account. The Sobel test gives a z-value of 7.80 (p = 0.000). For WoM, a similar result is obtained: the influence of brand values (BV) on word-of-mouth (WoM) is also perfectly mediated by brand attachment (BAtt★): the Sobel test gives here a z-value of 8.29 (p = 0.000).

The test demonstrates that brand attachment mediates the relationship between brand values and brand behaviour. Consumers feel more attached to brands with a higher perceived value content. This increased brand attachment then creates a higher intention to buy or use the brand, and a higher probability that the consumer engages in positive word-of-mouth.

5.6 Conclusion

The value proposition of a brand represents the values that are promised by the brand. We demonstrated in this chapter that this value proposition, as perceived by the consumer, should be described in terms of the same values as the value system of the consumer. Moreover, we demonstrated that the perceived value proposition of a brand has the same logic, and the same structure, as the consumer's value system: the brand value profile consists of a circular structure of values, in which certain values reinforce each other, and other values conflict with each other. In general terms, the perceived value profile of a brand can be modelled according to the structure illustrated by the Value Compass in Figure 4.1.

This chapter also contained an analysis of the impact of brand values on brand behaviour. This analysis demonstrated the following:

*   Brand values influence consumer behaviour,
*   The influence of brand values on behaviour is mediated by brand attachment.

Since the influence of brand values on consumer behaviour was found to be perfectly mediated by brand attachment, the analysis focused on the relation between brand values and brand attachment. We found that brand values contribute positively to brand attachment: on average, 27.8 per cent of the variance in brand attachment can be explained by its brand values.

Notes

1   In our research, the student database of the Hanze University of Applied Sciences Groningen was used for three survey rounds: the selection of value items in Stage 2 of the development of the Value Compass (February 2010), the confirmation of the structure of the Value Compass in Stage 6 and 7 of the development of the Value Compass (March 2010), and the test of the BVM (September 2010). In each of these three surveys, a different random sample was drawn out of the database. The factor structure and factor loadings of the – full – version of the Value Compass were based on the results of the March 2010 survey. For the test of the BVM, a shortened version of the Value Compass was used. The factor structure and factor loadings of the short version of the Value Compass were based on the results of the September 2010 survey.

2   A model has good fit with RMSEA $\leq$ 0.08, and CFI $\geq$ 0.92. Box 3.3 in Chapter 3 provides extensive background information on CFA.

3   The evaluation of the other brands was not redundant. They were used to construct the brand value profiles that were used in examples presented later in this text.

4   Factor loading for brand affect is 1.0. As one-item construct, brand affect is 100 per cent represented by the item that was used to measure brand affect. Hence, assessment of the construct reliability of brand affect is irrelevant.

5   These weights were derived with CFA, by taking the factor loading of each dimension on the brand attachment construct.

6   The short version of the Value Compass consists of nine factors. However, Lisrel can perform a multigroup structural equation modelling procedure for models with factors consisting of more than one item, and the value types honesty and safety consist of only one item. To enable Lisrel to perform the analysis, these two closely related value types had to be combined into one factor.

7   Additional support can be found by looking at the change in CFI. A more constrained model is assumed equivalent to a less constrained model, if CFI deteriorates with less than 0.01 (Cheung & Rensvold, 2002), as is the case here: moving from model B to model C, ΔCFI = 0.000; from C to D, ΔCFI = –0.001, and from D to E, ΔCFI = –0.003.

8   For the examples, all brand evaluations were used, as was pointed out previously in Note 3.

9   An intention to buy does not automatically imply that the person will buy a BMW. The actual conversion of intention into actual behaviour depends on, for instance, the availability of the necessary budget.

References

Baron, R. M. & Kenny, D. A. (1986). The moderator–mediator variable distinction in social psychological research: conceptual, strategic and statisical considerations. *Journal of Personality and Social Psychology, 51*(6), 1173–1182.

Cheung, G. W. & Rensvold, R. B. (2002). Evaluating goodness-of-fit indexes for testing measurement invariance. *Structural Equation Modeling, 9*(2), 233–255.

Gutman, J. (1982). A means–end chain model based on consumer categorization processes. *Journal of Marketing, 46*(2), 60–72.

Hair, J. H., Black, W. C., Babin, B. J., Anderson, R. E. & Tatham, R. L. (2006). *Multivariate data analysis* (6th edition). Upper Saddle River, NJ: Pearson Prentice Hall.

Holbrook, M. B. & Hirschman, E. C. (1982). The experiential aspects of consumption: Consumer fantasies, feelings, and fun. *Journal of Consumer Research, 9*(2), 132–140.

Keller, K. L. (2008). *Strategic brand management: Building, measuring, and managing brand equity* (3rd edition). Upper Saddle River, NJ: Prentice Hall.

Preacher, K. J. & Leonardelli, G. J. (2008). *Calculation for the Sobel test*. Retrieved 22 July 2012, from Quantpsy.org: http://quantpsy.org/sobel/sobel.htm

Thomson, M., MacInnis, D. J. & Whan Park, C. (2005). The ties that bind: Measuring the strength of consumers' emotional attachments to brands. *Journal of Consumer Psychology, 15*(1), 77–91.

Wilkie, W. L. & Pessemier, E. A. (1973). Issues in marketing's use of multi-attribute attitude models. *Journal of Marketing Research, 10*(4), 428–441.

Chapter 6

Value congruence

Brand attachment is stronger with a stronger match between the individual's value system and the perceived brand value profile. This value congruence is more relevant when values are more central to the individual (Proposition 5).

6.1 Introduction

The previous chapter confirmed that brand values influence the buying intentions of consumers. Stronger brands, that is, brands that propose a higher value content, are more appreciated: consumers are more attached to these brands. Higher brand attachment, in turn, results in a higher intention to buy the brand, or to spread positive word-of-mouth about the brand.

The analysis, so far, ignored the potential of value congruence. According to Proposition 5, value congruence plays an important role for consumer behaviour: consumers are expected to be particularly interested in brands that express the same values as the consumer himself considers important. We can illustrate this with the example of the travel agency used in Section 5.4. This travel agency offered wild water rafting trips and backpacking holidays. Hence, the value profile of this travel agency will emphasize values such as fun and stimulation. Value congruence then implies that consumers with *fun* and *stimulation* as central values will be more attracted to this travel agency than consumers who value, for instance, *safety* or *convenience*.

In this chapter, the impact of value congruence on consumer choice is investigated. This analysis involves linkage 3 of the Brand Value Model in Figure 6.1. For the analysis, we used the data set described in Section 5.2.

Before analysing the impact of value congruence, it is important to establish whether there is a direct relation between personal values and brand attachment. In other words, is it possible that consumers with certain value priorities have a natural tendency to prefer branded goods over non-branded goods? If a similar direct relation exists, then it needs to be taken into account when assessing the influence of value congruence. The possibility of this direct relation is explored in Section 6.2. Section 6.3 then gives the test results for the first part of Proposition 5: *brand attachment is stronger with a stronger match between the*

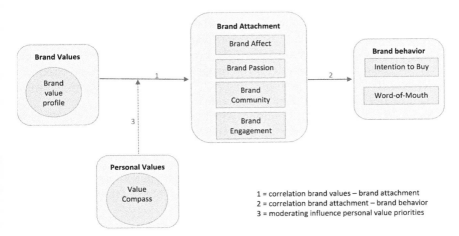

Figure 6.1 Brand Value Model (BVM)

individual's value system and the perceived brand value profile. Section 6.4 focuses on the second part of this proposition: *value congruence is more relevant for those values that are more central to the individual.*

6.2 Personal values and brand attachment

An individual's value orientation says something about his personal values, the things he considers important in life. Some people, for instance, have a stronger orientation to family values, others to security or prestige. If somebody places high priority on family values, he might show more interest in brands that help creating a cosy atmosphere. But a certain personal value orientation is not expected to create a strong positive or negative attitude toward branded products in general. Family-oriented people might be sensitive to family-oriented brands, but not all brands contain family values. Hence, we cannot establish a liking or disliking of family-oriented people toward brands in general. Consequently, no correlation is expected between an individual's value orientation and his general disposition toward brands.

There is, however, an exception to this expectation. It has been suggested that people purchase and use brands (in part) to construct their self-concept, and to differentiate themselves from others (Edson Escalas & Bettman, 2005). Consumers buy products and services for themselves, but they also express who they are through their brand choices. It is important to keep in mind that the value of a brand has been described as the differential effect that the brand has on consumer response, as compared to a similar but non-branded product (Keller, 1993). This differential effect might be related to its expected superior quality (in terms of product characteristics or performance), or its aesthetic appeal (e.g., stylish design). But the added value of a brand, the expected superiority of a branded product as opposed to a non-branded product, might also stimulate prestige-seeking behaviour: people can impress others by using brands that display status and wealth (Vigneron & Johnson, 1999). It has also been proposed that prestige-sensitive people prefer higher priced products (Richins, 1994; Vigneron & Johnson, 1999), and branded products generally exhibit higher prices than their non-branded equivalents.

Summarized, brands signal prestige, which makes brands susceptible to what has been labelled prestige-seeking consumer behaviour (Vigneron & Johnson, 1999). Consumer decision-making processes are partly influenced by this prestige-seeking consumer behaviour. Especially prestige-sensitive people engage in this type of consumer behaviour, resulting in a higher preference of prestige-sensitive consumers for branded products. This leads to the following hypothesis:

$H_{6.1}$: The personal value *prestige* correlates positively with brand attachment

As indicated above, we do not expect a significant correlation with brand attachment for the other personal value types.

Test of Hypothesis 6.1

METHOD

The relation between personal values and brand attachment is explored with the data obtained in the survey described in Section 5.2. Here, we present the analysis and the outcomes.

ANALYSIS

A stepwise regression analysis was executed on the results of the survey. Brand attachment was used as the dependent variable, and the nine personal value types as independent variables:

$$BAtt^\star = b_0 + \sum_{i=1}^{9} \left(b_i \times PV_i \right),$$

where: $BAtt^\star$ = (Log-transformed) Brand Attachment,

PV = Personal Value for value type i.

The brand attachment construct is a summary construct structured according to the output of the CFA analysis in Chapter 5. Each personal value type is a weighted average of its marker values, with weights derived from the factor loadings, as specified in Sections 4.5 and 5.2.

A preliminary analysis showed non-normality and heteroscedasticity in the model. As in the previous tests, a transformation procedure was executed, in which the dependent variable BAtt was transformed in its natural logarithm: BAtt* = ln (BAtt). The transformed model satisfied the assumptions of homoscedasticity and normality, and consequently was used to test the relation between personal values and brand attachment.

RESULTS

The model yields a small but significant result: $F(3,315) = 10.517$; $p < 0.001$. Even though significant, the explanatory power of the model is low: adjusted $R^2 = 0.057$. Three personal values were observed to influence brand attachment. As predicted, prestige-sensitivity has a positive impact on BAtt. The related value beauty also shows a positive correlation with Batt. We also found a relation that was not hypothesized: the personal value honesty correlates negatively with brand attachment. The other value types do not show significant regression coefficients.

In a series of simple regressions, each with one of the PVs as independent variable and BAtt as dependent variable, the results of the stepwise regression were confirmed. The personal values beauty, prestige and honesty showed a significant relation with brand attachment:

- *beauty, $t(313) = 2.985$, $p = 0.003$; $R^2 = 0.022$,*
- *prestige, $t(313) = 3.711$, $p < 0.001$; $R^2 = 0.034$,*
- *honesty, $t(313) = -2.539$, $p = 0.012$; $R^2 = 0.015$.*

For the other personal values, no significant relation was found.

The results confirm hypothesis 6.1. Prestige-sensitive people are significantly more attached to branded products. As proposed earlier by Vigneron and Johnson (1999), prestige-sensitivity makes people relate to brands, leading to a more positive brand attachment. Consequently, the potential of creating brand connections (e.g., brand communities) can be expected to be (somewhat) higher with prestige-sensitive individuals. But we have to take into account that prestige-sensitivity does not have a large impact on brand attachment: only 3.4 per cent of the reported variance in brand attachment is explained by prestige-sensitivity. Contrary to our expectations, the findings indicate two other small, but significant, relations between consumer values and brand attachment. Consumers that value *beauty* are, similar to prestige-sensitive consumers, more attracted to brands; an orientation toward *honesty*, on the other hand, results in a lower brand attachment. For the other value types, there is no significant impact of an individual's value orientation on brand attachment.

The observed relations are small but significant. The outcomes demonstrate that impact of an individual's value orientation on his consumer behaviour follows the pattern of compatibilities and conflicts proposed by the Value

Compass: promotion of self-interests (neighbouring value types *beauty* and *prestige)* stimulates the attachment to brands, whereas the opposing value type honesty results in a lower appreciation of brands (see Figure 6.2). The observed effects are significant, but relatively small.

It is important to highlight that these effects do not take the possibility of value congruence into account. A customer's value priorities might not create strong love or rejection for branded products in general, but his value orientation might lead to an attachment to those brands whose value profile matches with his own value priorities. The influence of value congruence is explored in the next section.

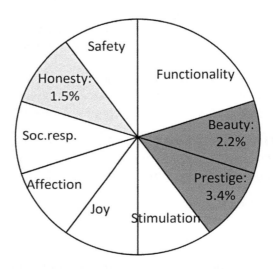

Figure 6.2 Personal values with a significant impact on brand attachment: percentages reflect explained variance (positive relations with dark accentuation, negative relation light)

6.3 Value congruence

Brand attachment is stronger with a stronger match between the individual's value priorities and the perceived brand value profile. (Proposition 5A).

In Section 2.8, self-congruence was defined as the match between an individual's self-concept and the image of the brand. Consumers form affect-laden relationships with brands that match their personality, a match that provides a means to create or support the consumer's identity. The influence of self-congruence on the relation between the individual and the brand was confirmed in a number of studies, see Section 2.8. Particularly noteworthy is a study by Kressmann *et al.* (2006). In this study, a model was developed that demonstrates the effects of self-congruence on brand loyalty. Brand personality aspects were used in this study as indicators for brand image. Respondents had to rate brands on these brand personality aspects (e.g., '*Indicate to what extent the personality attribute intelligent applies to the brand BMW*'). After doing so, they had to apply the same personality aspects to themselves ('*To what extent do you consider yourself to be intelligent?*'). Self-congruence was computed in this study by using the absolute difference scores between each brand personality rating and its corresponding self-image rating, and then averaged across all personality attributes for each respondent:

$$\text{self-congruence} = \frac{\sum_{i=1}^{n} |BI_i - SI_i|}{n},$$

where: BI_i = brand image aspect i,
SI = self-image aspect i,
n = number of image aspects.

By using this model, Kressmann *et al.* (2006) found that self-congruence has a positive influence on the relation between the individual and the brand.

In Section 2.8, value congruence was defined as a specific application of self-congruence. Value congruence implies that brands are more relevant to the individual if the perceived brand values have a better match with his individual values. Hence, we expect value congruence to have a positive influence on brand attachment. Following the previously used example of the travel agency offering exciting holidays like wild water rafting, we can imagine that a person who values adventure and excitement will experience value congruence and, consequently, will feel attached to this travel agency. On the other hand, a consumer who likes fully organized holidays in the sun in a safe all-inclusive resort probably feels value incongruence with this agency. This consumer will likely avoid this travel agency. This leads to the following hypothesis:

H $_{6.2}$: Value congruence results in higher brand attachment.

To test the effect of value congruence, a variant of the model of Kressmann *et al.* is used. Instead of self-image aspects, we focus on the value types of the Value Compass. As demonstrated previously (in Section 5.4), the brand value profile has the same structure as the consumer's value system, and contains the same value types. Therefore, the score for each brand value can be compared with the score for the corresponding consumer value. For instance, measuring the effect of value congruence on brand attachment in the example of the travel agency would imply comparing statements such as '*Excitement is important for me*' with a statement like '*The travel agency represents excitement*'. Following this procedure, congruence can be calculated in a similar vein as in the model of

Kressmann *et al.* (2006), by replacing the brand image and self-image aspects with brand values and personal values:

$$\text{value congruence} = \frac{\sum_{i=1}^{n} \left| BV_i - PV_i \right|}{n} \ ,$$

where: BV_i = brand value type i,
PV_i = personal value type i,
n = number of value types.

Test of Hypothesis 6.2

METHOD

The effect of value congruence on brand attachment is explored with the data obtained in the survey described in Section 5.2. Below, we describe the results of the test of the hypothesis.

ANALYSIS

A regression analysis was executed on the results of the survey. Brand attachment was used as the dependent variable, and value congruence as independent variable:

$$BAtt\star = b_0 + b_1 \times VC,$$

where: $BAtt\star$ *= (Log-transformed) Brand Attachment,*

$$VC = \text{value congruence, defined as } VC = \frac{\sum_{i=1}^{9} \left| BV_i - PV_i \right|}{9} .$$

As in the previous analysis, log transformation was applied to correct for non-normality and heteroscedasticity. Value congruence is calculated as the difference between the scores on the brand value type and the corresponding personal value type, for each of the nine value types of the shorter version of the Value Compass. The value type scores are a weighted average of their marker values, with weights derived from the factor loadings (see Sections 4.5 and 5.2).

A low value of VC implies high value congruence. For instance, a brand with a high prestige value (high BV) is expected to be valued by a person who considers prestige important (high PV). In this case $|BV - PV|$ will be low. Higher value congruence, hence a lower score on VC, is expected to result in a higher brand attachment. Consequently, a negative coefficient for b_1 is expected.

RESULTS

The effect of value congruence on brand attachment was found to be significant: t = −7.117, p < 0.001. The effect is meaningful: (adjusted) R² = 0.168, which means that 16.8 per cent of the variance in brand attachment is explained by value congruence.

The regression presented above was on an aggregate level, taking all value types together. Further regression analyses were executed for each value type of the Value Compass separately. For instance, for the value type safety, we used the model:

$$BAtt^\star = b_0 + b_1 \times VC_{safety},$$

where VC_{safety} was calculated as $BV_{safety} - PV_{safety}$.

The further analyses demonstrated a congruence effect for each value type of the Value Compass, tested significantly with p < 0.001. Consequently, we can conclude that a higher brand attachment is observed when the values attributed to a certain brand match the personal values of the respondent.

Hypothesis 6.2 is confirmed. The test demonstrates that value congruence, the match between the values proposed by a brand and the personal value priorities, results in a stronger brand attachment.

6.4 The moderating effect of value centrality

Value congruence is more relevant when values are more central to the individual (Proposition 5B).

The previous section demonstrated the relation between value congruence and brand attachment: consumers experience a stronger relationship with a brand when there is a match between their personal values and the brand values. In case of a mismatch (value incongruence), there is a negative influence on brand attachment. A similar effect was reported by the few other studies that focused on value congruence (Torelli *et al.*, 2008, 2012; Zhang & Bloemer, 2008, 2011).

A moderating effect related to congruence was proposed by Kressmann *et al.* (2006) when they incorporated the perceived importance of an attribute in their self-congruity construct. In their model, the effect of self-congruence is stronger when the attribute is a more important aspect of the individual's personality. Proposition 5B points to a similar effect for the BVM: the effect of the consumer's value priorities on behaviour is expected to be stronger when the values are more central to the individual. The following extreme situations can be expected:

- A certain value (e.g., *prestige*) is not central to the consumer in a certain setting (e.g., when considering whether to buy a car). Whether the car offers prestige or not will then be less relevant to this individual. The prestige value of the car has little influence on this consumer's brand attachment: the expected influence of value congruence on behaviour is limited.
- A certain value (e.g., *prestige*) is central to the individual in a certain setting (e.g., when considering whether to buy a car). Then, the prestige value of the car is expected to have a stronger influence on brand attachment. Two situations are possible:

1   The car offers prestige: value congruence. The brand attachment is expected to be positively influenced, because the prestige value of the car is important to the individual.
2   The car offers no prestige: value incongruence. The brand attachment is expected to be unaffected, or even negatively affected by the lack of prestige of the car.

In conclusion, we expect that the importance of personal values moderates the effect of value congruence on brand attitude:

$H_{6.3}$: **The effect of value congruence on brand attachment is stronger for those values that are more important to the individual.**

Test of Hypothesis 6.3

METHOD

A moderator is a variable that influences the direction and/or strength of the relation between an independent and a dependent variable (Baron & Kenny, 1986; Hair et al., 2006). The significance of a moderator effect can be determined with multiple regression analysis, by comparing the explained variance of the unmoderated equation with the variance explained by the moderated equation. For the analysis we used the data obtained in the survey described in Section 5.2.

ANALYSIS

To test for the moderating effect of PV on the relation between VC and BAtt[1], the following models were used:[2]

1   *Unmoderated equation:* $BAtt^\star = b_0 + b_1 \times PV + b_2 \times VC,$

2   *Moderated equation:* $BAtt^\star = b_0 + b_1 \times PV + b_2 \times VC + b_3 \times MODPV,$

where: $BAtt^\star$ = *(Log-transformed) Brand Attachment,*

PV = *Summated Personal Value Score over the nine value types, defined as*

$$PV = \sum_{i=1}^{9} \frac{PV_i}{9} ,$$

VC = *Value congruence,*

$MODPV$ = *moderating effect of personal values:*

$$MODPV = \sum_{i=1}^{9} \frac{PV_i \times VC_i}{9} ,$$

VC_i = *congruence with respect to value type I, defined as*
$BV_i - PV_i$

To determine the significance of the moderator effect, the unmoderated equation was estimated, and then compared with the moderated equation. A moderator effect is present if there is a significant increase in R^2 by adding the moderator effect $b_3 \times MODPV$. Significance of a moderator effect can be related to the coefficient b_3: a significant b_3 indicates a significant moderator effect.

In the analysis of the moderator effect, PV and VC were centred (i.e., for both PV and VC, the mean value was subtracted from each individual rating). This was done because the interaction effect in the moderator is highly correlated with the other two variables in the equation, resulting in unacceptable multicollinearity in the regression. Centring the moderating variable reduces problems associated with multicollinearity, without affecting the model fit and the explained variance (Frazier, Barron & Tix, 2004).

Results

The results confirm the hypothesis. For the unmoderated model, R^2 is 16.8% ($F_{(2,244)}$ = 25.907; $p < 0.001$), whereas the moderated model results in a higher explained variance of 18.1% ($F_{(3,243)}$ = 19.143; $p < 0.001$). The moderator effect MODPV is significant ($t_{MODPV}(245)$ = −2.192; p = 0.029), but with an increase in explained variance of only 1.6 per cent, the effect is relatively small.

To further investigate, an analysis was executed for each value type separately. The results gave a significant moderator effect (MODPV) for four of the 11 value types:

- beauty, $t(313)$ = −3.41; p = 0.001,
- prestige, $t(317)$ = −2.63; p = 0.009,
- functionality, $t(300)$ = −2.52; p = 0.012,
- stimulation, $t(285)$ = −2.60; p = 0.010.

A significant moderator effect was not found for the other value types. It seems that the moderator effect is stronger for values that put more emphasis on promoting personal interests and for utilitarian values, and absent in values motivating to care for and take care of others. Further research is necessary to elaborate on this point.

The results of the analysis support the hypothesis to a certain extent. For a number of value types, personal values moderate the influence of value congruence on brand attachment. For these values, the impact of value congruence on brand attachment is higher when these values are more important for the consumer. This effect is particularly true with values promoting the pursuit of self-interest.

6.5 Conclusion

Consumer values influence brand choice: consumers attempt to connect with those brands that reflect what the consumer himself considers important. This effect was referred to as value congruence, defined as the match between the values of the consumer and the values proposed by the brand. Indeed a significant effect of value congruence on brand choice was found: consumers are more attached to brands whose brand values match with their own values, whereas the perceived absence of important values results in a lower brand attachment. The congruence effect was found to be particularly relevant for values that are central to the consumer. Values that are less important for a consumer have a more limited influence on brand attachment.

Besides the effect of value congruence, we also found, to a limited extent, that prestige-sensitive consumers show a higher attachment to brands in general. Apparently, prestige-sensitivity makes people more susceptible to brands. A similar relation was found with respect to the value type *beauty*. Individuals for whom the opposing value *honesty* is an important value, on the other hand, have a somewhat lower tendency to attach themselves to brands.

Notes

1   As in the test of hypothesis 6.2, the log-transformed variable BAtt★ was used as indicator for brand attachment.
2   Formally, a moderator is the product of two variables of interest (Baron & Kenny, 1986), here PV and VC. However, we are not interested here in the interaction on aggregate level, but in the interaction on the level of value types. Consequently, we used a slightly adapted version of the moderator, in which we first calculated the moderator effects for each of the separate value types, and then averaged these across all value types to create the total moderating effect.

References

Baron, R. M. & Kenny, D. A. (1986). The moderator-mediator variable distinction in social psychological research: conceptual, strategic and statisical considerations. *Journal of Personality and Social Psychology, 51*(6), 1173–1182.

Edson Escalas, J. & Bettman, J. R. (2005). Self-construal, reference groups and brand meaning. *Journal of Consumer Research, 32*(3), 378–389.

Hair, J. H., Black, W. C., Babin, B. J., Anderson, R. E. & Tatham, R. L. (2006). *Multivariate data analysis* (6th edition). Upper Saddle River, NJ: Pearson Prentice Hall.

Keller, K. L. (1993). Conceptualizing, measuring, and managing customer-based brand equity. *Journal of Marketing, 57*(1), 1–22.

Kressmann, F., Sirgy, M., Herrmann, A., Huber, F., Huber, S. & Lee, D.-J. (2006). Direct and indirect effects of self-image congruence on brand loyalty. *Journal of Business Research, 59*(9), 955–964.

Richins, M. L. (1994). Special possessions and the expression of material values. *Journal of Consumer Research, 21*(3), 522–533.

Torelli, C. J., Özsomer, A., Carvalho, S. W., Keh, H. T. & Maehle, N. (2008). A measure of brand values: cross-cultural implications for brand preferences. *Advances in Consumer Research Conference*. San Francisco, CA.

Torelli, C. J., Özsomer, A., Carvalho, S. W., Keh, H. T. & Maehle, N. (2012). Brand concepts as representations of human values: Do cultural congruity and compatibility between values matter? *Journal of Marketing, 76*(7), 92–108.

Vigneron, F. & Johnson, L. W. (1999). A review and a conceptual framework of prestige-seeking consumer behavior. *Academy of Marketing Science Review, 1*(1), 1–15.

Zhang, J. & Bloemer, J. M. (2008). The impact of value congruence on consumer-service brand relationships. *Journal of Service Research, 11*(2), 161–178.

Zhang, J. & Bloemer, J. M. (2011). Impact of value congruence on affective commitment: Examining the moderating effects. *Journal of Service Management, 22*(2), 160–182.

Chapter 7

Brand values versus brand personality

The brand values concept provides a meaningful alternative to the brand personality concept (Proposition 6).

7.1 Introduction

Both values and personality traits can be used to describe people. In the previous chapters, we referred to values as guiding principles in people's lifes. An important aspect in this description was the focus on behaviour: values motivate people to behave in a certain way. Hence, values are connected with behavioural motives. Personality definitions generally have a different emphasis; they focus on character aspects or traits that describe the individual. This is the case, for instance, in the definition provided by Guilford, 'The individual's unique pattern of traits' (Guilford, 1959, p. 8), or in the emphasis on personality traits in the Five-Factor Model (McCrae & Costa, 1996). To sum up, traits give a characterization of individuals in terms of relatively enduring patterns of thoughts, feelings and actions.

Both concepts are also applied to assess the attractiveness of brands. Keller (2008) referred to personality traits and to values as determinants of brand image. In managerial practice, the core meaning of a brand is frequently described in terms of its brand values. In marketing theory, however, the use of personality traits to describe brands prevails. The most popular brand concept is Aaker's brand personality framework (Aaker, 1997). When it comes to values, marketing theory relies on models developed for the analysis of human psychology, in particular the value theories of Rokeach (1973) and, to a lesser extent, Schwartz (1992). As opposed to the development of the brand personality framework to describe the personality of a brand, no value-based brand concept has been developed so far. As we noted in Chapter 2, a further complication in the discussion of brand values and brand personality in marketing theory is that the distinction between both concepts has become blurred.

The aim of this study is to apply the values concept to marketing, and to introduce a meaningful value-based brand concept. To satisfy this purpose, we developed the Value Compass, by using recent insights from values theory and applying them to a consumer behaviour context. This process was described in the previous chapters. We also aim to distinguish brand values and brand personality, and to establish to which degree the use of brand values provides a meaningful alternative to the brand personality framework. This chapter presents the comparison of the two concepts. Section 7.2 discusses the Value Compass and the brand personality framework from a theoretical point of view, and describes the differences between both. This review leads to predictions concerning the relation between brand values and brand personality with consumer choice. These predictions are subsequently tested. Section 7.3 describes the test design and Sections 7.4 and 7.5 present the results of the test. We conclude this chapter with a summary of the main findings in Section 7.6.

7.2 Comparison of the Value Compass and the brand personality framework

Following the increasing attention for the symbolic meaning of a brand (e.g., Hirschman & Holbrook, 1982; Whan Park, Jaworski & MacInnis, 1986), Aaker introduced the concept of brand personality in 1997, as a framework to measure the symbolic meaning that consumers attribute to brands: *The objective [. . .] is to develop a theoretical framework of brand personality dimensions [. . .] and a reliable, valid, and generizable scale that measures these dimensions* (Aaker, 1997, p. 347). This brand personality framework was more extensively described in Chapter 2.

The brand personality scale developed by Aaker (1997) intends to measure the personality of the brand. This is less comprehensive than the intentions behind the Value Compass. With the Value Compass, both consumer values and brand values can be described and measured. Moreover, the Value Compass provides an instrument by which the influence of brand values on consumer behaviour can be assessed. Thus, the intentions behind both instruments are somewhat different. But are these differences in intentions related to actual differences in the two concepts? To generate a deeper understanding of brand values and brand personality, they are compared below. This comparison involves the following aspects:

1   the theoretical foundations of brand personality and brand values,
2   the conceptual structure of both concepts,
3   the universality of both concepts,
4   the relation with consumer behaviour.

Origins of brand values and brand personality

In both the brand personality framework and the Value Compass, aspects of psychology are applied to brands. There are, however, limits to the personification of brands: the words used to describe human characteristics or human values may not all be relevant to brands. Consequently, these human characteristics have to be adapted to fit a brand context (Azoulay & Kapferer, 2003). For the Value Compass, this adaptation was realized through a selection process. The values in the Value Compass originated from a comprehensive list of human values, a list that was created following a lexical approach (De Raad & Van Oudenhoven, 2008). Next, values were selected based on the extent to which they apply to a consumer behaviour context. As a result, a brand value system was developed with a conceptual structure resembling the structure of the human value system as described by Schwartz (1992).

Aaker's brand personality framework was derived from the Big Five theory of personality, and adapted to fit a branding context. Aaker generated her set of personality traits on the basis of a number of sources:

- literature review of scales used in psychology to measure the Big Five;
- personality scales used by marketers (academics and practitioners);
- a free association task performed by respondents who were asked to indicate which personality traits they associated with brands.

Out of this set of personality traits, respondents selected those traits that they considered descriptive for brands. According to Aaker (1997), three of her brand personality dimensions relate – to some extent – to three of the Big Five human personality dimensions. Sincerity taps into traits of agreeableness and conscientiousness. Excitement includes items like sociability, energy and activity, just as extraversion does. Competence captures traits found in conscientiousness and extraversion. Aaker does not relate the other two dimensions of brand personality, sophistication and ruggedness, to any of the Big Five dimensions.

Azoulay and Kapferer (2003) pointed out that the personality concept in some of Aaker's sources has a global, extended meaning, covering a variety of separate constructs. This includes personality traits, but also values, or reflections of the typical or stereotypical buyer. This global view on the personality construct is reflected in the broad definition that Aaker used for the brand personality concept: *the set of human characteristics associated with a brand*. As a result, the brand personality framework seems to cover a variety of human characteristics, involving more than just personality traits. In fact, conceptual lack of clarity of her brand personality construct was recognized by Aaker, when comparing the brand personality framework with the Big Five dimensions of human psychology: '. . . *whereas Sincerity, Excitement, and Competence tap an innate part of human personality, Sophistication and Ruggedness tap a dimension that individuals desire but not necessarily have*' (Aaker, 1997, p. 353). By implying a more value-like characterization of sophistication and ruggedness, the distinction between personality traits and values in the brand personality framework becomes fuzzy. To avoid conceptual lack of clarity, Azoulay and Kapferer advocated the use of a stricter definition of the use of brand personality: *the set of human personality traits that are both applicable to and relevant for brands* (Azoulay & Kapferer, 2003, p. 151).

The conceptual structure of brand values and brand personality

The Value Compass and the brand personality framework are structured differently. The Value Compass consists of 11 (or, in the short version, nine) value types. Aaker's brand personality framework consists of five dimensions, thereby paralleling the structure of the Five-Factor Model. The larger number of value types, as compared to brand personality dimensions, offers the potential of a richer and more differentiated analysis. This is amplified by the existence of a structure. Similar to the conceptual structure of the human value system, as specified by Schwartz (1992), the Value Compass is structured as a value system consisting of compatible and conflicting values. The circular structure of this value system explicitly takes the relations between values into consideration. Consequently, conclusions can be drawn from the importance of each value in a brand value profile, but also from the combinations of these values. For instance, it is possible to analyse to what extent the combination of certain values produces a consistent brand value profile, depending on the compatibilities and conflicts of the motivations expressed by these values. The relations among the five dimensions of Aaker's brand personality framework, on the other hand, are not specified. The absence of a structure linking these dimensions prevents the possibility of interpreting combinations of brand personality dimensions (e.g., evaluating the consistency of a certain pattern of brand personality traits).

Universality of the Value Compass and the brand personality framework

Both the value system developed by Schwartz and the personality trait dimensions of the Five-Factor Model were replicated in cross-cultural studies (McCrae & Costa, 1997; Schwartz, 1994; Schwartz & Bardi, 2001). This, however, does not imply that brand concepts derived from these constructs can be applied across societies. As was discussed in Chapter 2, the brand personality framework shows only limited cross-cultural validity. The cross-cultural validity of the Value Compass will be investigated in Chapter 8.

The relation with consumer behaviour

As was described in the introduction of this chapter, values are behavioural motives; they refer to '*what people consider important*' (Bilsky & Schwartz, 1994, p. 790). Personality traits describe what a person is like (Bilsky & Schwartz, 1994): traits characterize individuals in terms of what they think, feel or do, rather than considering the intentions behind these thoughts, feelings or actions.

Now, let us relate values and personality traits to consumer behaviour. Consumer behaviour is motivated by a discrepancy between what consumers have and what they want to have: consumers try to obtain something they did not have before. This wish of wanting something desirable can also be found in values, as they represent the goals that define what consumers would like to have, as in the example of the consumer looking for an exciting holiday because fun and stimulation are central values to him (and apparently his life is not yet stimulating enough so he needs this holiday to get his desired level of stimulation).

But to what extent can we say the same about personality traits? Personality traits provide a description of an individual, but they do not provide a reference to the discrepancy between what a person is like and what he would like to be. And, unlike values, traits do not provide explicit guidance for the actions that should be taken to decrease this discrepancy. And since consumer behaviour is focused on alleviating discrepancies, we argue here that personality traits do *not necessarily* constitute a motivating force for consumer behaviour. We can illustrate this with an example of a smart and intelligent individual who managed to become successful. In terms of Aaker's personality trait dimensions, this individual exhibits a high rating on the personality trait competence (see Figure 2.6). Due to his competent personality, he managed to progress to a higher position in the company where he works, earning a good salary, and being appreciated, sometimes even admired, by his co-workers. As a consequence of his societal position, he might be surrounded by brands that match a successful lifestyle, for instance, fashionable clothing matching the dress code of his professional position. But the successful position of this individual is related to his competences, not to his values. If being successful would be an important value to him as well, then we can indeed expect him to consistently desire brands that express success, according to the value congruence effect explained in the previous chapter. On the other hand, it is also possible that this individual does not value success, despite the fact that he is successful.[1] In that case, he does not necessarily desire brands expressing success.

In sum, consumer behaviour is expected to be more strongly related to what we consider important (realizing the goals symbolized by our values) than to what we are (our personality traits). We frame this in the form of the following hypothesis:

$H_{7.1}$ Values have a stronger influence on brand attachment than personality traits

This hypothesis was tested in a comparative study of brand values and brand personality traits. The design of this study is presented in the following section.

7.3 Method

The previous chapters demonstrated the structure of the Value Compass, and showed how the values in the Value Compass guide consumer behaviour.

In these chapters, we uncovered three mechanisms by which values are linked with behaviour:

1   The effect of brand values: brands are perceived to represent values. These brand values positively influence brand choice.[2]
2   The value congruence effect: the match between the value proposition of the brand and the value system of the consumer was shown to have a positive influence on brand choice.
3   The value centrality effect: the effect of value congruence on behaviour was found to be stronger for values that are more central to the individual. In other words, more important values have a stronger influence on brand choice.

The relation between values and consumer behaviour is the combined effect of these three mechanisms. An appreciation of the influence of values on consumer behaviour, as compared to the influence of personality traits on consumer behaviour, needs to take these mechanisms into account.

A comparative test was developed to analyse the impact of values and personality traits on behaviour. Two test versions were used. In one test version, respondents evaluated their own values and the values of a number of selected brands. In the other test version, respondents assessed their own personality and the brand personality of the selected brands. Both test versions were assessed in a survey distributed among a sample of Dutch students, in the form of an online questionnaire. As in the previous studies, the student database of the Hanze University of Applied Sciences Groningen, The Netherlands, was used to select students. Students were drawn randomly out of this database. The selected respondents received an email, followed by two reminders, with a request to fill out the survey. Respondents could access the survey by clicking on the link they could find in the email. When respondents followed this link, they were randomly assigned to either the value-based test version, or the test version based on personality traits. The software Surveymonkey was used to publish the survey online, and to collect the responses. The survey was available from 21 March 2011 until 31 March 31 2011.

Test design version A: values and consumer behaviour

In version A, respondents were confronted with two brands, Audi and IKEA. These brands were conveniently selected for the purpose of this test; they do not intend to give a representative coverage of consumer brands. Respondents evaluated their own values, the brand values of both brands, and finally their attachment toward these two brands. The design of test variant A was identical to the test design described in Section 5.2. Below, we briefly summarize this design.

Personal value priorities

Respondents rated their own value priorities on a 5-point scale, by answering the following question: '*How important is this value for you when you have to make a choice between products or services?*'. The shortened version of the Value Compass was used (see Table 5.1). As in Section 5.2, the respondent's score for each value type is the weighted average of the value items representing this value type, with weights identical to those used in the short version of the Value Compass (weights derived in the September 2010 survey round).

Brand values

As specified above, two brands were included in this test: Audi and IKEA. Each respondent evaluated one of these two brands; brands were randomly assigned to respondents. Respondents rated the brand values of IKEA and Audi on a 5-point Likert scale, by answering to the following question: '*A brand can represent certain values. Could you indicate to what extent the following brand represents these values (for instance, 'Audi represents strength')?*' Both brands were evaluated with the same value items as were used to evaluate the personal value priorities.

Brand attachment

Brand attachment was measured with items representing the four dimensions of brand attachment: brand affect, brand love, brand community and brand engagement. For a complete overview of these items, we refer to Table 5.2 in Chapter 5.

Test design version B: personality traits and consumer behaviour

Test version B was constructed in a similar style as version A, with the same brands, IKEA and Audi. However, in version B respondents evaluated personality traits, as opposed to the values that were evaluated in test version A. Respondents first evaluated their own personality traits, then they assessed to what extent they perceived these traits as belonging to the brand personality of the two brands. Finally, they assessed their brand attachment.

Personality traits

Respondents assessed their own personality based on a number of personality traits. The personality traits from Aaker's brand personality scale were used for this assessment. In her scale, Aaker's scale includes 42 traits that can be used to describe the personality of a brand, representing the five personality dimensions distinguished by Aaker: sincerity, excitement, competence, sophistication and ruggedness (see Figure 2.4). The majority of these traits can also be used to describe a human personality. In a qualitative pretest, however, a number of items proved to be ambiguous or difficult to interpret when applied to a person. This concerned the following traits: small-town, real, wholesome, secure, corporate, western and rugged. These problematic traits were excluded. Respondents were asked to evaluate their own personality with the remaining 35 traits: '*Please indicate how much each of these characteristics gives a good description of yourself*'. Ratings were obtained on a 5-point Likert scale.

The ratings for each personality trait were used to create individual scores for each of Aaker's five personality dimensions. Aaker does not give an indication how she calculated the average scores for the five personality dimensions from the individual ratings on personality traits. However, she specified that '*these traits had high item-to-total correlations on (. . .) their factors (ranging from 0.50 to 0.97), thereby ensuring high internal consistency*' (Aaker, 1997, p. 352).[3] With these high item-to-total correlations, we decided to define the trait dimensions as the unweighted average of the scores of the personality trait items by which they are represented.

Brand personality

As in the previous test version, the two brands Audi and IKEA were submitted. Both brands were evaluated with the same 35 personality traits as were used to evaluate the individual's personality profile. Brand personality traits were measured with a 5-point Likert scale. In the test, we used the same instruction as the one used by Aaker (1997) to construct her brand personality scale: '*We would like you to think of a brand as a person. This may sound unusual, but think of the set of human characteristics associated with each brand. For example you might think that the human characteristics associated with Pepsi Cola are fun, interesting and exciting. We're interested which personality traits or human characteristics come to mind when you think of IKEA*' (p. 350). The scores for the brand personality traits were used to construct the five dimensions of brand personality, again by taking the unweighted average of item scores.

BRAND ATTACHMENT

To measure brand attachment, exactly the same items were used as in test version A.

RESPONSE

A total of 804 students followed the link to the survey during the survey period. These students were randomly assigned to one of the two test versions. 256 respondents completed the test version based on brand values and 234 respondents completed the test version with brand personality.

ANALYTICAL METHOD

As stated in the introduction to this section, three mechanisms link values to consumer behaviour:

1   The brand values in the brand value profile stimulate brand attachment.
2   Value congruence stimulates brand attachment.
3   Value centrality makes the congruence effect more relevant.

For the relation between personality and behaviour, we expect the existence of similar mechanisms: the influence of brand personality traits and the influence of personality trait congruence on behaviour, and the influence of personality trait strength on the relevance of the trait congruence. The relation between values and behaviour was analysed with the results of test version A, and the relation between personality and behaviour with the results from version B.

Results were analysed by means of regression analysis. First, the results of test version A were used to analyse the relation between values and behaviour, for each of the three mechanisms. Brand attachment, as proxy for behaviour, is used as the dependent variable, and the value constructs (brand values, value congruence and value centrality) were the independent variables. The next step was a regression analysis on the results of test version B: the mechanisms that link personality traits (brand personality traits, trait congruence and trait strength) to behaviour. Finally, by applying Fisher's r-to-z transformation, the strength of the values–attachment relation was compared with the strength of the personality trait–attachment relation, for each of the three mechanisms.

The results of the test of hypothesis 7.1 are described in Section 7.5. But before turning to these results, we first summarize a number of descriptives of the test outcomes.

7.4 Values and personality traits: comparison of descriptives

Descriptives for personal values

In test version A, respondents evaluated first their personal value priorities, before they were asked to assess the brand values of IKEA and Audi. Table 7.1 presents means, standard deviations and confidence intervals of these personal values, for each value type. Value types in this table are ranked by importance, by using the sample mean as indicator for the importance of the value priority.

Descriptives for personality traits

In test version B, people assessed their own personality with the personality traits of Aaker's brand personality framework. Tables 7.1 and 7.2 presents the descriptives resulting from this assessment.

Table 7.1 Test results for version A: personal value priorities

Value type	Mean	Std. deviation	n	95% conf. interval
Honesty	4.056	1.026	233	[3.912, 4.200]
Safety	3.878	.951	240	[3.745, 4.012]
Enjoying life	3.846	.844	228	[3.727, 3.965]
Functionality	3.786	.743	228	[3.682, 3.891]
Affection	3.656	.849	231	[3.536, 3.775]
Beauty	3.393	.876	235	[3.270, 3.516]
Social responsibility	3.361	.849	235	[3.242, 3.481]
Stimulation	3.289	.761	232	[3.181, 3.396]
Prestige	3.167	.869	226	[3.053, 3.281]

The mean trait ratings are, in general, lower than mean ratings for value priorities. We have to take into account that value priorities of the Value Compass were specifically selected for their relevance for consumer behaviour. Through this selection procedure, only relevant value items, that is, value items with a higher mean importance, were selected for the Value Compass. Personality traits, on the other hand, were selected by Aaker for the extent to which they associate with brands, not because of their importance to the average individual. This difference in selection procedures forms an explanation for the higher mean ratings of value types.

Individual variation in trait levels between respondents, as expressed by the standard deviation, is also smaller than the interpersonal variation in value priorities. The larger variation in value priorities between individuals of the same population, as compared to the variation in personality traits, makes the Value Compass a more suitable instrument to detect priority differences in a population, for instance, for segmentation purposes.

Table 7.2 Test results for version B: descriptives for the personality trait dimensions

Personality trait dimension	Mean	Std. deviation	n	95% conf. interval
Sincerity	3.702	.467	210	[3.625, 3.780]
Competence	3.400	.500	229	[3.318, 3.483]
Excitement	3.243	.440	175	[3.170, 3.316]
Ruggedness	3.052	.693	205	[2.937, 3.167]
Sophistication	2.949	.582	215	[2.853, 3.045]

7.5 Brand values versus brand personality

As explained previously, the following mechanisms are expected to link brand values and brand personality to behaviour:

* a direct influence of brand values respectively brand personality on brand attachment;
* a congruence effect;
* a centrality effect.

Hypothesis 7.1 predicts that the combined effect of these mechanisms is stronger for values than for personality traits.

Test of hypothesis 7.1

$H_{7.1}$ **Values have a stronger influence on brand attachment than personality traits**

DESIGN

To test the hypothesis, a number of models were estimated. These models were related to the mechanisms described above. This resulted in the following analytical design:

Regression analysis was used to estimate the models. In all models, brand attachment was the dependent variable. For the analysis of the influence of values on brand attachment, the short version of the Value Compass (with nine value types) was used as analytical model. The five personality trait dimensions of Aaker's brand personality framework were used in the analysis of the influence of personality traits on brand attachment.

The structure of each model was based on the designs described in the previous chapters: the models related to the first mechanism have the same structure as the model described in Section 5.5, the congruence models are similar to the congruence model in Section 6.3, and the moderating effect of value centrality and trait strength was tested according to the design described

Table 7.3 Test design

	Test version A (influence of values)	Test version B (influence of traits)
Mechanism I brand attachment related to:	Brand values (IA)	Brand personality (IB)
Mechanism II brand attachment related to:	Value congruence (IIA)	Personality trait congruence (IIB)
Mechanism III Congruence effect moderated by:	Value centrality (IIIA)	Trait strength (IIIB)

in Section 6.4. Comparison of the strength of the correlations in the values-attachment relations with the trait-attachment relations was done with Fisher's r-to-z transformation.

As in the studies in the previous chapters, the models showed heteroscedasticity. Therefore a transformation procedure was used. With this procedure, brand attachment (BAtt) was transformed in its natural logarithm: BAtt* = ln (BAtt). The transformed models satisfy the assumptions of linearity, homoscedasticity and normality. Below, we report results based on the log-transformed variable BAtt.

Table 7.4 Comparison of the effect of brand values and brand personality on brand attachment[4]

Model I. The influence of brand values versus brand personality traits on brand attachment	Test version A (influence of values)	Test version B (influence of traits)
Brand attachment related to:	Brand values (IA)	Brand personality (IB)
Significance of correlation, model I	$F(9,171) = 17.269$; $p < 0.001$	$F(5,123) = 10.460$; $p < 0.001$
Explained variance (R^2) model I:	$R^2 = 0.449$	$R^2 = 0.270$
Significance of difference in R:	$z_{difference} = 2.01$ two-tailed probability $p = 0.044$	
Model II. Congruence effect: the influence of value congruence versus trait congruence on brand attachment	Test version A (influence of values)	Test version B (influence of traits)
Brand attachment related to:	Value congruence (IIA)	Personality trait congruence (IIB)
Significance of correlation, model II	$F(1,162) = 22.557$; $p < 0.001$	$F(1,93) = 22.128$; $p < 0.001$
R^2 mechanism II (congruence effect):	$R^2 = 0.117$	$R^2 = 0.184$
Significance of difference in R:	$z_{difference} = 0.79$ two-tailed probability $p = 0.430$	
Model III. Centrality effect: the influence of value centrality versus trait strenght on brand attachment	Test version A (influence of values)	Test version B (influence of traits)
Brand attachment related to:	Value centrality (IIIA)	Personality trait strength (IIIB)
R^2 change through mechanism III (centrality effect):	R^2 change = 0.195	R^2 change = 0.015
Significance of difference in R:	$z_{difference} = 2.65$ two-tailed probability $p = 0.008$	

RESULTS

Brand values have a strong and significant effect on brand attachment: explained variance of 44.9% (Model I in Table 7.4). The strength of brand personality traits also relates significantly to brand attachment, although the explained variance is lower: $R^2 = 27.0\%$. Comparison of correlations with Fisher's r-to-z transformation shows that brand values have a significantly stronger effect on brand attachment (in terms of explained variance) than the traits of Aaker's brand personality framework: the z-score of the difference between the brand values–attachment correlation and the brand personality–attachment correlation is significant.

Model II in Table 7.4 presents the congruence effect for both brand values and brand personality traits. The variance explained by brand personality is somewhat higher, but the difference is not significant.

Model III in Table 7.4 presents the moderating influence of value centrality on the match between personal values and brand values. Adding the effect of value centrality to the model increases the R^2 with 19.5 per cent: a significant increase. As explained earlier, this implies that when a consumer evaluates a brand, he will pay particularly importance to those values that are important to him. Brand values that are unimportant to the consumer have a significantly lower impact on his brand attachment. This effect is different with respect to brand personality. The analysis shows no significant moderator effect. If a brand possesses a brand personality that matches with the personality of the consumer, it has a positive effect on brand attachment; a mismatch between the consumer's personality and the brand personality results in a lower brand attachment. But, as opposed to what we saw in our analysis of brand values, we cannot make a distinction between more important and less important personality traits. Model III in Table 7.4 demonstrates that the value centrality effect is important, and significantly stronger than the (almost absent) trait strength effect.

The analysis shows that brand personality and brand values both influence brand attachment: consumers prefer brands with a stronger brand personality, and brands with a stronger value profile. For both constructs, the importance of this influence depends on the consumer. Consumers prefer brands whose brand values correspond with their own values, and they also prefer brands with a brand personality profile that matches their own personality structure. This makes both constructs useful indicators for the relation between the brand and its consumers.

There is a difference, however. We argued in Section 7.2 that the relation between values (*what people want to be*) and consumer behaviour is more straightforward than between personality traits (*what people are*) and behaviour, and, consequently, we expected a stronger relation between values and behaviour than between personality and behaviour. The analysis confirmed this expectation. By comparing the Value Compass with Aaker's brand personality framework, we found that the variance in attachment explained by brand values is significantly higher than when brands are described in terms of their brand personality.

Another difference between values and personality involves the congruence effect. Value congruence results in brand attachment: if a consumer perceives values in a brand that he considers more important, this will result in a higher brand attachment. Similarly, a match between the brand personality and the consumer's personality also results in higher brand attachment. As was already demonstrated in the previous chapter, value centrality moderates the extent to which value congruence has an effect on brand attachment: values in the brand profile that are more relevant to the consumer will have a stronger effect on his feelings toward the brand. Consequently, when considering the effect of brand values on brand attachment, we can focus on those values that are important to the consumer. As opposed to values, personality traits cannot be ranked in order of importance. In contrast with the observed value centrality effect, we did not find a comparable effect with respect to personality traits. Consequently, when evaluating the relation between brand personality and behaviour, we cannot distinguish between more or less important personality traits and all personality traits have to be taken into consideration.

The stronger impact of brand values on brand attachment can be related to conceptual differences between values and personality traits. A possible additional cause relates to the origins of the brand personality framework: Aaker developed her model in the USA and, as we addressed before, it was shown to have limited universality. This could make the items in the brand personality model less suitable for the evaluation of brands in other cultural contexts such as, in this study, the Dutch context. This suggestion, obviously, calls for evidence of the cross-cultural validity of the Value Compass. This will be investigated in Part IV of this book.

7.6 Conclusion

Anthropomorphism refers to seeing the human, and human characteristics, in non-human forms and events (Aggarwal & McGill, 2007). Although the complexity of the word anthropomorphism suggests a rare phenomenon, the personification of brands has been of central interest to marketers. Brands are perceived to possess humanlike characteristics, and marketers intentionally encourage this by instilling these human characteristics to brands (see e.g., Aaker, 1997; Keller, 2008; Torelli et al., 2012). The relevance to branding of one of these psychological concepts, values, has been emphasized extensively in this research. But values are not the only brand concept taken from psychology. In this chapter we compared the Value Compass with one of these brand concepts, Aaker's brand personality framework.

An important difference between both concepts relates to their structure. The consumer values of the Value Compass are structured as a dynamic system of compatible and conflicting values. Consequently, the impact of a certain value on behaviour should always be considered in relation to the impact of other values. In a branding context, this emphasizes the importance of taking into account the complete set of brand values associated with a brand. The brand personality traits in Aaker's framework, on the other hand, are treated conceptually as independent factors. Hence, using a brand personality concept can go no further than a list of personality traits associated with the brand, without clear guidelines for assuming consistencies or conflicting elements in the brand personality profile.

From a conceptual point of view, personality and values are related but different concepts. Values refer to *what people consider important*. Values guide behaviour, they motivate action to realize a certain goal. Personality traits, on the other hand, describe *what people are like*. We argued that this conceptual difference makes consumer values a better antecedent for consumer behaviour than the consumer's personality traits. This was tested by comparing the influence of values and consumer behaviour with the influence of personality on consumer behaviour. In this comparison, we found that values, as defined by the Value Compass, indeed have a stronger impact on consumer behaviour than personality traits as defined by Aaker's brand personality framework.

Since most brands operate in an international context, it is important to analyse brands with concepts that can be used in an international context. The currently most central models in values theory (Schwartz's value theory) and in personality theory (the Five-Factor Model) have both been validated in cross-cultural studies. However, Aaker's brand personality framework only has limited cross-cultural validity. The brand personality framework has even been criticized as a 'too American' framework (Azoulay & Kapferer, 2003). This can be circumvented of course by creating other brand personality frameworks more suitable to non-American contexts, but this does not improve the elegance of the framework. So far, we have not yet addressed the cross-cultural validity of the Value Compass. Due to the importance of the international perspective for branding, we turn to this in the next part of this study.

Notes

1   This is not a hypothetical situation: the individual in this example is successful because of personality traits related to intelligence, not because he values success. Chances are that he might start valuing what he does not have, perhaps the warm family life that he misses because of his professional success, and tries to organize his consumption patterns accordingly.

2   The influence of brand values on brand choice is mediated by brand attachment. The analyses in Chapter 5 and 6 confirmed the impact of brand values on the mediator variable brand attachment.

3   The item-to-total correlations emerging from test version B of our study are roughly similar to the correlations found by Aaker; they vary from 0.445 (for *original*) to 0.888 (for *glamorous*).

4   The explained variances with respect to the influence of brand values, value congruence and value centrality are different from the explained variances found in Chapters 5 and

6. A possible reason is related to the brands used in the survey: in Chapter 7, only the brands Audi and IKEA were tested, whereas a set of 16 brands was used for the analysis in Chapters 5 and 6.

References

Aaker, J. L. (1997). Dimensions of brand personality. *Journal of Marketing Research, 34*(8), 347–356.

Aggarwal, P. & McGill, A. L. (2007). Is the car smiling at me? Schema congruity as a basis for evaluating anthropomorphized products. *Journal of Consumer Research, 34*(4), 468–479.

Azoulay, A. & Kapferer, J.-N. (2003). Do brand personality scales really measure brand personality? *The Journal of Brand Management, 11*(2), 143–155.

Bilsky, W. & Schwartz, S. H. (1994). Values and personality. *European Journal of Personality, 8*(3), 163–181.

Guilford, J. P. (1959). *Personality*. New York, NY: McGraw-Hill.

Hirschman, E. C. & Holbrook, M. B. (1982). Hedonic consumption: Emerging concepts, methods, and propositions. *Journal of Marketing, 46*(3), 92–101.

Keller, K. L. (2008). *Strategic brand management: Building, measuring, and managing brand equity* (3rd edition). Upper Saddle River, NJ: Prentice Hall.

McCrae, R. R. & Costa, P. T. (1996). Toward a new generation of personality theories: Theoretical contexts for the five-factor model. In J. Wiggins, *The five factor model of personality* (pp. 51–87). New York, NY: The Guilford Press.

McCrae, R. R. & Costa, P. T. (1997). Personality trait structure as a human universal. *American Psychologist, 52*(5), 509–516.

Rokeach, M. (1973). *The nature of human values*. New York, NY: The Free Press.

Schwartz, S. H. (1994). Are there universal aspects in the structure and contents of human values? *Journal of Social Issues, 50*(4), 19–45.

Schwartz, S. H. (1994b). Beyond individualism/collectivism: New cultural dimensions of values. In U. Kim, H. C. Triandis, Ç. Kâgitçibasi, S.-C. Choi & G. Yoon, *Individualism and collectivism: Theory, method, and applications* (pp. 85–122). Thousand Oaks, CA: Sage Publications.

Schwartz, S. H. & Bardi, A. (2001). Value hierarchie across cultures: Taking a similarities perspective. *Journal of Cross-Cultural Psychology, 32*(5), 268–290.

Torelli, C. J., Özsomer, A., Carvalho, S. W., Keh, H. T. & Maehle, N. (2012). Brand concepts as representations of human values: Do cultural congruity and compatibility between values matter? *Journal of Marketing, 76*(7), 92–108.

Whan Park, C., Jaworski, B. J. & MacInnis, D. J. (1986). Strategic brand concept-image management. *Journal of Marketing, 50*(4), 135–145.

Part IV

The Value Compass and culture

Chapter 8

Cross-cultural validity of the Value Compass

8.1 Introduction

Values and culture are strongly linked: '*The concept of culture is a value concept. Empirical reality is culture for us because, and to the extent that, we relate to it to value-ideas*' (Weber, 1904). The interrelatedness of both concepts is also evident within a more contemporary definition, in which culture is defined as '*a system of attitudes, values and knowledge that is widely shared within a society and is transmitted from generation to generation*' (Inglehart, 1997, p. 15). Culture has a tremendous influence on how reality is perceived. Hofstede (2001), by using the onion as a metaphor, recognizes different layers of depth in his understanding of culture. Starting at the surface, we come across the most visible elements of a culture, expressed in symbols (such as national flags, dress codes or architectural styles). Below the symbols one can identify heroes (e.g., William of Orange, Benjamin Franklin, Mao or Napoleon) and rituals (e.g., cross-cultural differences in lunch and dinner rituals). Values in this model are the deepest manifestation of culture. But if values, the motivations underlying human behaviour, are so deeply entrenched within culture, the question can be raised to which extent a system of values can be applied across different cultures. This question will be addressed in this chapter. We will argue that, although the importance of values can be different across societies, the system organizing these values is cross-culturally valid.

Values have been regarded as a response to universal biologic needs and social and institutional demands (Schwartz & Bilsky, 1987). This implies, on the one hand, a universal element: human genetical structure and human basic needs are similar across our planet. On the other hand, different societies are faced with different natural and social challenges. And, when further zooming in, within each society, different (groups of) individuals are faced with their own specific challenges. This makes values a human universal, but also a cultural concept, and a characteristic of each individual within a culture. Hence, we can expect universal aspects in value orientations, differences in value orientations between societies and individual differences in value orientation.

It is important here to distinguish between two major orientations in cross-cultural studies: a structure-oriented focus and a level-oriented focus (Van de

Vijver & Leung, 1997). A study with a structure-oriented focus analyses the relationships among variables, and the similarities and differences in these relationships across cultures. For instance, a study attempting to demonstrate the universality of a construct has a structure-oriented focus. Schwartz provided evidence that his value theory can be used to describe values across different cultures (Schwartz, 1992; Schwartz, 1994; Schwartz & Sagiv, 1995; Schwartz et al., 2001). Hofstede (2011) also assumed cross-cultural validity of his six-dimensional cultural model. Universality of a concept, however, does not imply that the concept is equally important everywhere. For instance, the hedonic value of a brand can be more important in culture A, whereas the functional aspect of the brand is more relevant in culture B, irrespective of the fact that in both cultures hedonic and utilitarian values form conflicting value types.

Cross-cultural validation of a concept (structure-oriented) is necessary before one can attempt to focus on differences in importance of that concept across cultures, which would be the aim of a level-oriented study. The distinction between a structure-oriented and a level-oriented approach is also evident in Hofstede: the conceptual structure of his values concept (in his case: the six cultural dimensions) is similar across societies, but there are deeply entrenched cultural differences in the levels of importance of the different values. Following this line of reasoning, we also expect for the Value Compass that the model *structure* is similar across societies, but the importance of values (the *levels*) can differ between societies. This is expressed by Proposition 7:

> **Compatibilities and conflicts between consumer values are similar across cultures. There are, however, cultural differences in the importance of consumer values.**

The intention of this treatment is the development of a value system, which is not constrained to one society, but can be used cross-culturally to assess brand values and brand choice. Since the proof of the pudding is in the eating, this intention needs to be validated. So far, the Value Compass was developed and validated for one European country, the Netherlands. This chapter is devoted to a cross-cultural assessment of the Value Compass. For this assessment, the following questions will be addressed:

- To what extent do people from different cultures use the same values when they evaluate brands?
- To what extent is the structure of interrelations between these values similar across cultures?
- To what extent are these values equally important across cultures?

Investigating the universality of a concept involves a number of methodological considerations. The chapter starts with a discussion of these considerations. The design of the cross-cultural study of the Value Compass is described in Section

8.3, and the results are discussed in the Sections 8.4, 8.5 and 8.6. These results are divided in a structure-oriented and a level-oriented treatment. The structure-oriented treatment investigates the cross-cultural validity of the Value Compass. In the level-oriented treatment, differences of value priorities between societies are examined.

8.2 Methodological considerations in cross-cultural testing

For a valid cross-cultural comparison, it is necessary that what is being compared is the same in all studied countries (Berry *et al.*, 2011). For instance, equality in Dutch society is a concept referring to a non-hierarchical relation between individuals: individuals have access to the same opportunities. But is this conceptualization the same in other countries? And does a high score for equality in one country mean the same thing as an equally high score for equality in another country? This section raises a number of methodological issues related to the generalizability of cross-cultural studies. Treatment of these issues is necessary before we can proceed with the cross-cultural assessment of the Value Compass.

Universality assumes that a psychological concept can be generalized to describe the behaviour of people in any culture (Berry *et al.*, 2011). In other words, test results obtained in one country are comparable to the test results from another country. Universalism can be opposed to relativism. Relativism assumes human behaviour to be strongly influenced by culture: a concept developed in one culture cannot be transferred to other cultures. This implies, in its most extreme form, that test results obtained in one country cannot be compared with results obtained in another country. The distinction between universalism and relativism is one of the central issues in cross-cultural psychology. As discussed previously, most value systems assume a universal structure (Hofstede, 1980, 2011; Schwartz, 1992; Triandis, 1995).

Bias and equivalence

In a cross-cultural study, comparability of results is threatened by bias. Bias is a generic term for nuisance factors threatening the validity of cross-cultural comparisons. Different sources of bias can be identified, of which the following are relevant to cross-cultural studies: method bias, item bias and construct bias (e.g., Van de Vijver, 2011; Van de Vijver and Leung, 1997, 2011). Method bias is a source of bias arising from the research method used. It relates to, for instance, cross-cultural differences in the samples used for the test, differences in the way the test is administered, or unfamiliarity of the respondents with the type of measurement (or with the concept of survey in itself). Item bias relates to problems with a specific test item, for instance, if the test item means different things for respondents from different cultures.

Even when following the appropriate translation procedures, values can have a meaning specific to a particular society or culture. For instance, to what extent is the German value *Gemütlichkeit* equivalent to the Dutch value *gezelligheid*, or to the English value *cosiness*? Finally, there is construct bias if the meaning of a construct differs across cultures. An example is the conceptualization of human relations. Western culture emphasizes equality in relationships. Confucianism, on the other hand, with its strong focus on loyalty and respect, created an environment in which human relations are characterized by fundamental inequality. Confucianist relations are hierarchical, obligatory bonds of mutual devotion: from son to father, from wife to husband, from younger brother to elder brother, from ruled to ruler[1] (Kutcher, 2000). This different conceptualization of relationships potentially influences the way that values such as care, harmony, respect or power are (cor)related to each other.

Bias threatens the equivalence of measurement outcomes across cultures (Van de Vijver & Leung, 2011). Equivalence refers to the level of comparability of measurement outcomes: a measurement instrument is called equivalent if test items are interpreted in the same way by two persons belonging to different cultures. A meaningful cross-cultural comparison is possible only when measurement equivalence of the instrument has been demonstrated (Berry et al., 2011).

Measurement equivalence: comparability of test outcomes

When comparing test results, the following levels of equivalence can be distinguished (Van de Vijver & Leung, 1997, 2011): construct equivalence, structural equivalence, metric equivalence and scalar equivalence. These levels of equivalence will be described here in more detail.

Construct equivalence implies that the same construct exists in all studied groups, is conceptualized in the same way in all groups, and is manifested in the same way for all groups. Construct equivalence of a certain value type implies a shared meaning of the value type across cultures, but it also concerns a shared meaning and understanding of the value items representing the value type. The discussion about the extent to which values such as *Gemütlichkeit*, *gezelligheid* and *cosiness* share the same underlying meaning, is a discussion about their construct equivalence. Evidence for the construct equivalence of a value type can be provided by cross-culturally assessing the meaning associated with the value type and with the items by which it is described.

An instrument administered in different cultural groups shows *structural equivalence* if, in addition to construct equivalence, the construct consists of the same factors in all groups. In terms of the Value Compass, structural equivalence means that the Value Compass consists of the same value types in all the cultures under consideration, and that these value types are represented in each culture by the same items. For instance, with structural equivalence we can assume that the value type *prestige* can be distinguished in all societies under consideration, and that it can be represented by the value items *being successful, power* and *status* in all these societies. It does not imply, however, that the underlying factor loadings are similar. In one culture, for instance, it is possible that *prestige* contains a relatively strong power element, whereas in another culture the status aspect is more important.

Metric equivalence asserts that, in addition to structural equivalence, there is also equality of factor loadings. With metric equivalence, respondents interpret and use a measurement instrument (e.g., the Value Compass) in the same way across cultures, in the sense that differences between outcomes can be compared. This implies that value priority rankings can be compared across cultures. The second part of Proposition 7 – *there are cultural differences in the importance of consumer values* – can be tested after metric equivalence of the Value Compass has been demonstrated. It is then possible, for instance, to determine whether prestige is a relatively more important motivation in a certain culture, as compared to its importance in other cultures.

Metric equivalence, however, does not allow for absolute comparisons such as '*prestige is more important in culture A than in culture B*'. A higher score for prestige in a country can indeed imply that this value is more important in the country, but it is also possible that respondents in this country in general give relatively high scores in surveys. If we want to make absolute comparisons between countries, then *scalar equivalence*, or full-score equivalence, is required. Scalar equivalence means that the measurement scale is identical across the cultures in the cross-cultural comparison. It implies, for instance, that a score of 4 on a Likert scale obtained from a person in country A has exactly the same meaning as the same score from an individual in country B. Scalar equivalence is difficult to establish. For instance, the way people complete a survey is affected by differences in communication style. Some people consistently give more positive answers, or more extreme answers, whereas others will have the tendency to centre around the middle value of a scale.

Communication styles show consistent differences between cultures, thereby influencing cross-cultural comparison. Two types of culture-dependent communication styles can be identified (Cheung & Rensvold, 2000): extreme response bias and acquiescence bias. Extreme response bias is the extent of moderate responding versus extreme responding. A study by Marin, Gamba and Marin (1992), for instance, showed that the tendency to use both extremes of a response scale is higher among Hispanic Americans than among non-Hispanic Caucasian Americans. Extremity is reflected in a relatively higher standard deviation. Acquiescence is the tendency of respondents to give positive answers regardless of the content of the questions (Smith, 2004). Acquiescence is reflected in a relatively higher country average rating on, for instance, Likert-scaled questions. Acquiescence was shown to be related to individualism-collectivism and to power distance. More positive answers in response to personally relevant items are found in nations that are high on Hofstede's dimensions of collectivism or power distance (Smith, 2011).

Differences in communication style are a characteristic of a specific national culture (Cheung & Rensvold, 2000; Smith, 2011). But these differences are also a form of bias that complicates cross-cultural comparison (Hofstede & Hofstede, 2005; Leung & Bond, 1989). Averaging or standardization procedures can be used to reduce or eliminate unwanted cross-cultural differences in response styles (Fischer, 2004; Leung & Bond, 1989; Van de Vijver & Leung, 1997). These procedures enable cross-cultural comparison, but they do have statistical consequences. Most importantly, averaging or standardizing results creates scores that are not statistically independent of each other. Despite this statistical complication, and the observation that differences in response styles in themselves constitute an aspect of cultural difference, the benefit of enabling cross-cultural comparison is, according to Smith (2011), a persuasive argument in favour of eliminating cross-cultural differences in response style through standardization procedures.

Model structure equivalence

Measurement equivalence as discussed so far asserts that test outcomes can be compared across cultures. However, to demonstrate universality of the Value Compass, this is not enough. Unlike, for instance, the brand personality framework, the Value Compass is not a model consisting of a number of unrelated dimensions. The Value Compass also specifies relations between dimensions: it is a circular structure of compatible and conflicting value types. The consequence is that some value types correlate stronger with each other than other value types. If we want to test the first part of Proposition 7 – *the structure of the Value Compass is similar across cultures* – then we have to take the interrelations between value types into account. Cross-cultural validation of the structure of the Value Compass requires, in addition to the equivalence tests described above, also a test of the equivalence of the interrelations between value types. There are a number of methods available to explore these interrelations.

Confirmatory factor analysis (CFA) provides the possibility to test and compare the structure of models. In CFA, a test of the equivalence of conceptual models, for instance, the structure of the value system in country A as compared to this structure in country B, implies a stepwise procedure (Hair *et al.*, 2006; Van de Vijver & Leung, 1997). In each step of this procedure, the equivalence criteria are tightened.[2] The first step would be a test of the construct equivalence, then in subsequent steps structural equivalence, metric equivalence and finally model structure equivalence are tested.

Interrelations can also be analysed visually, by looking at the positions of values in the value space. The value space is a graphic representation of the interrelations between values. An example is the value space of the Value Compass, presented in Figure 3.1. Equivalence of model structure implies, that the arrangement of values in the value space is similar across countries. This visual inspection has been used, for instance, in the development of the portrait values questionnaire (PVQ) (Schwartz *et al.*, 2001). The PVQ was developed as an alternative method to measure the universality of the theory of human values. In the PVQ, short verbal portraits of different people were used to measure value priorities. Each portrait represented the importance of a value. Indications for value priorities were obtained by asking people to compare these portraits to themselves. Validation of the PVQ, as compared to Schwartz's value survey (SVS), was done by a visual comparison of the value spaces resulting from both models: based on test outcomes, Schwartz *et al.* created a value space containing the value types according to Schwartz's value survey, and a value space containing the arrangement of the value types with data obtained from the PVQ. By comparing the two structures, Schwartz *et al.* found evidence for the match between the PVQ and the SVS.

8.3 Design of the cross-cultural study

The cross-cultural study of the Value Compass includes validation of the existence of the value types of the Value Compass across a number of countries, validation of the model structure, and a visual inspection of the value spaces in the countries in the test. The countries from which the sample was taken, the test design, and the method of analysis are described below.

Sample

Cross-cultural validity of the Value Compass was tested by submitting the values of the Value Compass to samples from different cultures. As in Hofstede's work, countries were used as indicators of culture. Surveys were distributed to respondents in a number of geographically dispersed European countries. These countries were selected in such a way that a regional spread across the continent was realized. In this way, some of the cultural variation within Europe could be taken into account. In Northwestern Europe, in addition to the Dutch survey described previously, a sample was drawn in Germany. In Southern Europe, Italy was included as a representative of Latin, Catholic culture. Bulgaria in Southeastern Europe constitutes the Slavic, Orthodox country in the test. Finally, we included one of the Baltic countries, Lithuania. To test the validity of the Value Compass in a non-western culture, the Value Compass was also submitted to a sample collected from China.

A difference in background characteristics of respondents affects value priorities (Section 4.5). Therefore, it is important to use groups with comparable age and sociodemographics in cross-cultural tests. The tests of the Value Compass, described in the previous chapters involved student samples from the Netherlands. To enhance comparability, the research population in the other countries in this cross-cultural study also consisted of students in higher education.

For the Dutch results, the outcomes of the analysis described in Chapter 5 were used. As mentioned in that chapter, the student database of the Hanze University of Applied Sciences Groningen was used to select students. Students were drawn randomly out of this database. The German sample was obtained in the same vein, by a random selection of students out of the databases of the following German universities: Fachhochschule Hamburg, Fachhochschule Potsdam and Hochschule der Medien Stuttgart. For the Italian sample, the student database of IULM (Università di Lingue e Scienze della Comunicazione, Milano) was used. Due to the limited response from this source, it was supplemented in a later stage by surveys distributed as hard copy to randomly selected students of Bocconi Università, Milano. For the other countries in the test, Bulgaria, Lithuania and China, we had, unfortunately, no direct access to student databases. Consequently, a different sampling procedure had to be used: in these countries, volunteers distributed hard copies among randomly selected students in higher education.

Design

For a valid cross-cultural comparison, not only differences in sample characteristics, but also differences in test design should be minimized. Therefore, all questionnaires were identical to the one described in Chapter 5, containing personal value ratings, brand value ratings and indicators for brand attachment.[3]

For the results of the Netherlands, the outcomes of the survey described in Chapter 5 were used. This survey was based on the short version of the Value Compass. As was described in Chapter 5, respondents rated the relevance of each value item in a consumer choice context on a 5-point scale, by answering the question 'How important is this value for you when you have to make a choice between products or services?'. The ratings for the value items were used to construct value types. The respondent's score for each value type was derived from the weighted average score of the value items representing this value type, with weights derived from their factor loadings. We used the factor loadings that had been derived from the outcomes of the test described in Chapter 5 (see Section 5.2).

In the surveys in the other countries, the short version of the Value Compass was also used. Questions in all surveys were identical, and the same set of value items was used in each survey. To construct value types, in each country we used the same factor loadings as were used in the Dutch sample. By using identical factor loadings, we forced the value types to have the same structure in each tested country, thereby enabling a comparison of the goodness-of-fit of this structure across the tested countries.

To ensure culturally more homogeneous samples, we only used questionnaires filled out by students originating from the country in which they were sampled (e.g., the Italian survey results contain only the answers from Italian nationals; students from non-Italian origin were filtered out). In Section 4.5

Table 8.1 Sample design specifics for the international study of the Value Compass

	Survey period	Sample size (n)	Language in which the survey was administered	Sampling method
Bulgaria	2011, Nov. 25–Dec. 24	150	Bulgarian and English	Hardcopy
Germany	2010, Nov. 1–Dec. 15	450	English	Online
Italy	2010, Nov. 11–Dec. 3 2011, Apr. 26–May 2	340	Italian and English	Online and hardcopy
Lithuania	2010, Nov. 1–Dec. 15	280	English	Hardcopy
Netherlands	2010, Sep. 12–Sep. 30	850	English	Online
China	November 2010	180	Chinese (Mandarin) and English	Hardcopy

we found that gender effects potentially influence the ordering of value priorities. To correct for these gender effects, the results for each sample were weighted toward an 'ideal' distribution of 50 per cent males and 50 per cent females.

In the Netherlands, Germany and Lithuania, the average English language proficiency of higher education students was considered sufficiently high to distribute the survey in English. In Italy, China and Bulgaria, countries in which the English language proficiency is generally more limited, a bilingual survey was distributed. Surveys were translated into Italian, Chinese and Bulgarian, by using a translation-back translation procedure. As indicated previously, in the Netherlands, Germany and in part of the Italian sample, students were sampled through the database of their universities. These students received an email containing a link to the online survey. Where this distribution method was not feasible, the surveys were distributed as hardcopy. Differences in test administration are a potential source of bias. Although, as indicated previously, test results can be standardized in comparative studies to control for these differences, we have to be aware of them when interpreting results. Table 8.1 summarizes details about the language of the survey, the period in which the survey was administered, the sample size per country, and the sampling method used. For the sample size, only the students who completed their personal value priorities were counted as respondents.

Method of analysis

Meaningful cross-cultural comparison is possible only with equivalence of the measurement instrument. Following the discussion in the previous section, measurement equivalence of the Value Compass can be demonstrated by testing for the following levels of equivalence:

1   *Construct equivalence.* The purpose of the first step in the equivalence study is to find support for the existence of each value type of the Value Compass, across all countries in the test. This implies a cross-cultural examination of each of these value types. This examination can be found in the next section.

2   *Factor structure equivalence* or *structural equivalence.* With evidence of factor structure equivalence, we can assume that the Value Compass is composed of the same value types, and that these value types consist of the same items, across all countries in the test. Section 8.5 describes the analysis of factor structure equivalence, together with the analysis of metric equivalence.

3   *Metric equivalence* or factor loading equivalence. Metric equivalence implies equal factor loadings for the value types of the Value Compass, across countries. Evidence of metric equivalence allows for *cross-cultural comparison of the rank ordering* of value priorities. If, however, we want to make a direct *comparison of value ratings* across cultures, scalar equivalence is required. As explained in the previous section, we do not expect scalar equivalence of the Value Compass, due to cultural differences in response styles. To take these differences in response style into account, a standardization procedure needs to be implemented. Section 8.5 presents supportive evidence for the metric equivalence of the Value Compass, by means of confirmatory factor analysis. After presenting this evidence, countries are compared with standardized results, to allow for a direct comparison of value priority ratings.

4   *Model structure equivalence.* A central element of the Value Compass is its structure: values are arranged in a circular pattern that represents the relations between values. Model structure equivalence implies that we find the same pattern of relations between values across countries. In Section 8.6, confirmatory factor analysis is used, in combination with a visual inspection of the value space, to test model structure equivalence of the Value Compass.

Equivalence can be tested by looking at goodness-of-fit. We will do this by examining the RMSEA and the CFI, for each step in the stepwise procedure. These statistics were described in more detail in Box 3.3. The following criteria were used to test goodness-of-fit:

- RMSEA ≤ 0.08 indicates good fit; RMSEA ≥ 0.10 indicates poor fit; a moderate fit is indicated by RMSEA values between 0.08 and 0.10.
- CFI ≥ 0.92 indicates good fit; CFI ≤ 0.90 indicates poor fit; a moderate fit is indicated by CFI values between 0.90 and 0.92.

An alternative goodness-of-fit test in the stepwise procedure is to compare the fit of a more constrained model with the less constrained model from the previous step. Because of increasing restrictions, the fit of a more restricted model deteriorates as compared to a less restricted model. Equivalence can be assumed if deterioration in CFI (Δ CFI) of the more restricted model is smaller than or equal to 0.01 (Cheung & Rensvold, 2002). Equivalence is rejected if Δ CFI is larger than 0.01.

The equivalence tests of the Value Compass are discussed in the following sections. Each section first presents the analysis of equivalence, and then continues with the results of the cross-cultural comparison that can be performed at that level of equivalence.

8.4 Construct equivalence of the Value Compass

The first step in the analysis is the examination of the construct equivalence of the Value Compass. Construct equivalence implies that the value types of the Value Compass, and the value items representing these value types, can be identified in all countries in the test, and have the same meaning in all these countries. An analysis of the cross-cultural meaning of value types necessitates an extensive study of the semantics of each concept, which is beyond the purpose of this study. To compensate for this deficiency, a number of statistical indicators are used to give an indication of the extent to which each value type emerges as a distinct value type in every country in the test. More specifically, this includes the following:

- Cross-cultural analysis of the internal consistency of a value type. In the Value Compass, a value type is represented by a number of value items. These value items give meaning to the value type. A high internal consistency implies that these items are highly correlated, in other words, they share the same meaning. Cronbach's alpha is a commonly applied reliability measure. A slightly different indicator, frequently used in confirmatory factor analysis, is construct reliability. For both Cronbach's alpha and construct reliability, a value of 0.7 or higher indicates a high internal consistency.
- Cross-cultural analysis of discriminant validity. High discriminant validity of a value type ensures that the value type represents a unique aspect of the Value Compass not expressed by the other value types. Mathematically, with a discriminant validity larger than one, the variance extracted by the value type is larger than the covariance it shares with other value types, implying that the value type can be considered to be distinct from these other value types (Hair et al., 2006). A detailed explanation of discriminant validity and construct reliability was presented in Box 3.3.

Construct equivalence of the value types was assessed with a cross-cultural analysis of the discriminant validity and the internal consistency of each value type, by means of confirmatory factor analysis (CFA). The results of this assessment are presented in Table 8.2 and 8.3.

Table 8.2 Cross-cultural comparison of discriminant validity of value types

Value type	NL	GE	IT	LT	BG	CH
Functionality	2.07 (safety)	1.32 (safety)	1.47 (safety)	1.27 (beauty)	2.59 (beauty)	1.52 (joy)
Safety**	NA	NA	NA	NA	NA	NA
Honesty**	NA	NA	NA	NA	NA	NA
Social responsibility	2.34 (care)	2.39 (care)	2.92 (care)	2.38 (care)	3.14 (care)	1.54 (care)
Affection	1.16 (joy)	1.38 (joy)	1.24 (joy)	1.25 (honesty)	1.51 (stim.)	0.98 (joy)*
Enjoying life	1.34 (care)	1.52 (care)	1.11 (stim.)	1.46 (stim.)	1.63 (stim.)	0.93 (beauty)*
Stimulation	1.41 (joy)	1.54 (joy)	0.90 (joy)*	1.11 (prestige)	1.16 (joy)	1.21 (joy)
Prestige	1.41 (beauty)	1.56 (beauty)	1.94 (joy)	1.24 (stim.)	2.01 (beauty)	0.89 (beauty)*
Beauty	1.71 (prestige)	2.17 (prestige)	1.39 (joy)	1.69 (funct.)	2.47 (prestige)	1.12 (joy)

* Value below threshold level of 1.0, indicating poor discriminant validity.
** The value types safety and honesty are represented with one value item, hence, indicators for the discriminant validity for these two value types do not apply

Table 8.3 Cross-cultural comparison of internal consistency of value types

Value type	Number of items in the value type	NL	GE	IT	LT	BG	CH
Functionality	3	0.713	0.749	0.687 *	0.648 *	0.525 *	0.659 *
Safety*	1	NA	NA	NA	NA	NA	NA
Honesty**	1	NA	NA	NA	NA	NA	NA
Social responsibility	3	0.828	0.819	0.854	0.732	0.836	0.694 *
Affection	3	0.763	0.725	0.722	0.625 *	0.736	0.571 *
Enjoying life	3	0.819	0.762	0.714	0.729	0.757	0.614 *
Stimulation	3	0.737	0.698 *	0.626 *	0.652 *	0.623 *	0.576 *
Prestige	3	0.727	0.600 *	0.625 *	0.706	0.650 *	0.532 *
Beauty	3	0.802	0.726	0.782	0.757	0.724	0.685 *

* Value below threshold level of 0.7, indicating poor internal consistency.
** The value types safety and honesty are represented with one value item, hence, indicators for the internal consistency for these two value types do not apply

Table 8.2 presents the extent to which the value types can be identified as distinct constructs in each country. Similar to the procedure followed in stage 7 of the development process of the Value Compass in Chapter 2, the test of discriminant validity was focused on those value types that are most similar, hence, on neigbouring value types: for each value type, the discriminant validity is listed as compared with the most closely related value type. For instance, in the Italian sample, most closely related to the value type *functionality* is *safety*. Consequently, the discriminant validity between these two value types is listed in the table. The assessment shows that the value types of the Value Compass can, indeed, be identified as separate constructs across the countries in the test, at least for the European countries. In only four cases, the value types do not show adequate discriminant validity. Three out of these four cases are related to the outcomes of the Chinese sample.

Table 8.3 presents the assessment of construct reliability. This assessment demonstrates that, again with the exception of the Chinese sample, most value types show acceptable internal consistency. If we exclude the results of the Chinese sample, the construct reliability ranges from 0.525 (value type *functionality* in the Bulgarian sample) to 0.854 (value type *social responsibility* in the Italian sample), with a median of 0.726. This is substantially higher than the internal consistencies reported in a validation of the Schwartz Value Survey (Schwartz *et al.*, 2001).[4] Three value types, *functionality, prestige* and *stimulation,* contain a higher degree of variability than the other value types, at least in a number of the country samples. This is potentially caused by the procedure that was followed to construct value types. As noted previously, the value types of the Value Compass were formed by drawing partition lines in the value space. These partition lines created distinct regions in the value space, representing the value types of the Value Compass. The value items within each of these regions cover the full spectrum of meaning attached to the value type defined by the region. Some value types comprise a bigger region, hence, a larger variability. Following Schwartz *et al.* (2001), we consider the higher degree of variability of the value types *functionality, stimulation* and *prestige* as an indication of a broader spectrum of meaning attached to these value types. The high cross-cultural difference in variability of the value type *functionality*, ranging from CR = 0.525 in the Bulgarian sample to CR = 0.749 in the German sample, indicates a certain amount of cultural divergence in the interpretation of the items comprising this value type. An additional nomological analysis could be used to analyse this divergence, but this is beyond the purpose of this study.

Another possible reason behind the variability of the value type *functionality* is the nature of this value type: it was defined in the short version of the Value Compass as a combination of the value types *achievement* and *functionality*. Variability with respect to the value type *functionality* indicates that, when not constrained by practical considerations, the 'full' version of the Value Compass should be preferred to the short version.

The Chinese sample deviates substantially from the European results. None of the Chinese value types meet the norm of CR −0.7. The Chinese value types do not seem to represent well-defined entities. This, in combination with the limited discriminant validity of some of the Chinese value types, indicates that the value types of the Value Compass, in its present form, do not provide a good fit to the motivating forces underlying Chinese consumer behaviour.

Concluding, the results give evidence for the construct equivalence of the value types across the European samples, supporting the existence of these value types as distinct constructs in all European samples. Further support can be provided by supplementing these results with an analysis of the meaning associated with each of the value types, and the value items representing them, however, this is beyond the current purpose of this study. With this evidence of the cross-cultural existence of the value types, we can proceed with the next phase of the validation process: investigating to what extent these values can be combined in each country as a Value Compass. In the cross-cultural comparison, we include the outcomes of the European samples. Since the Chinese outcomes differ substantially from the European outcomes, a comparison with the Chinese data will be done in a separate analysis.

8.5 Metric equivalence of the Value Compass

This section comprises three subsections. In the first subsection, structural and metric equivalence of the Value Compass is assessed. Support for metric equivalence enables a cross-cultural comparison of value rankings. This comparison is provided in Section 8.5.2. In the last subsection, Section 8.5.3, a cross-cultural comparison of value ratings is provided, based on standardized outcomes.

8.5.1 Evidence of metric equivalence

We found support for the cross-cultural existence of the value types of the Value Compass in the previous section. Equivalence of constructs, however, does not imply equivalence of the model by which they are related to each other: the building blocks might be available in each tested country, but this does not necessarily result in an identical building style.

In this section we explore structural equivalence and metric equivalence of the Value Compass. Structural equivalence, also referred to as factor structure equivalence or configural equivalence (Hair *et al.*, 2006; Van de Vijver & Leung, 2011), implies that the Value Compass consists of the same value types in all countries. This is a precondition to metric equivalence. Metric equivalence ensures that the factor loadings in the Value Compass are identical across countries. With evidence of metric equivalence, we can compare value priority rankings across countries, and we can answer questions such as '*Is honesty a more important motivation for consumer behavior than prestige, in all countries in the test?*'.

Test: method, analysis and results

METHOD

The analysis of structural equivalence and metric equivalence is based on the outcomes of the surveys executed in the Netherlands, Germany, Italy, Lithuania, Bulgaria and China. Considering the somewhat problematic interpretation of the value types in the Chinese data, as presented in the previous section, a separate analysis was executed excluding the Chinese outcomes. The analysis and the results of the analyses are described below.

ANALYSIS

Equivalence was tested with Confirmatory Factor Analysis (CFA), by using the stepwise procedure described in Section 8.2. The software Lisrel was used to execute the analysis.

As a first step in this procedure, the structural equivalence of the Value Compass was examined. To find evidence for structural equivalence, we first needed to test, for each of the six countries, whether the values that motivate consumer behaviour can be organized as a value system consisting of eight value types (model A).[5] Then, in a nested model, this test was performed for all countries simultaneously (model B). This test provided evidence whether the Value Compass is represented in all countries with the same eight value types. With evidence for structural equivalence, we proceeded with the test of metric equivalence: a test of equivalence

Table 8.4 Metric equivalence of the Value Compass

Model	(Sub)hypothesis	χ^2	df	RMSEA	CFI	Decision
A – GE	Value Compass Germany consists of eight factors (n = 450)	715.4	202	0.075	0.944	
A – NL	Value Compass Netherlands consists of eight factors (n = 850)	952.9	202	0.070	0.963	
A – IT	Value Compass Italy consists of eight factors (n = 340)	684.7	202	0.084	0.943	
A – LT	Value Compass Lithuania consists of eight factors (n = 280)	533.6	202	0.077	0.972	
A – BG	Value Compass Bulgaria consists of eight factors (n = 150)	398.4	202	0.081	0.922	
A – CH	Value Compass China consists of eight factors (n = 180)	650.0	202	0.111	0.839	
B	Structural equivalence	2337.6	1212	0.072	0.956	Supported
C	Metric equivalence	2447.6	1287	0.071	0.955	Supported

Adding the extra constraint posed by metric equivalence results in Δ CFI = –0.001, as compared to structural equivalence. This is considerably smaller than the criterion value of Δ CFI = –0.01 (Cheung & Rensvold, 2002).

Table 8.5 Metric equivalence of the Value Compass across the European countries in the test

Model	(Sub)hypothesis	χ^2	df	RMSEA	CFI	Decision
B	Structural equivalence exists for all European countries	1691.0	1010	0.061	0.970	Supported
C	Metric equivalence exists for all European countries	1768.8	1070	0.060	0.970	Supported

Adding the extra constraint posed by metric equivalence results in Δ CFI < –0.001, as compared to structural equivalence. This is considerably smaller than the criterion value of Δ CFI = –0.01 (Cheung & Rensvold, 2002).

of factor loadings (model C). If metric equivalence is supported, the importance of value priorities between countries can be compared.

RMSEA and CFI were used as indicators of model fit, with equivalence supported if RMSEA ≤ 0.08 and CFI ≥ 0.92, and equivalence rejected with RMSEA ≥ 0.10 and CFI ≤ 0.90). Additional support for metric equivalence was found if the decrease in CFI, as compared to the model with structural equivalence, is smaller than or equal to 0.01.

RESULTS

The test results, including the Chinese results, are presented in Table 8.4.

The results support structural and metric equivalence of the Value Compass, across the countries in the test. The evidence across the European countries is strong. The existence of the value types in China, however, is less evident: both CFI and RMSEA do not meet the criteria for good fit of the Chinese model. Excluding China from the comparison gives an important improvement in the values of RMSEA and CFI, for both the test of structural equivalence and of metric equivalence (see Table 8.5).

The results support metric equivalence of the Value Compass. It needs to be emphasized, however, that the evidence for equivalence is strong for the European countries in the test, but rather weak for the Chinese sample. With support for metric equivalence, it is possible to use the Value Compass to examine the influence of consumer values on choice behaviour within the tested countries. This allows for statements such as '*In country A, honesty-related values are a more important motivation for brand choice than prestige-related values*'. It is also possible to compare the ranking of value priorities between countries, for instance, to analyse whether honesty is more important than prestige in other countries as well. This type of information can be of relevance to brands aiming to position themselves in several countries. The next subsection provides an overview of similarities and differences in value priority rankings in the tested countries.

Metric equivalence does not allow for statements such as *honesty is more important in country A than in country B*. For this type of direct comparison of the importance of values, we need metric equivalence of the Value Compass, but in addition, we also need to take differences in response styles into account. This is discussed in Section 8.5.3. The equivalence tests in this section do not ensure equivalence of model structure either. Evidence for the universality of the structure of the Value Compass (e.g., *Is honesty opposing prestige in all countries in the test?*) will be examined with the model structure equivalence test presented in Section 8.6.

8.5.2 Cross-cultural comparison of value priority rankings

Individual values are partly a result of a shared cultural background, and partly reflect unique individual experiences (Hofstede, 1980; Schwartz, 1994b; Schwartz & Bardi, 2001). The average of the value priorities within a country reflect this shared cultural background; individual variation around this average reflects unique personality and experience. Previously, we saw that different views emerged with regards to the relation between values and culture. On one extreme, culture has been defined as '*the collective programming of the mind that distinguishes the members of one group or category of people from others*' (Hofstede, 2011). In this view, culture is a major determinant of cross-cultural differences in societal values, and we can expect relatively high differences in the average value priorities between countries. On the other hand, there is the view that emphasizes values as a human universal. In this view, between-country differences in value priorities are limited. In support of this view, a number of studies showed only low to moderate variance in ratings of value priorities across samples from different cultures (Fischer & Schwartz, 2011; Schwartz & Bardi, 2001).

The basic difference between these opposing views does not concern the value dimensions themselves. Both Hofstede (2001) and Schwartz (1992, 1994) emphasize the cross-cultural validity of their value dimensions, and the way they are organized. The difference relates to the value levels. In Hofstede, cultures can be characterized by the importance given to certain values. Schwartz, on the other hand, puts more emphasis on the similarities in value priority levels.

The focus of our research is on consumer choice: the values of the Value Compass motivate consumers to like or to feel attached to brands. The question whether the importance of values is culture-related is relevant to consumer behaviour. If the ordering of values is culture-dependent, then brand choice is influenced by the cultural background of the consumer. With the evidence of metric equivalence for the Value Compass, as was demonstrated in the previous section – at least within a European context – value priorities between the tested countries can be compared. This was done by estimating the average value priority rating for each value type in each county, in a procedure identical to the procedure followed to construct the value profile of the Netherlands in Section 4.5. As first step in this procedure, the individual value type ratings were calculated as the weighted average of the scores the individual gave to the value items representing the value type. Weights were derived from the loadings of each item on its value type, as specified in the design section of this chapter. Metric equivalence implies equal factor loadings, hence, the same weights were applied for all countries in the test. Next, for each country, the sample mean for each value type was derived by averaging the results over all individuals. This sample mean was used as an estimate for the country average of the value type.

Table 8.6 presents country averages for the countries in the study, with, between parentheses, the value priority rankings within the country. Based on the European country averages, a European baseline ranking was established:[6] the average for each value type was calculated as the unweighted average of the country means of the European countries.

Metric equivalence allows for the comparison of value priority rankings (the numbers between parentheses in the table). When doing so, a striking pattern of similarities can be observed among the European countries. *Safety* and *honesty* are the most important values in all these countries, *prestige* and *stimulation* values are among the least relevant values. A significance test with Spearman's rho confirms that the rank orderings of value priorities in European countries are highly correlated ($p < 0.01$). In conclusion, a European hierarchy of value priority rankings emerges. Consumer behaviour activates the same values across Europe, ordered in a similar hierarchy of importance. There are a couple of deviations from the European baseline rank ordering. For instance, *honesty* is the most important value in Germany and the Netherlands, whereas *safety* is slightly more important in Italy, Lithuania and Bulgaria. Italians give a relatively high importance to beauty, and consumption in the Netherlands is more hedonically motivated.

The ranking of Chinese value priorities differs significantly from the European value priority levels. In China, as in the European countries, *safety* and *honesty* are the most important values, and *stimulation* the least important. Chinese consumers show a high feeling of responsibility for future well-being. An expression of this sense of responsibility can be observed, for instance, in the Chinese tendency to save more money to provide for the future and the studies of their (grand)child(ren) (Horioka & Wan, 2007). Personal pleasure and (immediate) care for close family, on the other hand, are less relevant for the Chinese consumer. In comparison with European consumers, Chinese consumers tend to favour the aesthetic value (the looks) of a product more than its function. Chinese consumption also seems more oriented toward expressing or confirming status. As was pointed out in the previous sections, the observed differences between the Chinese and the European value hier-

Table 8.6 Cross-cultural comparison of value priorities (Spearman's rho tested with European baseline)

Rank ordering, European baseline		BG	GE	IT	LT	NL	CH
1. Honesty	4.148	4.431 (2)	3.971 (1)	4.204 (2)	4.025 (2)	4.109 (1)	3.819 (2)
2. Safety	4.087	4.450 (1)	3.792 (2)	4.210 (1)	4.104 (1)	3.880 (2)	4.259 (1)
3. Functionality	3.946	4.324 (3)	3.691 (3)	4.035 (3)	3.910 (3)	3.771 (4)	3.540 (8)
4. Enjoying life	3.783	3.926 (5)	3.493 (4)	3.733 (5)	3.887 (4)	3.875 (3)	3.625 (5)
5. Affection	3.620	3.820 (7)	3.473 (5)	3.462 (7)	3.674 (5)	3.670 (5)	3.553 (7)
6. Soc.resp.	3.556	3.936 (4)	3.449 (6)	3.513 (6)	3.557 (6)	3.325 (6)	3.700 (3)
7. Beauty	3.513	3.895 (6)	3.166 (7)	3.744 (4)	3.456 (8)	3.303 (7)	3.646 (4)
8 Stimulation	3.340	3.756 (8)	3.053 (8)	3.241 (9)	3.380 (9)	3.271 (8)	3.154 (9)
9. Prestige	3.336	3.651 (9)	3.012 (9)	3.355 (8)	3.527 (7)	3.134 (9)	3.618 (6)
Country statistics:							
Mean value scores		4.021	3.456	3.722	3.724	3.593	3.657
Standard deviation value scores		0.821	0.948	0.928	0.879	0.892	0.850
Spearman's rho (r$_s$)[1]		0.900	1.000	0.850	0.933	0.983	0.500
Test of rank correlation		p < 0.01	p = 0.00	p < 0.01	p < 0.01	p < 0.01	p = 0.178

1 The rank ordering for each country is compared with the European baseline rank ordering

archy needs to be interpreted with caution, considering the limited equivalence. On the other hand, these outcomes strengthen the evidence that a different importance is attached in China to partly different values.

Even within Europe, in spite of the observed similarities in importance *rankings*, there are sizeable differences in value *ratings* between countries. The importance of safety values, for instance, differs from 4.45 in Bulgaria to 3.88 in the Netherlands. Substantial differences in value ratings can be observed for the other value types as well. However, these differences cannot be directly compared. As pointed out previously, it is not possible to draw any conclusions regarding similarities and differences in the absolute levels of value ratings without correcting for response style. We return to this point in the next section, but first we proceed with a comparison between value priorities for human behaviour in general, as uncovered by Schwartz (1992), and the motivations that guide consumer behaviour, according to the Value Compass.

The overview above presents evidence for a largely similar ordering of the values of the Value Compass across Europe. A consensus in ordering of value hierarchies was also found for the values in the Schwartz value theory (Schwartz & Bardi, 2001): some value types (e.g., benevolence, self-direction, universalism) appeared in this study as consistently more important across societies than other value types (e.g., tradition, power). Table 8.7 shows the pan-cultural baseline of rankings of the value types of Schwartz's value system (Schwartz & Bardi, 2001). This baseline was established with a sample taken from 54 countries.

Below we will compare the hierarchical ordering of values in both systems, although we have to keep in mind that, due to the difference in value activation (life in general in Schwartz's value theory, consumer behaviour in the Value Compass), not all value types are comparable between the Value Compass and Schwartz's value theory.

A first observation is that there are similarities between the two value priority rankings. Values related to *honesty* (benevolence in Schwartz's system) and *safety* (security) are important in both baseline rankings, whereas *prestige* (power) and *stimulation* are relatively unimportant. There are also differences in the two value hierarchies. Consumer behaviour is more strongly driven by concerns for *safety* and pleasure (*enjoying life*). These two value types are relatively more important in the Value Compass than the comparable values security and hedonism in Schwartz's value theory. Universalism (*social responsibility*), on the other hand, is less important for consumer behaviour: people seem to be more concerned about the well-being of all people and of nature as general idea (in Schwartz's value system) than when these values are actually applied during the consumer's decision making process. This possibly provides an explanation for the observed gap between the general attitude toward caring for the environment, and the actual display of pro-environmental (consumption) behaviour (e.g., Kollmuss & Agyeman, 2002): people – when asked – seem to care more for the environment than what becomes evident from their behaviour.

Table 8.7 Pan-cultural ordering of value priorities (Schwartz & Bardi, 2001)

Mean ranking	Value type	Mean rating
1	Benevolence	4.72
2	Self-direction	4.42
3	Universalism	4.42
4	Security	4.38
5	Conformity	4.19
6	Achievement	3.85
7	Hedonism	3.73
8	Stimulation	3.08
9	Tradition	2.85
10	Power	2.35

8.5.3 Cross-cultural comparison of value ratings

The previous results showed a high degree of similarity in value priority *rank ordering* across countries. We could see, for instance, that *security* and *honesty* are important values in all cultures in the sample. A number of culture-specific deviations from the general pattern were visible as well. *Beauty*, for instance, is a more important motive for behaviour in Italy than in Germany.

The general agreement in value hierarchies across cultures is consistent with the cross-cultural agreement in value priority orderings in Schwartz's value theory (Schwartz & Bardi, 2001). A study of Fischer and Schwartz (2011) took this a step further by revealing relatively small country differences in average value score *ratings*: country effects seem to account for little variance in most value items. The results of Fischer and Schwartz highlight that individual differences rather than country culture are the critical source of influence on response to value items.[7] These outcomes seem to oppose other findings (e.g., Hofstede, 1980; Markus & Kitayama, 1991; and Triandis, 1995) that emphasize the variability of values across societies.

Below, we will present a comparison between countries of the importance *ratings* of the consumer values of the Value Compass. As argued earlier, a direct comparison of value ratings between countries is possible only after correcting for differences in response styles. An example illustrates this. The value type *social responsibility* ranks the sixth position in both Italy and Germany: this value has a similar priority in both countries. *Social responsibility* receives a rating score of 3.45 in Germany and 3.51 in Italy. Although the rating score in the Italian sample is higher, with these results it is not possible to state that *social responsibility* is relatively more important in Italy. The Italian sample as a whole has a tendency to give more positive answers: the country average value score in the Italian sample is 3.72 as compared to 3.46 in the German sample. This tendency complicates the comparison: is *social responsibility* more important in Italy, or is the higher Italian score caused by the fact that Italians give more positive answers anyway?

As was explained earlier, cultural differences in response styles can be caused by acquiescence bias or extreme response bias. In our results, method bias is also a possible cause: sampling procedures varied to a certain extent between countries (online versus hardcopy surveys). In order to eliminate the effects of these types of bias, a standardization procedure is applied to the data.

Procedure to create standardized value type ratings per country

The country scores for each value type were adjusted by using within-culture standardization (Fischer, 2004). With this adjustment procedure, the value types are standardized within each country, by setting the mean response of the country at zero and the standard deviation at one, as done in z-transformation. The standardized value type scores for each country were obtained with the following calculation:

$$\text{Standardized score for value type i } (PV_i) = \frac{PV_i - \text{mean country score}}{\text{standard deviation country score}}$$

Scores were taken from Table 8.8. For instance, the standardized score for honesty in Bulgaria was calculated as:

$$\text{Standardized score for honesty} = \frac{4.431 - 4.021}{0.821} = 0.523 \ .$$

With this standardization procedure, differences between countries in mean value type scores (due to acquiescence bias) and differences in standard deviations between countries (due to extreme response bias) are eliminated.

Standardization does not influence the value priority ranking, but it does enable comparison of the similarities and differences of value ratings between countries (Fischer, 2004). The standardized score for each value type reflects the relative importance of the value type in a country, as compared with its importance in other countries. Table 8.8 presents an overview of the standardized value ratings for each country in the test, and the standardized ratings for the European baseline.

Table 8.8 Cross-cultural comparison of standardized value ratings

European baseline rating		BG	GE	IT	LT	NL	CH
1. Honesty	0.498	0.499 (2)	0.543 (1)	0.519 (2)	0.342 (2)	0.578 (1)	0.191 (2) *
2. Safety	0.430	0.523 (1)	0.354 (2)	0.526 (1)	0.432 (1)	0.322 (2)	0.708 (1) *
3. Functionality	0.272	0.369 (3)	0.248 (3)	0.337 (3)	0.212 (3)	0.200 (4)	−0.138 (8) *
4. Enjoying life	0.089	−0.116 (5)	0.039 (4)	0.012 (5)	0.185 (4)	0.316 (3)	−0.038 (5)
5. Affection	−0.093	−0.245 (7)	0.018 (5)	−0.280 (7)	−0.057 (5)	0.086 (5)	−0.122 (7)
6. Soc. resp.	−0.164	−0.104 (4)	−0.007 (6)	−0.225 (6)	−0.190 (6)	−0.300 (6)	0.051 (3) *
7. Beauty	−0.213	−0.153 (6)	−0.306 (7)	0.024 (4)	−0.305 (8)	−0.325 (7)	−0.013 (4) *
8. Stimulation	−0.406	−0.323 (8)	−0.425 (8)	−0.518 (9)	−0.391 (9)	−0.361 (8)	−0.592 (9)
9. Prestige	−0.411	−0.451 (9)	−0.468 (9)	−0.395 (8)	−0.224 (7)	−0.515 (9)	−0.046 (6) *

* indicates a relevant but small difference, with 0.2 < d < 0.5.

The consequence of standardization can be demonstrated by once again comparing the scores for *social responsibility* between Germany and Italy. Standardization does not influence the ranking of value priorities: *social responsibility* still ranks in sixth position. But, by removing the differences in response patterns, we can see that *social responsibility* is actually a relatively more important value in Germany than in Italy. This conclusion would not have been possible from the unstandardized scores.

The cross-cultural analysis of the Value Compass reveals differences in importance ratings of values across cultures. The size of these differences can be interpreted by using Cohen's rule of thumb (Cohen, 1992): the effect size of a standardized difference between two items is relevant but small if this difference is at least 0.20 but lower than 0.50, medium if at least 0.50 and lower than 0.80, and large if at least 0.80.[8] From Table 8.8, a number of differences can be observed. According to Cohen's rule of thumb, however, all the differences between European countries have to be classified as small. For instance, if we compare Germany and the Netherlands, there are relevant but small differences with respect to *enjoying life* (more important in the Netherlands than in Germany) and *social responsibility* (more important in Germany than in the Netherlands). A comparison between Italy and Germany shows relevant differences for *care & affection* and *social responsibility* (both value types more important in Germany), and for *beauty* (more important in Italy). The Chinese outcomes, however, deviate substantially from the European outcomes: six out of nine value type have a relevant difference in importance with the European baseline, although even in this comparison the differences should all be classified as small.

By using standardized value ratings, it is possible to cross-culturally compare results. This is illustrated in the following example, which presents a graphic visualization of a cross-cultural comparison of value ratings.

Example: visual presentation of country differences in value priorities

Figure 8.1 provides a comparison of the three Western European countries in the sample: Italy, Germany and the Netherlands. The figure demonstrates the similarity of value patterns across (Western) European cultures. The value priorities of the three countries are highly correlated. Beneath this baseline of similarities, a number of cultural differences can be identified. The Dutch prefer to enjoy life, Italians emphasize beauty and Germans favour a more responsible consumption pattern.

We can tentatively relate these differences to underlying cultural dimensions, as were uncovered by Hofstede.[9] Italy, for instance, is a country characterized by masculinity and high power distance, which can be reflected in the relatively high importance of values motivating behaviour to create a difference with others (*prestige* and *beauty*). However, not all differences can be directly related

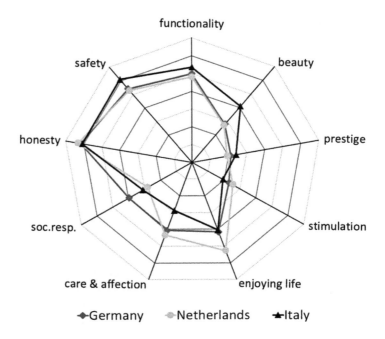

Figure 8.1 Value Compass: comparison of Italy, Germany and the Netherlands

to Hofstede's cultural dimensions. For German consumers, for instance, *social responsibility* is an important consideration, much more so than the Netherlands. Hofstede's cultural dimensions do not provide a clear-cut explanation here. In terms of cultural dimensions, there is only one important difference between both countries: Germany is masculine, whereas the Netherlands is a feminine country (see Figure 2.7 in Chapter 2). *Social responsibility* is not typically a property of masculine countries. A more likely correlation is expected between the value type *social responsibility* and Hofstede's dimension long-term orientation. However, on this dimension, Germany and the Netherlands only differ slightly, with the Netherlands having a somewhat higher long-term orientation.

Culturally more distant countries can be expected to show larger differences in value priority ratings. This is illustrated by the comparison of China and the Netherlands in Figure 8.2.

The comparison of the Western Dutch and the Eastern Chinese society reveals considerable differences in value priorities. The closely related value types safety and honesty are relatively important in both societies, but the search for safety is a more central concern for Chinese consumption behaviour, whereas the Dutch are more preoccupied with the honesty of the brands they chose.

functionality

safety

beauty

honesty

prestige

soc.resp.

stimulation

care & affection

enjoying life

◆China   ⬤Netherlands

Figure 8.2 Value Compass: comparison of the values of China and The Netherlands

Social responsibility seems more important in China than in the Netherlands, whereas for Dutch consumers the relation with friends and family is relatively important when consuming. This can explain the importance of gift giving (birthdays, Saint Nicolas) in Dutch society to confirm and stimulate these relations. The higher relevance in China of the value type *social responsibility* is possibly connected to the Chinese long-term orientation. But it is more complex to explain why Chinese culture places less value on *care & affection* than Dutch culture. This seems to conflict with the interdependent self-concept in Asian culture, but it is in accordance with the masculinity in Chinese and the femininity in Dutch culture and with the difference in power distance in both cultures. Schwartz, in his value-based cultural analysis makes a similar observation concerning the Chinese care for close others: China is a culture that legitimates hierarchical differences, but it is not a prototypical collectivist society if we view collectivism as the commitment to promote the well-being of close others (Schwartz, 1994b).

The value types beauty and prestige are more relevant for Chinese than for Dutch consumers. For Chinese buying behaviour the aesthetic and prestige aspects of a product or service seem at least as important as its functionality: Chinese buy products to make a difference with others or to show their (low or high) position in society. Consummator activities (like gift giving or restaurant visit) then establish or demonstrate this societal status. This matches with the importance of power distance in Chinese society. In the Netherlands a visit to a restaurant will be more motivated by having a good time with friends and family, or just having fun. A brand profile emphasizing hedonic values (joy, stimulation) connects better with the individualistic Dutch consumer than with Chinese consumers: consumption for immediate pleasure in the Netherlands as opposed to consumption (or investment) in China to create a higher quality of life in the future.

The divergence in outcomes can be explained by 'real' differences, but the difference between the Chinese and the Dutch (and other European) outcomes can also be related to differences in the content and meaning associated with these values. The translation and back translation procedure used to create the Chinese equivalence for the values of the Value Compass ensured the selection of more or less comparable value items, but the associations of Chinese respondents with each of these value items can still be different from their European interpretation. This aspect is important for a generalization of the Value Compass beyond the European (or western) context, but is not further explored here.

8.6 Model structure equivalence of the Value Compass

The metric equivalence of the Value Compass, as demonstrated in the previous section, implies that we can cross-culturally compare value priorities. Additional evidence is needed showing that the interrelations between values in the Value Compass, their conflicts and compatibilities, are similar in each country in the test. This evidence is provided with the test of model structure equivalence of the Value Compass. This test is presented in this section. It comprises two subsections. Section 8.6.1 presents an analysis based on confirmatory factor analysis. In Section 8.6.2, model structure equivalence is analysed by means of a visual inspection of the value spaces of each country in the test.

8.6.1 Evidence of model structure equivalence

The Value Compass is a dynamic value system of compatible and conflicting values. Some value types, for instance, *prestige* and *beauty*, can go hand in hand and reinforce consumer behaviour, whereas other values such as *prestige* and *honesty* work in opposite directions. This interrelated structure is an important feature of the Value Compass. This structure was demonstrated with the results of the Dutch sample. Evidence of the universality of this structure is needed before it can be generalized to other countries.

The analysis of model structure equivalence focuses on the interfactor co-variance equivalence: the extent to which compatibilities and conflicts between value types are the same across countries. After establishing equivalence of model structure, one further analysis can be executed: a test of the equivalence of error variances of value types. The combination of factor loading equivalence (metric equivalence), interfactor covariance equivalence and error variance equivalence represents what is referred to as tight cross-validation (Hair *et al.*, 2006). In this section, we describe the analysis of model structure equivalence and tight cross-validation of the Value Compass. The analysis is presented below.

Test: method, analysis and results

METHOD

The analysis of model structure is based on the outcomes of the surveys carried out in the Netherlands, Germany, Italy, Lithuania, Bulgaria and China. The analysis and the results of the analysis are described below. The analysis is carried out for all the countries in the test. Due to the limited fit of the model for the Chinese sample, an additional test is carried out for only the five European countries.

ANALYSIS

Equivalence was tested with Confirmatory Factor Analysis (CFA), by using the stepwise procedure described in Section 8.2. The first two steps, assessment of structural equivalence (model B) and metric equivalence (model C), were already executed in the previous section. Here we focus on an examination of the model structure of the Value Compass, by means of the following steps:

- *Factor loading and interfactor covariance equivalence (model D). Model D implies model structure equivalence: the system of conflicts and compatibilities between value types is equivalent across the countries in the test.*
- *Factor loading, interfactor covariance and error variance equivalence (model E). Model E represents the tight cross-validation of the Value Compass.*

Lisrel was used to execute CFA. RMSEA and CFI were used as indicators of model fit, with equivalence supported if RMSEA $\leq$ 0.08 and CFI $\geq$ 0.92, and equivalence rejected with RMSEA $\geq$ 0.10 and CFI $\leq$ 0.90. Additional support for equivalence is found if ΔCFI $\leq$ 0.01, as compared to the previous model in the sequence.

RESULTS

The test results are presented in Table 8.9. RMSEA, CFI and ΔCFI were used as indicators.
Model D, model structure equivalence, is supported by the analysis. The analysis demonstrates that the structure of the Value Compass is a universal structure. Model E, tight cross-validation, is also supported by the test results, although the fit significantly decreases as

Table 8.9 Tight cross-validation of the Value Compass

Results including the Chinese sample							
Model	(Sub)hypothesis	χ^2	df	RMSEA	CFI	Δ CFI	Decision
B	Structural equivalence	2337.6	1212	0.072	0.956	–	Supported
C	Metric equivalence	2447.6	1287	0.071	0.955	–0.001	Supported
D	Model structure equivalence	2848.4	1467	0.072	0.947	–0.008	Supported
E	Tight cross-validation of the Value Compass	3386.4	1582	0.080	0.930	–0.017	Partly supported

Results for the five European countries in the test (excluding the Chinese sample)							
Model	(Sub)hypothesis	χ^2	df	RMSEA	CFI	Δ CFI	Decision
B	Structural equivalence, European countries in the sample	1691.0	1010	0.061	0.970	–	Supported
C	Metric equivalence, European countries	1768.8	1070	0.060	0.970	0.000	Supported
D	Model structure equivalence, European countries	2055.0	1214	0.062	0.964	–0.006	Supported
E	Tight cross-validation of the Value Compass, European countries	2490.8	1306	0.071	0.949	–0.015	Partly supported

compared to model D, both when including and excluding the Chinese sample. This implies differences in the error variance between countries. A detailed inspection of the output (not presented here, results are available from the author) showed that the substantial decrease in fit due to unequivalence in error variance is mainly associated with the Lithuanian and Bulgarian samples. A potential cause is the way the surveys were administered. Distribution was in hard copy in Bulgaria and Lithuania, and partly or completely digitally in the other European countries in the test. We conclude that model structure equivalence of the Value Compass is supported by the data, with substantial but not conclusive evidence for error variance equivalence of the Value Compass.

Equivalence of model structure is supported by the analysis. The analysis demonstrates that the structure of the Value Compass, in terms of compatibilities and conflicts between value types, is a universal structure: this structure can be assumed to be the same across the European countries in the test.

As mentioned before, the Chinese results indicate that caution is necessary with generalizing this model structure to non-western countries, although the results from the Chinese sample do not contradict the European results.

Additional evidence is needed before the Value Compass can be generalized to China, or to other non-western countries.

So far, model structure equivalence of the Value Compass was tested with CFA. An alternative approach is a visual inspection of the structure of the Value Compass by means of multidimensional scaling. This is presented in the next subsection.

8.6.2 Model structure equivalence: visual inspection of the value space

The Value Compass essentially is a value space visualizing the relations between values. Distances between values in this visualization reflect conceptual differences. Values sharing a similar underlying motivation can be grouped together in distinct regions in a value space. These overarching groups are the value types of the Value Compass. The structure of the Value Compass was developed in Chapter 3, and schematically represented in Figure 4.1. In the previous sections we found supportive evidence for the generalizability of this structure: across the European countries in the test, we can assume the same overarching value types, with the same structure of compatibilities and conflicts between them.

The structure of the Value Compass was derived by means of confirmatory factor analysis. However, it is also possible to investigate the structure by a visual comparison of the value spaces of different countries. Following the results of the previous analysis, we would expect these value spaces to have a similar structure, that is, the structure predicted by Figure 4.1. The outcomes of the comparison of value spaces are presented below. This comparison can be seen as providing additional support to the results of the equivalence tests presented in the previous sections.

Cross-cultural comparison of the structure of the value space

METHOD

The analysis of model structure is based the outcomes of the surveys carried out in the Netherlands, Germany, Italy, Lithuania, Bulgaria and China. The analysis and the results of the analysis are described below. Multidimensional scaling (MDS) was used to verify whether the value structure of each country in the test matches the schematic structure of the Value Compass.

ANALYSIS

The method used by Schwartz et al. (2001) to validate the structure of the PVQ (Portrait Values Questionnaire) was used to compare the structure of the Value Compass across countries.

For each country in the test, the nine value types were represented in a value space, by means of multidimensional scaling. The distribution of value types for the Netherlands defined the theoretical structure of the Value Compass. The value type functionality was arbitrarily ranked 1. The rankings for the other value types were assigned counterclockwise: safety received rank 2, honesty rank 3, and so on (see Figure 8.3). This procedure was repeated for all the countries in the test. Spearman's rho (ρ) was used to test the match in rank ordering; orderings were tested against the Dutch 'baseline' rank ordering.

RESULTS

The value space for the Netherlands, with vectors drawn from the origin of the value space to the point representing each value type is presented in Figure 8.3.

The findings support cross-cultural generalizability of the value system structure. We can see in Table 8.10 that, for all European countries in the test, correlations of the structure of

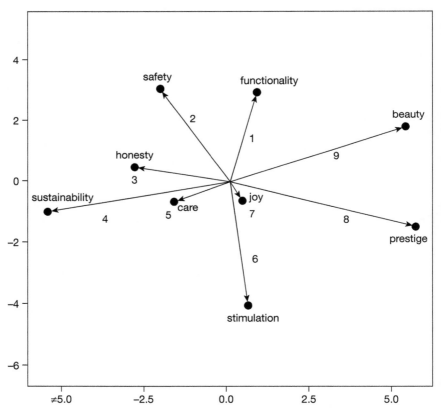

Figure 8.3 Value type structure of the Value Compass, the Netherlands

Table 8.10 Ordering of value types in the value space

Value type	NL	GE	IT	LT	BG	CH
Functionality	1	1	1	1	1	1
Safety	2	2	2	4	4	2
Honesty	3	4	3	2	2	6
Social responsibility	4	3	4	3	3	3
Care & affection	5	5	5	5	5	5
Stimulation	6	7	6	6	6	4
Enjoying life	7	6	7	8	8	7
Prestige	8	8	8	7	7	8
Beauty	9	9	9	9	9	9
Spearman's rho (r_s)	–	0.967	1	0.933	0.933	0.883
Test of rank correlation (NL is baseline)		$p < 0.001$	$p = 0$	$p < 0.001$	$p < 0.001$	$p = 0.003$

value relations with the 'baseline' structure are highly significant ($p < 0.001$). The baseline structure is also confirmed for the Chinese sample, although the Chinese results represent some serious deviations from the baseline.

The graphical arrangements of the value spaces for each country support the results of the equivalence test in the previous section: values are arranged according to a similar pattern across Europe. This is an important finding. We can assume that consumer values can be described in the same terms across all European countries in the test, interacting in the same way when influencing consumer behaviour.

We need to mention that we found supportive evidence for the structure of the Value Compass, *within Europe*. The Chinese data present, to a certain extent, a similar structure as the European outcomes. However, these data also show some important deviations from the 'European' structure of the Value Compass. Especially the interrelations of the value types *honesty* and *stimulation* diverge markedly in the Chinese data.

8.7 Conclusion

Many brands operate in a cross-cultural or global context. Comparability of, for instance, the extent to which a brand's value proposition is perceived in the same way across borders, is important. Consequently, brands need to be analysed by means of instruments that can be used in a cross-cultural context. For the cross-cultural validation of the Value Compass, the following levels of equivalence were examined: construct equivalence, metric equivalence and model structure equivalence. With an analysis of the outcomes of samples originating from a number of European countries (Bulgaria, Germany, Italy, Lithuania and the Netherlands), we found the following results:

- Substantial construct equivalence of the value types of the Value Compass: the value types appear to be meaningful constructs in each of the studied countries; well represented by their value items.
- Support for metric equivalence of the Value Compass, which implies that the Value Compass can be used in each of the studied countries for the evaluation of consumer values. Metric equivalence also implies that importance rankings of values can be compared across these countries.
- Support for model structure equivalence, which implies that the structure of the Value Compass, as found in Chapter 2, can be applied across these European countries.

With these results, we conclude that consumer values and brand values are described in the same terms across Europe, according to the structure proposed by the Value Compass.

When making comparisons across countries, however, it needs to be taken into account that results are influenced by differences in communication style. For instance, Italian respondents consistently gave a higher rating to their personal values than German respondents. In a direct comparison of international outcomes, differences in results due to differences in response style need to be eliminated. Consequently, a standardization procedure has to be applied before international outcomes can be directly compared. After standardizing our response data, we found a high consensus in the ordering of importance of consumer values across Europe: values are consistently more important (e.g., *safety, honesty*) or less important (e.g., *prestige, stimulation*) in motivating brand choice, across the tested countries.

Despite this general consensus, we found a number of consistent differences in importance *ratings* of values between European countries. For instance, pleasure-oriented values were more important in the Netherlands, beauty-oriented values more important in Italy and social responsibility more important in Germany.

The analysis was replicated with results of a non-European country: China. The Chinese results appeared to diverge significantly from the European baseline value priority ordering. Deviations between Chinese and European results, however, need to be interpreted with caution: the outcomes also yielded only limited evidence of measurement equivalence between the European and the Chinese results. We conclude that additional evidence is needed before the Value Compass can be generalized to non-western societies.

Notes

1   Confucianism specifies five human bonds: from son to father, from wife to husband, from younger brother to elder brother, from ruled to ruler and from friend to friend. Only the fifth, and least important, Confucianist bond, the one from friend to friend, does not have a hierarchical aspect.

2   This procedure was also followed to test hypothesis 5.1, the equivalence of the structure of the brand value profile and the structure of the Value Compass.

3   In the surveys distributed in China and Bulgaria, only the personal value priorities were evaluated. The surveys used in the other countries also included an evaluation of brand values and brand attachment. The results for the brand values and for brand attachment are not included here. However, the interested reader can contact the author for the detailed results.

4   A previous reference to this study was made in Chapter 2. In their study, Schwartz *et al.* reported internal consistencies ranging from 0.45 to 0.76, with a median of 0.66. In the study by Schwartz *et al.*, Cronbach's alpha was used as an indicator. Cronbach's alpha and the construct reliability indicator used in Table 8.3 yield largely similar outcomes.

5   As in the test of hypothesis 5.1, the comparison of the structure of the brand value profile with the structure of the Value Compass, the value types *honesty* and *safety* had to be combined in one factor to enable Lisrel to perform the analysis. The other value types are the value types of the short version of the Value Compass: *care & affection, social responsibility, enjoying life, stimulation, prestige, beauty* and *functionality*.

6   With a sample of five European countries, the sample size is too small to construct a true European baseline value hierarchy of the Value Compass. Formally, we should refer to the average value priority ranking of the five European countries in the study. However, we justify the reference to a baseline here considering the high general agreement in the observed hierarchical ordering of values between countries.

7   In the study of Fischer and Schwartz, only conformity values appeared to have important cross-cultural differences. However, conformity values are not activated toward consumer behaviour: the value types *tradition* and *conformity* do not have a corresponding value type in the Value Compass (see Section 4.4).

8   Formally, Cohen's d is calculated as $d = (x_1 - x_2)/s$, where X is an absolute group mean and s is the standard deviation of the baseline group, whereas in our comparison one standardized group mean is compared with another standardized group mean: $x_1/s_1 - x_2/s_2$. However, standard deviations for the value types in the tested countries are fairly similar, which makes $x_1/s_1 - x_2/s_2$ largely equal to $(x_1 - x_2)/s$. Consequently, we will refer to Cohen's d as indication for effect sizes.

9   Differences between cultures can be caused by several (combinations of) factors. With the limitation of the number of countries in the sample, any explanation of causes of cross-cultural differences is tentative. For an adequate analysis of the reasons behind similarities and differences in value ratings between cultures, a larger number of countries are necessary.

References

Berry, J. W., Poortinga, Y. H., Breugelmans, S. M., Chasiotis, A. & Sam, D. L. (2011). *Cross-Cultural psychology: Research and applications.* Cambridge, UK: Cambridge University Press.

Cheung, G. W. & Rensvold, R. B. (2000). Assessing extreme and acquiescence reponse sets in cross-cultural research using structural equations modeling. *Journal of Cross-Cultural Psychology, 31*(2), 187–212.

Cheung, G. W. & Rensvold, R. B. (2002). Evaluating goodness-of-fit indexes for testing measurement invariance. *Structural Equation Modeling, 9* (2), 233–255.

Cohen, J. (1992). A power primer. *Psychological Bulletin, 112*(1), 155–159.

Fischer, R. (2004). Standardization to account for cross-cultural response bias: A classification of score adjustment procedures and review of research in JCCP. *Journal of Cross-Cultural Psychology, 35*(3), 263–282.

Fischer, R. & Schwartz, S. (2011). Whence differences in value priorities? Individual, cultural, or artifactual sources. *Journal of Cross-Cultural Psychology, 42*(7), 1127–1144.

Hair, J. H., Black, W. C., Babin, B. J., Anderson, R. E. & Tatham, R. L. (2006). *Multivariate data analysis* (6th edition). Upper Saddle River, NJ: Pearson Prentice Hall.

Hofstede, G. (1980). *Culture's consequences: Comparing values, behaviors, institutions and organizations across nations.* Thousand Oaks, CA: Sage.

Hofstede, G. (2001). *Culture's consequences: Comparing values, behaviors, institutions, and organizations across nations* (2nd edition). Thousand Oaks, CA: Sage.

Hofstede, G. (2011). Dimensionalizing cultures: The Hofstede model in context. *Online Readings in Psychology and Culture, 2*(1). http://dx.doi.org/10.9707/2307–0919.1014.

Hofstede, G. & Hofstede, G. (2005). *Cultures and organizations, software of the mind.* New York, NY: McGraw-Hill.

Inglehart, R. F. (1997). *Modernization and postmodernization: Cultural, economic and political change in 43 countries.* Princeton, NJ: Princeton University Press.

Kollmuss, A. & Agyeman, J. (2002). Mind the gap: Why do people act environmentally and what are the barriers to pro-environmental behavior. *Environmental Education Research, 8*(3), 239–260.

Kutcher, N. (2000). The fifth relationship: dangerous friendships in the confucian context. *The American Historic Review, 105*(5), 1615–1629.

Leung, K. & Bond, M. H. (1989). On the empirical identification of dimensions for cross-cultural comparisons. *Journal of Cross-Cultural Psychology, 20*(2), 133–151.

Marin, G., Gamba, R. J., & Marin, B. V. (1992). Extreme response styles and acquiescence among Hispanics. *Journal of Cross-Cultural Psychology, 23*(4), 489–509.

Markus, H. R. & Kitayama, S. (1991). Culture and the self: Implications for cognition, emotion, and motivation. *Psychological Review, 98*(2), 224–253.

Schwartz, S. H. (1992). Universals in the content and structure of values: theoretical advances and empirical tests in 20 countries. In M. Zanna, *Advances in experimental social psychology* (Vol. 25, pp. 1–65). New York, NY: The Free Press.

Schwartz, S. H. (1994). Are there universal aspects in the structure and contents of human values? *Journal of Social Issues, 50*(4), 19–45.

Schwartz, S. H. (1994b). Beyond individualism/collectivism: New cultural dimensions of values. In U. Kim, H. C. Triandis, Ç. Kâgitçibasi, S.-C. Choi & G. Yoon, *Individualism and collectivism: Theory, method, and applications* (pp. 85–122). Thousand Oaks, CA: Sage Publications.

Schwartz, S. H. & Bardi, A. (2001). Value hierarchie across cultures: Taking a similarities perspective. *Journal of Cross-Cultural Psychology, 32*(5), 268–290.

Schwartz, S. H. & Bilsky, W. (1987). Toward a universal psychological structure of human values. *Journal of Personality and Social Psychology, 53*(3), 550–562.

Schwartz, S. H. & Sagiv, L. (1995). Identifying culture-specifics in the content and structure of values. *Journal of Cross-Cultural Psychology, 26*(1), 92–116.

Schwartz, S. H., Melech, G., Lehmann, A., Burgess, S., Harris, M. & Owens, V. (2001). Extending the cross–cultural validity of the theory of basic human values with a different method of measurement. *Journal of Cross-Cultural Psychology, 32*(5), 519–542.

Smith, P. B. (2004). Acquiescent response bias as an aspect of cultural communication style. *Journal of Cross-Cultural Psychology, 35*(1), 50–61.

Smith, P. B. (2011). Communication styles as dimensions of national culture. *Journal of Cross-Cultural Psychology, 42*(2), 216–233.

Triandis, H. C. (1995). *Individualism & collectivism*. Boulder, CO: Westmore.

Van de Vijver, F. J. (2011). Bias and real differences in cross-cultural differences. In F. J. Van de Vijver, A. Chasiotis & S. M. Breugelmans, *Fundamental questions in cross-cultural psychology* (pp. 235–257). Cambridge, UK: Cambridge University Press.

Van de Vijver, F. J. & Leung, K. (1997). *Methods and data-analysis for cross-cultural research*. Newbury Park, CA: Sage.

Van de Vijver, F. J. & Leung, K. (2011). Equivalence and bias: A review of concepts, model, and data analytic procedures. In D. Matsumoto & F. J. Van de Vijver, *Cross-cultural research methods in psychology* (pp. 17–45). New York, NY: Cambridge University Press.

Weber, M. (1949, original 1904). *The methodology of the social sciences*. Translation, Edward A. Shils and Henry A. Finch, New York, NY: The Free Press.

Part V

Conclusion

Chapter 9

Summary and conclusions

9.1 Introduction

The values concept is used in psychology to identify the motivations underlying behaviour. Marketeers borrowed this concept, and used it to define what they call brand values. However, as sometimes happens with borrowed concepts, the contents of the concept and the way it is applied can become detached from its original meaning. In psychology, the human value system is perceived as an integrated structure: actions in the pursuit of any value have consequences that can be consistent with some values, but conflicting with other values. In marketing, however, values are generally not treated as an integrated value system guiding behaviour. The view on values in marketing theory is still strongly influenced by Rokeach: values are considered end-states of being, a set of rather abstract motivations that give meaning and importance to the benefits of consumption (Gutman, 1982). With values being rather abstract motivations, the concept did not seem readily applicable to explain consumer behaviour, and attention has shifted to other, more 'tangible' imagery aspects such as brand associations and brand benefits. Within branding theory, the distinction between values and personality has become fuzzy (Aaker, 1997; Keller, 2008): we signalled a tendency to use brand personality, a *personality instrument*, as indicator of brand *values*. With this study we intend to align the use of values in marketing with the theoretical foundations of the values concept. Our aim was to develop a value system with relevance to consumer behaviour. Three objectives were defined:

- the development of the Value Compass, a value system activated toward consumer choice,
- the assessment of the effect of values on consumer choice,
- the assessment of the cross-cultural validity of the Value Compass.

Below, the outcomes of our study are summarized (Section 9.2). The limitations of the study are discussed in Section 9.3. The contributions to values theory and to marketing theory are highlighted in the Sections 9.4 and 9.5, respectively. Managerial implications are further specified in the final section of this chapter.

9.2 Summary of findings

This research was devoted to values, and the influence they have on consumer behaviour. Our study of consumer values was guided by seven propositions. Here, we present the main results pertaining to each proposition.

> *Values are guiding principles. Values motivate people to make choices that improve their quality of life (Proposition 1).*

Economic indicators such as per capita income are widely used as indicators for the quality of life. However, there is an increasing awareness of the importance of other indicators, emphasizing the general feeling of happiness or subjective well-being of the individual. This growing concern is visible in academics (e.g., Deci & Ryan, 2008; Diener, 2000), but is finding its way into policy guidelines as well (e.g., United Nations, 2011). The emphasis on a more individual, subjective appreciation of quality of life shifts our attention to how a higher quality of life can be attained. This brings us to values. Values are the individual beliefs that a certain end goal is more desirable than another goal, beliefs that can motivate the individual to take action to pursue this goal (Rokeach, 1973; Schwartz, 1992). Values, in other words, guide the individual in making choices that improve his perceived quality of life. The overall quality of life, however, is quite generic, and can lead to defining abstract, broadly defined goals such as *freedom* or *tolerance*. Choices, on the other hand, are generally made in a specific context. In order to make values into a useful guide to behaviour, it makes sense to specify the context. With that purpose in mind, the Value Compass was developed.

> *A consumer choice situation, being a specific choice context, activates a specific (sub)set of values. This set of values, referred to as the Value Compass, is structured as a dynamic value system of compatible and conflicting values (Proposition 2).*

This study was focused on consumer behaviour. We found that, indeed, consumers take their own values into consideration when they develop a certain attitude toward a brand, or when they make choices.

With the stepwise approach described in this study, the values guiding consumer choice were revealed. The development of the Value Compass started with a comprehensive list of values, which was composed by means of a lexical approach (De Raad & Van Oudenhoven, 2008). This comprehensive list was submitted to a jury. The jury selected the value items that, according to their judgement, make sense in a consumer choice context. In two survey rounds,

Table 9.1 The values of the Value Compass

Care & affection	Intimacy	Honesty	Safety
caring for someone	cosiness	honesty	feeling of security
family life	intimacy	keeping a promise	protection
friendship	romance	loyalty	safety
harmony	sensuality		

Enjoying Life	Stimulation	Prestige	Beauty
enjoying life	adventure	leadership	beauty
excitement	being active	power	elegance
fun	being sportive	status	good-looking
pleasure	courage	being successful	sense of beauty

Functionality	Achievement	Social responsibility
efficiency	innovation	being environment-friendly
functionality	intellect	providing for a better world
precision	progress	recycling
reliability	smart-solutions	

those value items were selected that appear most representative for consumer behaviour. Exploratory factor analysis with principal component analysis demonstrated that these value items can be categorized in 11 value types. Confirmatory factor analysis confirmed these value types, and helped to define the marker values for each value type:

By using multidimensional scaling, consumer values were found to be organized as a value system with a structure resembling the one found by Schwartz (1992): the Value Compass is organized as a value system in which certain values reinforce each other, whereas other values conflict which each other. The circular structure of the Value Compass can be visualized in the form of a value space, which is schematically presented in Figure 9.1. In this value space, values sharing a similar motivational goal are grouped together into value types. Neighbouring value types are compatible with each other, whereas opposing value types represent conflicting motivations. The value space is organized along two central dimensions:

- *Promotion of self-interests versus Care for others*. This dimension represents values motivating people to promote their own personal interests or to make a difference with others, as opposed to values motivating choices aimed at living in harmony with others, caring for others, and taking care of others.
- *Fun versus Function*. This dimension represents values motivating people to improve their quality of life by making hedonic choices, as opposed to values motivating them to make utilitarian (functional) choices.

Within each dimension, different types of consumer values can be identified. The fun-dimension is represented by the value types *enjoying life* and *stimulation*, the opposing function-dimension by *functionality* and *achievement*. Self-interests are pursued by values related to *prestige* and *beauty*, whereas care for others is connected to *safety, honesty, social responsibility, affection* and *intimacy*.

The two dimensions of the Value Compass present a mix of classifications found in value theory and in marketing theory. The first dimension resembles the dimension self-enhancement versus self-transcendence in Schwartz's value theory. The second dimension, *Fun versus Function,* is connected to the utilitarian-hedonic distinction frequently found in consumer behaviour literature, but cannot be retraced in the value system designed by Schwartz.

> *The structure of the brand value system, the perceived value proposition of the brand, is similar to the structure of the consumer's value system (Proposition 3).*

The Value Compass as presented above represents consumer motivations. We can imagine, for instance, that some consumers give higher priority to hedonic motivations, whereas the behaviour of others might be more strongly influenced by concerns for prestige or status. Our research demonstrated that people perceive brand values according to a structure resembling the organization of their own value system. Consequently, the value profile of a brand can also be described by the structure proposed by the Value Compass, as presented in Figure 9.1.

> *Brand values stimulate the relationship between the consumer and the brand, by creating an emotional attachment to the brand. Brand attachment, in turn, results in an intention to buy or use the brand (Proposition 4).*

The influence of values on consumer behaviour is represented by the Brand Value Model in Figure 9.2. This model links brand values to brand attachment. Brand attachment, the emotional attachment to a brand, is an indicator of the relation between the consumer and the brand. It consists of a number of related dimensions: brand affect, brand passion, brand community and brand engagement. Brand attachment, in turn, is related to brand performance, as can be expressed by the intention to buy the brand, or the tendency to promote the brand through word-of-mouth.

In our study, we demonstrated the linkages proposed by this model. We showed that there is a positive correlation between brand values and brand attachment: brand values stimulate the emotional attachment to a brand. This implies that brands that manage to create stronger associations with their brand values generate a higher level of brand attachment. In line with marketing literature, we also demonstrated that a higher brand attachment leads to a higher performance of the brand.

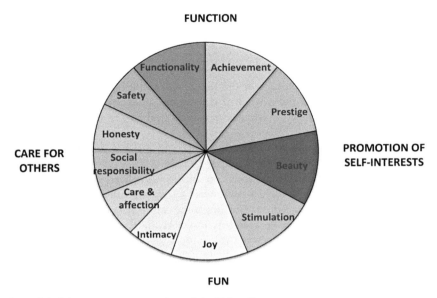

Figure 9.1 Schematic representation of the Value Compass

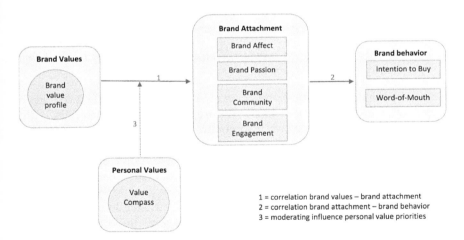

Figure 9.2 The Brand Value Model

Brand attachment is stronger with a stronger match between the consumer's value priorities and the perceived brand value profile. This value congruence is more relevant when values are more central to the consumer Propoition 5).

In itself, the conclusion that the performance of a brand is related to its strength, is not a novelty. The advantage of the use of the values concept, however, is that it enables us to map the impact of consumer values on brand attachment, thus on brand performance. This aspect is indicated by the dotted line in the Brand Value Model.

In our research, we confirmed earlier observations that prestige-sensitivity makes people more susceptible to liking brands (e.g., Vigneron & Johnson, 1999). Individuals with a stronger focus on impressing others, value types *prestige* and *beauty*, were shown to have a somewhat stronger tendency to be attached to brands. Individuals for whom the opposing value *honesty* is an important value, on the other hand, have a slightly lower tendency to attach themselves to brands. The influence of personal values on a general disposition to like or dislike branded products was found to be limited. This changes, however, when we consider the effect of value congruence.

Congruence is the match between the individual's self-concept and the image of the brand. The idea of congruence has been applied in combination with other brand concepts (e.g., Kressmann *et al.*, 2006; Sirgy, 1982). We defined value congruence as the match between the consumer's value priorities and the values proposed by the brand. We demonstrated a significant effect of value congruence: brands indeed realize a higher brand attachment if they manage to create a value profile that matches the value priorities of their consumers.

The brand values concept provides a meaningful alternative to the brand personality concept (Proposition 6).

Currently, the most popular brand concept in the marketing field is the brand personality framework (Aaker, 1997). We argued that brand personality is not a conceptually 'pure' concept: it incorporates a variety of separate constructs, including personality traits, but also values or reflections of the typical buyer (Azoulay & Kapferer, 2003). As a result, concept confusion has led brand personality to become an umbrella covering a variety of other concepts, including values.

We showed that, even when using a conceptually stricter definition of brand personality, the use of a brand values concept has some important advantages over the brand personality framework. The first advantage relates to conceptual structure. Values are structured as a dynamic system of compatible and conflicting values. Consequently, the impact of a certain value on behaviour should always be considered in relation to the impact of other values. This emphasizes the importance of taking into account the complete set of values associated with a brand. The Value Compass provides this opportunity: it creates a structure of relations between brand values. Brand personality traits, on the other hand, are treated conceptually as independent factors. Hence, using a brand personality concept can go no further than a list of personality traits associated with the brand, without clear guidelines for the interaction between elements in the brand personality profile.

The second advantage of the brand value concept concerns its relation with behaviour. Values refer to *what people consider important*. Values have an explicit and direct relation with behaviour: they motivate people to make choices. Personality traits, on the other hand, describe *what people are like*. We argued that this conceptual difference makes consumer values a better antecedent for consumer behaviour than personality traits. In our study, we made a comparison between the values of the Value Compass and the personality traits in Aaker's brand personality framework, and their relation with consumer behaviour. In this comparison, we found that values, as defined by the Value Compass, indeed have a stronger impact on consumer behaviour than personality traits as defined by the brand personality framework.

Compatibilities and conflicts between consumer values are similar across cultures. There are, however, cultural differences in the importance of consumer values (Proposition 7).

Most brands operate in an international context. Therefore, it is important to analyse brands by means of concepts that can be used in an international context. With respect to the brand personality framework, however, a number of studies pointed toward the limited cross-cultural of this framework (Aaker, Benet-Martinez & Garolera, 2001; Azoulay & Kapferer, 2003; Geuens, Weijters & De Wulf, 2009).

The cross-cultural validity of the Value Compass was tested with samples taken from a number of European countries: Germany, Italy, the Netherlands, Lithuania and Bulgaria. The analysis of the test results showed equivalence of the factor structure of the Value Compass, across these European countries. From this analysis we concluded that the Value Compass is a model that can be generalized across these countries.

Besides similarities in the structure of the Value Compass in a European context, the cross-cultural analysis also revealed a pattern of similarities in the importance ranking of value priorities. This suggests the existence of a European baseline ranking of value priorities. There are a few deviations from this baseline ranking, for instance, *beauty* is relatively important in Italy, *joy* relatively important in the Netherlands and *prestige* somewhat more important in Lithuania. Overall, however, the importance ordering of consumer values between European countries is highly correlated.

Application of the Value Compass beyond Europe seems to require further research. The test of the Value Compass with a Chinese sample revealed important deviations from the European structure.

9.3 Limitations

The outcomes of this study were based on an extensive study of the influence of values on consumer behaviour, with data collected in a number of geographically dispersed countries. Although the research provided us with interesting outcomes, there are a number of limitations that provide opportunities for further research.

A first limitation relates to the nature of the sample used for this research. Although we refer to the outcomes as being 'results from the Dutch sample', or 'results obtained from Germany', all data in this study were obtained from student samples. Since we took student samples in each country of the study, we ensured cross-cultural comparability of the outcomes across the countries involved. However, since the focus was on only one segment of the population, we cannot ensure generalizability to the whole population. This is a point of difference with, for instance, the sample used for the Schwartz Value Survey, where a more representative sample was taken from each country. To be able to truly generalize the outcomes of the Value Compass, we suggest this study is replicated in a more representative subset of the population.

A second limitation involves the sampled countries. The choice of countries in the cross-cultural analysis was aimed at providing a regional distribution across Europe, but western societies outside Europe, such as the United States or Australia, were not included. Information from these societies, or from the European countries not included in the sample, would provide additional evidence for the generalizability of the Value Compass. Only one non-western society, China, was entered in the analysis. We observed that the results from the Chinese sample presented a number of deviations from the other outcomes. Additional data are needed to find out if this is related to incidental factors surrounding this Chinese sample or to the sampling procedure used, or that consumer behaviour in Chinese society truly differs from a European or western setting. Since China is hardly representative for non-western societies in general, it is also important to replicate the test of the Value Compass in other non-western societies.

We also need to mention that the sampling method itself had a possible impact on our results. In some of the sampled countries, the survey was distributed as an online survey, whereas in other countries – due to practical considerations – the survey was administered to either part of the sample or to the whole sample in the form of a hardcopy. Although we corrected for differences in response style by using a standardization procedure, the difference in sampling is a potential source of bias. Similarly, the language in which the survey was presented to the respondents potentially causes bias. Even with a translation – back translation procedure, a translated item can be associated with a somewhat different meaning than the original item. Finally, we need to point out that the database used to generate our value items originates from the Netherlands, creating the potential of a culturally biased selection of value items.

The rationale for the development of the Value Compass was that values activated toward a specific setting might be different from values related to life in general. Additionally, we argued that the closer we define values to a behaviour of interest, the stronger the link with that behaviour. Consumer behaviour was our behaviour of interest, and we developed the Value Compass as a model to understand consumer choice. Within the context of consumer choice, however, several choice settings can be identified. Hypothetically, each product category defines its own choice context. As an example, the decision to buy a car is a different choice context, with a different level of involvement, than the decision to buy a bottle of beer. It is possible that the impact of values on behaviour is not the same across consumer choice settings. In order to validate the generalizability of the Value Compass, we advise to investigate the relation between values and behaviour across different consumer behaviour settings.

9.4 Contribution to value theory

The value system that emerged from the studies of Schwartz (1992) represents values as guiding principles in life. In Schwartz's value system, values form a continuum of related motivations. This continuum takes the form of a circular structure, in which neighbouring value types express more similar, compatible motivations, whereas opposing value types are clearly distinct from each other and express conflicting motivations. Our research provided additional evidence for the structure in which human values are organized. When activating values toward a specific choice context, namely consumer choice, we found that a value system emerges with a circular structure resembling the one predicted by Schwartz (1992).

Schwartz specified that values are guiding principles for life in general, and that they transcend specific actions and situations (Schwartz, 2006). Individuals, however, do not just use their values as guiding principles for life in general; they make choices continuously, in a variety of settings. Each specific choice setting involves specific values (Seligman & Katz, 1996), and different situations activate different values (Verplanken & Holland, 2002). Consequently, we can only accurately assess the impact of values on behaviour if we specify the context. The study of the Value Compass highlighted this for consumer behaviour. For consumer behaviour we found a similar structure as predicted by Schwartz. Some value types in the Value Compass are highly similar to those defined by Schwartz (e.g., *safety, stimulation, achievement*). However, not all the value types in the Value Compass can be traced back to the ones defined by Schwartz. We observed that a consumer behaviour setting activates specific values not found by Schwartz (*beauty, intimacy, functionality*). Also, certain value types that were defined by Schwartz (e.g., *tradition, conformity*) appear less relevant to consumer choice: they are not represented in the Value Compass. When we look at the two dimensions organizing the Value Compass, we found that one of these dimensions, *promotion of self-interests versus care for others*, is similar to one of the dimensions organizing Schwartz's value system. However, the other dimension of the Value Compass, *fun versus function*, seems more typical to consumer behaviour and cannot be traced back to Schwartz (1992).

We found that values indeed influence consumer behaviour: consumers are induced to make choices consistent with their value priorities. Their choice motivation can be interpreted as a result of two sets of values: the value priorities of the consumer and the values that he perceives in the object (e.g., brand) of his choice. Apparently, consumers don't simply consider their own value system in isolation: they are actively looking for a match between their own values and the values proposed by the brand.

Finally, in previous studies, it has been suggested that individuals can hold perceptions of the value systems of others (e.g., Rohan, 2000). Our study takes this a step further. We showed that 'others' not only refers to other individuals; also inanimate ('non-living') objects and concepts such as brands are perceived to have a value system. We not only found that consumers believe that brands can be characterized by their brand values, our study also demonstrated that the perceived value system of a brand is characterized by a structure that resembles the individual's value system.

9.5 Contribution to marketing

The relevance of values to branding is not new to marketing literature: brand values have been referred to as associations that characterize the most important aspects of a brand (Keller, 2008), and many corporations profile their corporate values or brand values prominently. So far, however, brand values were generally conceptualized as a list of unrelated items. The construction of a brand image – the set of aspects, benefits or values with which the consumer associates a brand – then becomes a creative process for which the marketer has the choice between an undefined number of associations. Although this choice can be guided by a number of considerations, such as the choice for utilitarian benefits as opposed to hedonic benefits, a clear conceptual framework guiding this creative choice process seems to be lacking.

In a number of recent studies, a values-based brand concept was introduced and linked to consumer behaviour (e.g., Allen, Gupta & Monnier, 2008; Torelli *et al.*, 2012; Zhang & Bloemer, 2008). However, these studies used the value system developed by Schwartz (1992) a value system that is not activated toward consumer behaviour, and therefore less suitable to this context.

In our study, we proposed the Value Compass, a conceptual framework for a values-based explanation of consumer behaviour. The Value Compass is a comprehensive representation of consumer values: by using value theory, we showed that consumer values can be described as a circular structure consisting of values that reinforce each other, and values that conflict with each other. Additionally, we found that brand values can be described according to a structure strongly resembling the consumer's value system. This implies that the Value Compass also provides an instrument that can be used to describe (and to visualize) the value proposition of a brand.

By using the Value Compass, our analysis demonstrated a significant positive influence of values on consumer behaviour: brand values congruent with the consumer's value priorities stimulate emotional attachment to the brand which, in turn, leads to buying intentions or increased word-of-mouth. The Brand Value Model proposed in this book visualizes the relation between values and consumer behaviour.

In our study, the Value Compass was compared with one of the most commonly used brand concepts, the brand personality framework. We found that this brand personality framework has become an umbrella covering a variety of other concepts, including values (Azoulay & Kapferer, 2003). When comparing brand personality (even when based on a strict, conceptually 'pure' definition) with brand values, we found that the use of a brand values concept has a number of advantages. One of these advantages relates to the conceptual structure: the brand personality framework offers a list of unrelated brand personality aspects, whereas the Value Compass provides a structure by which a brand can be evaluated. Another point of difference concerns the extent to which the concept can be generalized across cultures. The brand personality framework seems to offer only limited cross-cultural validity, whereas the Value Compass was shown to provide a structure that can be used within, at least, a European context. A third advantage concerns the relation with behaviour. We found that there is a stronger, and conceptually more straightforward relation between the values of the Value Compass and consumer behaviour, as compared to the personality traits in the brand personality framework.

9.6 Managerial implications

Brand equity, the value of a brand, can be viewed from the consumer's perspective or from an organizational perspective (Keller & Lehmann, 2006). Taking the consumer's perspective, a brand is of value to consumers if it matches their demands. This perspective was taken throughout this study: we looked at the value proposition as perceived by the consumer, and the extent to which the brand value proposition matches the consumer's value orientation.

Brands can also be assessed from the organizational point of view. From this point of view, a brand delivers added value if it helps to attain the objectives the organization wishes to realize with the brand. Branding can be viewed as providing the brand with a value profile that maximizes its contribution to these objectives, by expressing to the consumer, or to other stakeholders, what the brand represents. Brand management can use the Value Compass as an analytical instrument, for the analysis of the current brand value profile, and the match of this value profile with the value system of the consumer. In case this analysis indicates the potential for improvement, the Value Compass can be used as a strategic instrument in the (re)design of the brand image, or as a structure that guides creativity, as it provides guidelines for the creation of a strong and consistent brand value profile.

References

Aaker, J. L. (1997). Dimensions of brand personality. *Journal of Marketing Research, 34*(8), 347–356.

Aaker, J. L., Benet-Martinez, V. & Garolera, J. (2001). Consumption symbols as carriers of culture: A study of Japanese and Spanish brand personality constucts. *Journal of Personality and Social Psychology, 81*(3), 492–508.

Allen, M. W., Gupta, R. & Monnier, A. (2008). The interactive effect of cultural symbols and human values on taste evaluation. *Journal of Consumer Research, 35*(8), 294–308.

Azoulay, A. & Kapferer, J.-N. (2003). Do brand personality scales really measure brand personality? *The Journal of Brand Management, 11*(2), 143–155.

Deci, E. L. & Ryan, R. M. (2008). Hedonia, eudaimonia and well-being: An introduction. *Journal of Happiness Studies, 9*(1), 1–11.

De Raad, B. & Van Oudenhoven, J. P. (2008). Factors of values in the Dutch language and their relationship to factors of personality. *European Journal of Personality, 22*(2), 81–108.

Diener, E. (2000). Subjective well-being: The science of happiness and a proposal for a national index. *American Psychologist, 55*(1), 34–43.

Geuens, M., Weijters, B. & De Wulf, K. (2009). A new measure of brand personality. *International Journal of Research in Marketing, 26*(2), 97–107.

Gutman, J. (1982). A means-end chain model based on consumer categorization processes. *Journal of Marketing, 46*(2), 60–72.

Keller, K. L. (2008). *Strategic brand management: Building, measuring, and managing brand equity* (3rd edition). Upper Saddle River, NJ: Prentice Hall.

Keller, K. L. & Lehmann, D. R. (2006). Brands and branding: Research findings and future priorities. *Marketing Science, 25*(6), 740–759.

Kressmann, F., Sirgy, M., Herrmann, A., Huber, F., Huber, S. & Lee, D.-J. (2006). Direct and indirect effects of self-image congruence on brand loyalty. *Journal of Business Research, 59*(9), 955–964.

Rohan, M. J. (2000). A rose by any name? The values construct. *Personality and Social Psychology Review, 4*(3), 255–277.

Rokeach, M. (1973). *The nature of human values.* New York, NY: The Free Press.

Schwartz, S. H. (1992). Universals in the content and structure of values: theoretical advances and empirical tests in 20 countries. In M. Zanna, *Advances in experimental social psychology* (Vol. 25, pp. 1–65). New York, NY: The Free Press.

Schwartz, S. H. (2006). Les valeurs de base de la personne: Théorie, mesures et applications. *Revue Française de Sociologie, 47*(4), 929–968.

Seligman, C. & Katz, A. N. (1996). The dynamics of value systems. In C. Seligman, J. M. Olson & M. P. Zanna, *The psychology of values: The Ontario symposium, 8* (pp. 53–76). New York, NY: Psychology Press.

Sirgy, M. J. (1982). Self-concept in consumer behavior: A critical review. *Journal of Consumer Research, 9*(3), 287–300.

Torelli, C. J., Özsomer, A., Carvalho, S. W., Keh, H. T. & Maehle, N. (2012). Brand concepts as representations of human values: Do cultural congruity and compatibility between values matter? *Journal of Marketing, 76*(7), 92–108.

United Nations (2011). *Happiness: Towards a holistic approach to development*. Retrieved 25 August 2011, from Resolutions adopted by the General Assembly at its 65th session: www.un.org/ga/search/view_doc.asp?symbol=A/RES/65/309&Lang=E

Verplanken, B. & Holland, R. W. (2002). Motivated decision making: Effects of activation and self-centrality of values on choices and behavior. *Journal of Personality and Social Psychology, 82*(3), 434–447.

Vigneron, F. & Johnson, L. W. (1999). A review and a conceptual framework of prestige-seeking consumer behavior. *Academy of Marketing Science Review, 1*(1), 1–15.

Zhang, J. & Bloemer, J. M. (2008). The impact of value congruence on consumer-service brand relationships. *Journal of Service Research, 11*(2), 161–178.

Appendix

Comprehensive list of 190 brand value items (in English and Dutch)

Value item, English	Value item, Dutch*
a comfortable life	R – een comfortabel leven
accessibility	toegankelijkheid
	accuraatheid
accuracy	nauwkeurigheid
adventure	avontuurlijkheid
advice	adviseren
ambition	S – ambitie
attention	aandacht
authenticity	echtheid
authority	S – autoriteit
beauty	S – schoonheid
artistic	kunstzinnigheid
attractive	aantrekkelijkheid
being calm	kalmte
being civilized	geciviliseerd zijn
being discrete	discreet zijn
being environmentally conscious	milieubewustzijn
being environment-friendly	milieuvriendelijkheid
being goal-oriented	doelbewustheid
being humane	humaan zijn
being idealistic about the future	toekomstideaal
being qualified	gekwalificeerdheid
being sportive	sportiviteit
being unique	individualiteit
being up-to-date	progressiviteit
being well-balanced	in balans zijn
being well-organized	georganiseerdheid
belonging to something	S – ergens bijhoren
carefulness	zorgvuldigheid
caring	verzorgdheid
	zorgzaamheid
certainty	zekerheid
charity	weldoen
cheerfulness	vrolijkheid
clarity	duidelijkheid
common-sense	nuchterheid

Value item, English	Value item, Dutch
competence	competentie
	deskundigheid
competition	competitie
confidence	vertrouwen
confidentiality	vertrouwelijkheid
convenience	comfort
cooperation	samenwerking
cosiness	gezelligheid
cosmopolitan	kosmopolitisch zijn
courage	moed
craftsmanship	ambachtelijkheid
	vakkundigheid
creativity	S – creativiteit
credibility	geloofwaardigheid
culture	cultuur
curiosity	S-nieuwsgierigheid
customer orientation	klantgerichtheid
daring	S – durf
delivering quality	kwaliteit leveren
development	ontwikkeling
diversity	diversiteit
down-to-earth	nuchterheid
dynamic	energiek zijn
efficiency	efficiëntie
elegance	elegantie
emancipation	emancipatie
enjoying life	levenslust
enjoying things	genieten van dingen
enjoyment	S – genieten van het leven
enthusiasm	enthousiasme
entrepreneurship	ondernemingsgeest
environmental protection	S – bescherming van de natuur
excitement	enthousiasme
experience	ervaring
expertise	expertise
family life	Familieleven
	gezinsleven
family tradition	Familietraditie
feeling of security	geborgenheid
feeling of superiority	onderscheidingsvermogen
femininity	vrouwelijkheid
feminism	Feminisme
fitness	fitheid
flexibility	flexibiliteit
freshness	frisheid
friendliness	vriendelijkheid
friendship	S – vriendschap
fun	lol
functionality	Functionaliteit
genius	genialiteit

Value item, English	Value item, Dutch
good manners	etiquette
good-looking	mooiheid
guts	lef
harmony	harmonie
health	S – gezondheid
high performance	prestaties leveren
homeliness	huiselijkheid
honesty	S – eerlijkheid
hospitality	gastvrijheid
hygiene	hygiëne
idealism	idealisme
imagination	fantasie
improvement of society	maatschappijverbetering
independence	S – onafhankelijkheid
	zelfstandigheid
individualism	individualisme
individuality	individualiteit
indulgence	genot
influence	S – invloed
ingenuity	vindingrijkheid
innocence	onschuld
innovation	vernieuwing
inspiration	Inspiratie
intellect	intellect
intimacy	intimiteit
keeping a promise	beloftes nakomen
knowledge	kennis
leadership	leiderschap
loyalty	S – loyaliteit
	trouw
masculinity	mannelijkheid
mobility	mobiliteit
musicality	muzikaliteit
nationalism	nationalisme
nature	natuur
non-violence	geweldloosheid
openness	openheid
optimism	optimisme
originality	originaliteit
passion	passie
peace	vrede
perfection	perfectie
physical exercise	lichaamsbeweging
pleasure	S – plezier
possession	bezit
power	krachtig zijn
precision	precisie
pregnancy	zwangerschap
pride	trots
privacy	privacy

Value item, English	Value item, Dutch
professional expertise	vakkennis
professionalism	professionaliteit
progress	vooruitgang
progressiveness	vooruitstrevendheid
prosperity	welvaart
protection	bescherming
providing for a better world	wereldverbetering
punctuality	punctualiteit
purity	puurheid
	zuiverheid
quality of life	kwaliteit van het leven
recreation	ontspanning
reliability	betrouwbaarheid
reputation	reputatie
resourcefulness	inventiviteit
respect	respect
respectability	aanzien
responsibility	S – verantwoordelijkheid
romance	romantiek
safety	veiligheid
satisfaction	tevredenheid
self-assurance	zelfverzekerdheid
self-confidence	zelfvertrouwen
sense of beauty	schoonheidsgevoel
sense of humour	humor
sensuality	erotiek
sexuality	sexualiteit
simplicity	eenvoud
sincerity	oprechtheid
smart solutions	slimheid
solidarity	solidariteit
sophistication	stijl
soundness	degelijkheid
spirituality	S – spiritualiteit
spontaneity	spontaniteit
stability	stabiliteit
status	status
style	stijl
successful	S – succes
sustainability	duurzaamheid
temperament	levendigheid
thinking ahead	vooruitdenken
cost efficiency	zuinigheid
to be active	actief zijn
to be expressive	expressief zijn
to be sociable	sociaal zijn
to laugh	lachen
to recycle	recyclen
tolerance	tolerantie
tradition	S – traditie

Value item, English	Value item, Dutch
trust	**vertrouwen**
truth	**waarheid**
unity with nature	**S – eenheid met de natuur**
usefulness	**bruikbaarheid**
varied life	**S – gevarieerdheid**
versatility	**veelzijdigheid**
vitality	**levenskracht**
	vitaliteit
wealth	**S – rijkdom**
well-being	**welzijn**
wisdom	**S – wijsheid**

*In this list, S implies that the value item was taken from Schwartz' value system, whereas R indicates that the values item comes from the Rokeach value survey.

Index

For Product Safety Concerns and Information please contact our EU
representative GPSR@taylorandfrancis.com
Taylor & Francis Verlag GmbH, Kaufingerstraße 24, 80331 München, Germany